Cases in Security Analysis and Portfolio Management

Steven E. Bolten

University of Houston

Holt, Rinehart and Winston, Inc.
New York Chicago San Francisco Atlanta
Dallas Montreal Toronto London Sydney

TP

PREFACE

Investments as a university subject is rapidly moving away from the descriptive towards the analytical and conceptual, much as Managerial Finance has done in the recent past. The typical course content has shifted from merely acquainting the student with the characteristics of the various types of financial assets, industry structures, and portfolios to conceptual frameworks around which the student can discipline his thoughts and through which he can understand the functioning and the evaluation processes of the securities markets. Theories of financial asset price determination have developed and been refined, portfolio management has grown into a rigorously and thoroughly explored economic function, and Investments in general has been integrated into the theory of Finance.

This sudden shift in the subject matter has brought with it some of the same problems as the shift in Managerial Finance. The most obvious of these has been to strain the student's ability to associate the concepts with the practice of the financial world. Partly because the student has been concentrating so hard on mastering the concepts and partly because the subject has been traditionally so pragmatic, he has not been able to bridge the gap. Some students claim the new Investments is too theoretical and chafe under the instruction, not realizing its value as a base of knowledge from which they can develop the tactics and the tools of analysis to cope with any emerging situation. Others complain the material is too quantitatively abstract to be applied.

These complaints are frequently mirrored in the student's performance. Some, particularly non-finance majors, have simply turned elsewhere for electives because they could find no useful relevance in the course. Many others have become languid in the course without ever having their interest sparked and, frankly, wondering where the subject fits. Still others, perhaps the most frustrating group of all, are the more capable students who become bewildered because they had not clearly focused or grasped one or two points as the concepts were constructed into an integrated framework or because they had not sharpened the analytical tools derived from the theory. Consequently, they either become exasperated in their effort to understand the material or discovered the course's relevance too late in the semester to provide the proper interaction with the instructor during the term.

The solution to the student's complains and the accompanying problems, and what this text provides, is a selection of relatively short cases, many based on actual situations, which illustrate point by point the application and the relevance of the conceptual frameworks to the practice of security analysis and portfolio management. Each case forces the student to relate a specific idea to a real situation and so master the concepts, sharpen his tools of analysis, and discover the relationship between the theory and the practice. Doing the cases, the student learns each point in its proper sequence before moving on to the next one and so maintains a proper pace with the class. Each case also forces the student to examine the data as if he were professionally involved in investments. This procedure exposes him to a sufficient number of cases so that he awakens to the recurring indicators that most analysts through experience find significant. In addition, once the student sees the relevance of the theory to the situation and how he can use the theory as a base for understanding the circumstances of different situations, his interest usually heightens and his resistance to mastering the theory melts away.

The cases are constructed to emphasize the more recently developed analytical techniques and evaluation frameworks, although not to the exclusion of other pertinent, but perhaps older, concepts. Each case is keyed directly to one specific topic or technique, such as the calculation of mutual fund viability, so that student is required to concentrate on that particular material. None of the cases is overly complicated or lengthy to prevent the student from sacrificing his study of the text with an inordinate amount of time on the cases. For the same reason, the student is given questions at the end of each case to direct his attention to the pertinent points.

To further stimulate the student's interest the cases are examined from the viewpoint of an external, practicing analyst. In keeping with realism none of the data are any more than that which is normally available to the average investor or analyst. Almost all the data are, therefore, external data on publicly held companies from sources readily accessible to the student, although in most instances the name has been changed or the data have been modified to simplify or complete the case. This realism should let the student vicariously relive the moments of decision. He will be able to pit his judgement against history and should learn to avoid the mistakes of others. As it is said: those who do not study history are doomed to repeat it.

This casebook is keyed to the standard Investment texts, and the cases are categorized by specific topics closely identified with the appropriate text material so the instructor may coordinate the two. A relatively large number of cases are offered, so the instructor may choose which are most appropriate for his purpose in conjunction with his text.

I would like to thank Jane Mottus and Mary Fitzsimmons for their typing effort.

Houston, Texas
January 1973

Steven E. Bolten

CONTENTS

vi

To the POOH

Case 1

JOHN CRAIG

Security Markets and Transactions

John Craig is a senior in college majoring in Finance. John has just turned 21 and has accumulated $3,000 in savings from his birthday presents and past savings, which he keeps on deposit in a local savings and loan association at 5% interest, compounded quarterly. While John has received several circulars from insurance companies trying to sell him life insurance as an investment, he does not own any policies. The only other asset John has is his 1968 Ford convertible which he recently purchased for cash from a used car lot at a very reasonable price. John has no steady girl friends and does not plan to be married in the near future. He is in perfect health, and has a very high draft lottery number, which will assure his not being drafted. He has spoken to several large manufacturing companies about employment after he graduates from college and his prospects for getting a job appear very good.

Ever since his course in Corporation Finance, John has been anxious to learn more about investing his accumulated savings in stocks to make his savings grow, but John has not been able to take an Investments course and is, therefore, somewhat ignorant of the procedures he should take to start his investment program or even what preliminary information he should have before buying stocks. John, therefore, went to the local branch of a national brokerage firm in his college town of Encino, California.

John had become aware of the local branch when they had advertised a free investment seminar for beginners, and he had noticed in the ad that they claimed to be members of the New York Stock Exchange and other leading stock and commodity exchanges.

The broker, Mr. Mark Lowry, greeted John and made him feel at home. John explained he was interested in opening an account but that he was a novice and needed an introduction to the mechanics. Mr. Lowry asked John his financial and personal position and then explained how to open an account. Mr. Lowry explained that John would have to pay a commission to the brokerage firm, part of which went to Mr. Lowry, for their services in purchasing the stock.

Mr. Lowry explained that his firm not only acted as a broker in purchasing and selling stocks but also brokered in commodities, bonds, mutual funds, and other securities, which John might also be interested in. Many of the bonds in the present market offered higher yields than John was getting on his deposit at the savings and loan association, and if John were willing to give up the liquidity that the savings and loan offered, he could get 7½% on the bonds of such quality companies as General Motors. In addition to bonds, John could purchase stocks, which Mr. Lowry explained, entitled John to receive any dividends which may be paid to the stockholders by the company and to any capital gains which could occur if the share price rose. Still a third alternative for John could be mutual funds which entitled John to participate in a diversified portfolio of securities and to any dividends or capital gains which occurred in the portfolio.

John was impressed with the list of possible investments available to him but wanted to know more about stocks in particular. He was especially interested in the stock of Amalgamated American Hotels, Inc. (AAH) which he had heard some of the students in Investments talking about. Mr. Lowry explained that with his $3,000, John could open either of two types of accounts. He could open a cash account in which John paid in full for the shares of AAH he bought. Since AAH was selling at $50 a share John could buy 60 shares. But, Mr. Lowry went on to explain, in addition to the $50 a share price, John would have to pay an odd-lot differential of one eighth of a point ($.125) a share because he was buying less than 100 shares or what is known as a round lot. Mr. Lowry explained that purchases or sales in other than multiples of 100 shares were handled through a firm specializing in odd lots and for their extra service John would have to pay the odd-lot differential. The one-eighth point was usually added on to the purchase price. In addition, John would have to pay a commission to the brokerage firm, part of which went to Mr. Lowry, for his services. John would be able to purchase fewer than 60 shares if he wished to invest no more than $3,000. However, if John wished, he could open a margin account in which John would have to put up 60% of the total purchase price in cash and the brokerage firm would loan him at 8% interest the other 40% toward the purchase of AAH shares. John would still, of course, have to pay a commission; and if he bought other than multiples of 100 shares, the odd-lot differential on the odd number of shares over the round lot multiple. Mr. Lowry then gave John the commission schedule reproduced below:

EXHIBIT 1

COMMISSION SCHEDULE
100 Share Lots

AMOUNT	COMMISSION
$100 but less than $800	2.0% + $ 6.40
$800 but less than $2,500	1.3% + $12.00
over $2,500	.9% + $22.00

EXHIBIT 1 (Continued)

AMOUNT Odd-lot (same as above less $2.00)	COMMISSION
MULTIPLE ROUND LOT ORDERS	
$100 but less than $2,500	1.3% + $12.00
$2,500 but less than $20,000	.9% + $22.00
$20,000 but less than $30,000	.6% + 82.00
$30,000 but less than $300,000	.4% + $142.00
$300,000 and over	negotiated
plus	
1st 100 shares to 1,000 shares	$6 per 100 shares
1,100 shares or over	$4 per 100 shares

If John purchased the shares of AAH on margin he would have to sign an hypothecation agreement and agree to have his securities held in "street name", i.e. in titular ownership of the brokerage firm; John would not come into the possession of his stock certificate, i.e. evidence of ownership. Mr. Lowry explained these agreements were necessary to enable the firm to borrow money which in turn was lent to John to buy the share of AAH, but that John would know he owned the securities because the firm would issue John notification of his purchase and provide a monthly statement of John's account.

John decided that he wished to place an order for AAH, and Mr. Lowry explained that the order could be placed in several ways. John could order a specific number of shares at the going market price, i.e., the price being asked by potential sellers, which Mr. Lowry found to be $50. If John placed this market type of order, he would be assured of buying the shares at the best possible price asked by sellers when his order reached the exchange, if it were a round lot or the price of the last round lot sale plus the odd differential if it were an odd lot. However, if John chose, he could limit the price he was willing to pay and instruct the broker's representative on the floor of the exchange to pay no more than the specified price. This type of order, Mr. Lowry explained, was a limit order. In addition, John could restrict the time in which the order could be executed by the broker's floor representative. Among the time options, John could limit the order to one day, a week, a month, or allow the order to remain in effect until he can-called it. John instructed Mr. Lowry to limit his order to $50 a share, and to execute it as soon as possible but without a specific time restriction.

Because AAH was traded on the Pacific Coast Stock Exchange as well as in the Over-the-Counter market, Mr. Lowry explained, he would try both markets to see if one had a lower price than the other. As it turned out, the Over-the-Counter market had a share price for AAH of 49 bid and 50 asked. Since Mr. Lowry's firm was not a dealer in the stock, he explained it would make no difference in which market the stock was purchased. John remained in the office until he saw the Pacific Coast exchange ticker (the electronic notification system) report AAH had traded with the following symbol on the ticker:

AAH
2000s50

QUESTIONS

1. Discuss John Craig's possible investment objectives in light of his financial and personal position. Phrase your discussion as if you were a broker establishing reasonable targets of expected return and appropriate risks. Refer to specifics in John's position to support your conclusions.

2. If John opened a cash account, what would John's total investment be, including any odd-lot differential and commission, if he did not exceed $3,000 in total and the purchase price was $50 a share?

3. If John were to open a margin account, how many shares of AAH could he buy? (ignore commission and odd lot differential costs for simplicity). What would be the value of John's cash account if AAH fell to $40? What would be the value of John's margin account if AAH fell to $40? Compare the margin account value to the cash account value after the fall in the share price and draw conclusions.

4. What is meant by hypothecation and "street name?" How can John receive delivery of the stock certificates if he chooses?

5. Give the specific order in the appropriate language and words, which John used to instruct Mr. Lowry to buy the AAH shares for his cash account.

6. Distinguish between the Over-the-Counter market and the Pacific Coast Exchange. What does Mr. Lowry mean by AAH bid 49-asked 50 and that his firm is not a dealer in the shares of AAH? How can the stock of AAH be traded in two different markets? Are there any other markets?

7. Distinguish among stocks, bonds, commodities, and mutual funds? Give specific examples of each. Discuss the advantages and the disadvantages of a corporate bond compared to a savings and loan deposit.

8. When does a stockholder receive capital gains? When are dividends paid shareholders?

9. Interpret the ticker symbol which John saw.

Case 2

THE GLEN GLUE OFFER

Securities Markets and Transactions

The Glen Glue Co. (GG), an established retailer of ladies apparel, had just undergone a change in management. The new management had pledged to start an aggressive acquisition program designed to diversify the company into many fields. As its initial expansion effort, GG made a tender offer on July 13 for the shares of McKeon Drug Distributors, Inc. GG offered to exchange five of its shares for each share of McKeon and obligated itself to accept at least one million shares if tendered, but gave itself the option to purchase, on a pro rata basis, all or any tendered shares in excess of one million. The offer expired in two weeks, unless extended by GG.

McKeon's board of directors reacted sharply to the offer, especially since it had not been notified in advance that the tender offer was to be announced. McKeon's management angrily denounced the tender as a raid to gain control of a well-managed company and to loot its assets at a ridiculously undervalued price. They maintained that the shares were worth much more than GG was offering and that it was not in the best interests of the stockholders to accept GG's offer.

McKeon, an established distributor of drugs and cosmetic items to independent drug stores has a substantial sales base of almost $300,000,000 annually, although as is often the case in the wholesale distribution industry, profit margins were low and net profit was not very large. McKeon's earnings, reproduced below, for the last several years had been rather flat, and the prospects for the company, even

Year	Earnings Per Share
1965	$2.75
1966	2.60
1967	2.80
1968	2.78
1969	2.65
1970	2.85
1971	2.83
1972	2.70

with the tender offer, appear to be more of the same. Increased competition from large drug chains who were promoting their own label brands and avoiding the distributor were beginning to cut into McKeon's profit margins and sales growth.

Historically, McKeon shares had sold between 15 to 16 times earnings and were selling at $40 a share on the New York Stock Exchange before the tender announcement. Dividends had averaged about 60% of earnings, and the present dividend was $1.70. Similar firms in the drug distribution industry sold at approximately the same price-earnings ratio and yield.

The main attraction for acquiring McKeon would appear to be the hope of increasing its profit margins with more than a proportionate increase in net profit, although the best estimates available indicate that even if GG gained control flat earnings and a constant dividend could be expected for several more years. McKeon had 4 million shares outstanding of which less than 500,000 were controlled by management and another million shares could be considered closely held off the market, but not necessarily in accord with management. This meant that if GG succeeded in acquiring a million shares it would have 25% of McKeon's stock and control of the company.

On the day of the tender offer, made just after 3:30 p.m. Eastern time, McKeon stock rose from $40 to $44 a share, and to $46.75 on the Pacific Coast Exchange. GG shares rose $1 to $10 on the New York Stock Exchange. The day after the tender offer, McKeon shares rose to $46.75 on the New York Stock Exchange.

On the day following the offer, Mr. Archibald Bull, an investor, sold 100 shares of McKeon stock short at $46.75 a share. Mr. Bull's broker made arrangements for Mr. Bull to borrow the 100 shares from one of the other clients who owned the stock. Mr. Bull put up an appropriate deposit with the broker to insure that he would repay the borrowed shares. Mr. Bull had evaluated the situation and had decided McKeon stock was not worth the $50 in GG shares being offered and that after the tender offer expired, he would be able to purchase the shares at a cheaper price and repay the shares he had borrowed at a profit.

Another investor, Mr. Briggs decided he saw a profit opportunity too. He sold 500 shares of GG stock short at $10 apiece and purchased 100 shares of McKeon at $46.75. It was Mr. Briggs' intention to arbitrage between the value of the two securities and to profit when he received his GG shares in exchange for his McKeon shares.

Shortly before the expiration of the tender offer, Mr. Bull's broker called to say that the client from whom Mr. Bull had borrowed the McKeon shares wanted to tender his shares for the GG shares and that he, the broker, could not find any other of his clients who was willing to loan Mr. Bull other shares of McKeon because all were planning on tendering their shares. Mr. Bull was then obliged to return the shares but could find no other person from whom to borrow them. Mr. Bull also soon discovered that when he went to buy the shares back in the open market in order to repay the ones he had borrowed, the price of McKeon stock had risen sharply to $49 a share while GG shares remained steady at $10. Mr. Bull had no choice but to pay $49 a share for the 100 shares of McKeon and to take a loss.

Shortly after the expiration date, GG announced it had received tenders for 2.5 million shares but that it was exercising its right to take only 1 million shares on a pro rata basis and was returning the rest. At that announcement, the price of McKeon stock sank to $42 a share while the price of GG shares remained at $10. Mr. Briggs sold the McKeon shares that were returned to him and covered his GG short position.

QUESTIONS

1. What is the dividend yield on McKeon stock before the tender offer?
2. Relate the price action in McKeon stock to the tender announcement, and to the period shortly before and shortly after the expiration date. What had happened to the marketability of the McKeon stock? What was the estimated floating supply before the tender and on the expiration date? Do you think this affected the price?
3. How did Mr. Bull intend to make a profit? What was Mr. Bull's loss? (ignore transaction costs).
4. Why did Mr. Bull lose money, despite the drop in McKeon's price to $42 after the tender offer expired? Why did Mr. Bull have to buy the McKeon shares when he did?
5. How did Mr. Briggs intend to profit? What was his expected profit (ignoring transaction costs)?
6. What was Mr. Briggs' loss?
7. Could the price of McKeon stock have risen above $50 during the tender offer? Why or why not?

Case 3

STUDENT EXERCISE

Information Sources

Go to your school and/or local library and find what sources of financial information they carry in each of the categories described below. Give the name of the publication and a brief summary of the information contained therein.

1. Business Cycles
2. Chart Services
3. Commodity
4. General Economic Conditions
5. Bank Statistics
6. Stock Market Regulations
7. Convertible Bonds
8. Franchise Investments
9. Individual Company Statistics
10. Foreign Investments
11. Growth Stocks
12. Insider Reports
13. Insurance Stocks
14. Mutual Funds
15. Financial Newspapers and Magazines
16. Technical Indicators
17. Over-the-Counter Securities
18. Warrants
19. Trade Journals

Case 4

MR. SCHANE AND OTHERS

Compounding

Mr. Schane considers himself a lucky man. He is now retired from his plumbing business in which he had been employed for the last forty years. He is financially comfortable although not rich and prefers to measure his wealth in terms of his family. His wife, Mary, is still alive and his two daughters are both happily married to professional men in the state. But the pride of Mr. Schane's life is his three grandchildren, Maggie and Bess, both 5, and Jane, 3 years old. Both he and Mrs. Schane want to make sure their grandchildren will have the advantages of a college education, something which neither of them had. To Mr. Schane's way of thinking there is no finer legacy he could leave his children than that of knowledge.

With this idea in mind, Mr. Schane went to his friend, Mr. Whitcomb, the manager at the local savings and loan association where Mr. Schane had an account. Mr. Whitcomb suggested that a savings account, held in trust for his grandchildren until their eighteenth birthday, would be a most appropriate way of providing financial assistance for their education. Mr. Whitcomb pointed out that at the present dividend rate of 5%, the initial deposit would grow to a suitable nest egg for the grandchildren's education. Mr. Schane agreed and opened a $1000 account for each of the grandchildren.

Dr. Eason

When Dr. Eason was 55 years old and still practicing dentistry, he had taken out a $10,000 lump sum investment plan with the Lion Mutual Fund, as part of his retirement program. He had made arrangements for the fund to reinvest all the dividends and capital gains distributions in additional shares of the fund. At the time of the initial purchase, the fund's share price was $10. Now, ten years later at his retirement, the share price is $12.50, and the number of shares Dr. Eason owns is now 1,200. However, during the ten year period, the price of the shares has fluctuated from a low of $9.37 to a high of $14.87, and the dividends which Dr. Eason had reinvested for him varied from a low of $.02 a share to a high of $.33 a share during the ten years.

At the same time he bought the mutual fund, Dr. Eason also purchased two bonds of American Telephone and Telegraph, which promised to pay him 8% ($80 a year on the $1,000 cost per bond) each year for the next 40 years. When Dr. Eason received the semi-annual interest check of $80 from the company, he gave it to his wife for spending money, and she did spend it. Upon his retirement, Dr. Eason still owned the bonds, which were selling on the New York Bond Exchange for $1,000 each.

Mrs. Alfred

Mrs. Alfred, a widow, is a secretary at the local college. Before her husband's untimely demise, they had planned to go on a cruise to celebrate their 25th anniversary, and had started, on their 20th anniversary, a save-a-cruise account at the local national bank. In conjunction with the savings counselor at the bank, they had estimated that if they put $100 on each anniversary in the account for the next five years, they would have enough for the cruise. The savings counselor had calculated this on the basis of the 4% the bank annually paid on these special savings accounts.

Despite her husband's death, Mrs. Alfred had decided to continue the account and to take that cruise on what would have been her 25th anniversary. When the time came she planned to withdraw the entire amount in the account and spend it all on the cruise; she felt her husband would have wanted it that way.

Mr. Nall

Mr. Nall, an assistant professor of Finance at the state university, is 45 years old and has begun to plan for expected retirement at age 65. His goal is to retire to the hill country 50 miles east of the university and to take up fishing in a most serious fashion. He figures by that time his daughters will be through college and he and his wife will need only a limited income of $7,500 a year, even considering inflation, in addition to his other retirement programs such as social security and the university's pension plan, to make ends meet. He would like to leave the capital from which he expects to generate his retirement income as a legacy to his daughters and wants to live only on the income from his retirement fund and the $18,010 trust fund he receives on his 65th birthday. He calculates that at his retirement interest rates should be 7.5% on appropriate investments for his accumulated funds.

As his first move towards his goal, he is starting, at the end of this year, to put aside $2000 a year from now until his retirement.

QUESTIONS
1. When Mr. Schane's grandchildren reach 18, what will be the value of the account which Mr. Schane established for each?
2. What is the present investment worth of Dr. Eason's mutual fund shares? What has been the compound rate of return to Dr. Eason's mutual fund investment over the ten years he has held it? What has been the compound interest rate to his bond investment? Explain the difference between the two.
3. How much will Mrs. Alfred have to spend on her cruise?
4. How much capital does Mr. Nall need on his 65th birthday in order to receive $7,500 a year income at 7.5% interest? What compound rate of return does he need in order to reach his goal?

Case 5

YOUNG MR. NESS

Investment Mathematics

Mr. Ness, a recent 1972 MBA graduate of Harvard University, has just started his training as a security analyst with a respectable Wall St. firm. He has been instructed to keep his eyes and ears open and to learn from the old hands, who have been security analysts with the company for many years. Despite the fact that he has taken numerous courses in Finance and Investments and has an extensive academic background in the area, the firm still insisted he go through a trial period of training. One of the first assignments for young Mr. Ness was to evaluate the prospects of the First Industrial Corp., one of the nation's largest industrial equipment manufacturers, and to estimate an appropriate price for the stock and for its 8% subordinated debenture, due 1980.

Since this was only the first week of Mr. Ness's employment, he solicited the advice of the old hands before proceeding with his assigned project. First, he went to Mr. Engberg, the firm's most experienced analyst. Mr. Engberg told him the first step in the evaluation of any stock was to estimate as accurately as possible the company's earnings per share for the coming year. This estimate should then be compared to what the other firms on the "street" were estimating to make sure your own estimate was not too far afield. If it were outside the commonly accepted range, it was advisable to recompute one's own estimate and to look for errors. If you remained firmly convinced of the accuracy of your own estimate, the chances for profit were enhanced if you were later proved correct, because the market would have to adjust to your estimate from that which previously prevailed. However, Mr. Engberg assured Mr. Ness that divergences of any magnitude were rather rare and that usually all analysts knew within 24 hours of each other any significant change in the estimate.

Mr. Ness then asked Mr. Engberg how he arrived at his estimate of next year's earnings and what he did with it once he got it. Mr. Engberg explained that he derived his most accurate estimates from his interviews with management and that in the case of First Industrial Corp. his current estimate was $2.50 a share, the same as last year's earnings per share.

Mr. Engberg then told Mr. Ness to examine the stock prices of other firms in the same industry as First Industrial as a clue to what the share price should be in relation to earnings. Mr. Engberg gave him Table 1, which showed the price-earnings ratios for other firms in the industry as an example of what should be done. Mr. Engberg went on to explain that Ace Machinery and Alab Machinery were considered to be the leaders in the industry, particularly in the area of innovation and that both those companies were conservatively capitalized in comparison to First Industrial Corp. In his opinion, First Industrial should sell for a little less than either of the other two. However, because of their slower growth, Mr. Engberg considers Star Co. and James Machinery to be slightly less attractive than the average firm in the industry. All in all, Mr. Engberg considers First Industrial Corp. to be about average in the industry.

Thanking Mr. Engberg, Ness proceeded to quiz Mr. Samats on what he considered to be the appropriate method for evaluating First Industrial Corp. Mr. Samats explained that he belived it depends on the time horizon over which you intended to hold the stock. He maintained that the value of the stock today reflected what investors thought they would receive for the stock if they sold it at some time in the future plus any dividends they might receive while they held the stock. Mr. Ness arbitrarily proposed a one year holding period so Mr. Samats could illustrate what he meant. Samats said he expected First Industrial stock to be $26.50 by the end of the year and that he expected the firm would pay its usual dividend of $1.00 a share. Samats told Ness to use those estimates in calculating the present value, which should be the estimated worth of the stock.

Next, Mr. Johnson, another analyst at the firm, suggested that Ness devote his primary attention in his evaluation to First Industrial's dividend, for that was what really counted. He told Ness to compute the dividend yield and compare it to the yield on other stocks in the industry as he had done in Table 2. Johnson figured that First Industrial should yield at least the industry average and maybe a little more because of its history of slower growth in dividends than other stocks in the industry. He estimated First Industrial should yield about 4%, provided the pay-out ratio did not exceed 50%.

Mr. Gruber was more interested in the firm's growth than in its current dividend or earnings. He maintained that investors were willing to pay a premium on present earnings in order to capture the future increase in benefits promised by a growing dividend stream. Mr. Gruber told Ness that investors could be expected to capitalize the present dividend by a multiple which represented the present cost of funds to the firm less the firm's growth of dividends. Thus, the capitalization rate Ness calculated, represented the difference between the 10% cost of funds that Mr. Gruber figured was appropriate for the firm and the 6% historical growth rate of dividends for the firm. Mr. Gruber gave Ness the following formula for his use:

$$P = \frac{D}{r - g}$$

where P was the justified price, D was the current dividend, r was the firm's cost of funds, and g was the firm's historical growth rate of dividends. Ness was told that the formula would provide him with the evaluation tool he desired.

Mr. Ness then asked the most recent addition to the analytical staff besides himself for his comments. The young analyst, Mr. Mastra, confided that he meant no disrespect but that he thought the methods of analysis so far presented to Ness were not very good. He belived the market to be a much more accurate and reliable indicator of the present worth of any stock or bond based on what the market knew of the situation, and he assumed after seeing all the time and energy spent on gathering information that the market knew just about all there was to know at any one time. He firmly believed that any stock was accurately priced at the appropriate value in the market place until some factor which affected either the firm's prospects or the general market's present equilibrium became apparent. The only way Mr. Ness could hope to profit in the market was then to try to predict the future course of any changes. Mr. Mastra further went on to state that he believed the four major factors which most affected stock prices were changes in the firm's earnings prospects, in the prevailing interest rate, in the firm's operating environment, and in its capital structure. Mr. Mastra confided in Ness that he thought $25.00 a share was the right price for the stock unless some new information came to his attention to change his mind.

Finally, Ness went to the firm's bond analyst, Mr. Pasqua, to get his opinion on the value of the 8% subordinated First Industrial debenture of 1980. Mr. Pasqua instructed Ness to find out what other bonds of the same quality, according to the Moody's bond rating service, were yielding. Ness found that most subordinated debentures of comparable quality were yielding approximately 10% in the current market. Mr. Pasqua then asked Ness if he had learned about the present value of money when he was a student at Harvard; Mr. Pasqua had gone to Yale. Ness assured him he had. Then Mr. Pasqua told Ness the present value of the future interest payments and the return of principal at maturity discounted at the prevailing 10% rate should approximate the value of the debenture.

TABLE 1

PRICE EARNINGS RATIOS FOR INDUSTRIAL EQUIPMENT MANUFACTURERS

ISSUE	STOCK PRICE	ESTIMATED E. P. S.	P/E
Worth Mach.	$15	1.50	10X
Alab Mach	44	4.00	11X
Star Co.	27	3.00	9X
Cincin. Mach.	18	1.80	10X
Ace Mach.	66	6.00	11X
James Mach.	13.50	1.50	9X
First Indus.	25.00	2.50	—

TABLE 2

YIELD ON INDUSTRIAL EQUIPMENT MANUFACTURERS

	DIVIDENDS	YIELD
Worth	$ .60	4.0%
Alab Mach.	1.58	3.6
Star Co.	.95	3.5
Cincin. Mach.	.70	3.9
Ace Mach.	2.38	3.6
James Mach.	.80	5.9
First Industrial	1.00	—

QUESTIONS

1. What is the price-earnings ratio for First Industrial Corp? If everything else remained constant but Mr. Engberg's estimate of next year's earnings per share rose, what would you expect to happen to the stock price?
2. What is First Industrial's dividend yield? Is it appropriate under Mr. Johnson's criteria?
3. Compute the estimated stock price under Samats' method and under Gruber's method.
4. Compute the approximate price of the debentures under Mr. Pasqua's rules. If the interest rate fell to 8% for this class of debentures what would be the approximate price under Mr. Pasqua's rules?
5. Compare the evaluation techniques suggested by the various analysts in the case. Discuss the strengths and weaknesses of each.

Case 6

MR. MOYERS

Yield Calculations

Back on January 1, 1967, when Mr. Moyers, a young investment client of Bach and Co., member of the New York Stock Exchange and other leadings exchanges, first decided to open an account, he consulted with John Dippe, a Bach broker. Mr. Moyers explained he had almost $20,000, which was left to him by his great aunt, to invest. While he was naturally interested in seeing his capital increase, he, nevertheless, did not want to take large chances with his funds and wanted suggestions on "safe" stocks and bonds which Mr. Dippe felt would conserve his capital while providing income and some growth.

At that time Mr. Dippe's firm was underwriting a new bond issue for the General Telegraph and Telephone Co. (GTT), and Mr. Dippe was anxious to sell some of these to please his boss. In addition, the 4 7/8% sinking fund debenture due January 1, 1989 seemed like a logical choice for Mr. Moyers. The debentures were selling at par to yield the coupon rate of 4 7/8%. Mr. Dippe explained that Moyers could split his investment 50% in bonds and 50% in stocks if he bought ten of these GTT debentures. Mr. Dippe suggested that the other $10,000 be invested in a conservative stock, which offered current income and capital gains potential.

Dippe told Moyers what he considered to be the advantages of purchasing these bonds. He pointed out that if Moyers had put his money into a savings and loan account he would have only received the 4 1/2% then being paid in interest compared to the 4 7/8% coupon yield he could get on the GTT debenture. Also, he explained that if interest rates in general declined, the GTT debenture would increase in price and Moyers could, if he sold the debenture, reap a capital gain. Dippe also added, with less emphasis, that an increase in interest rates would depress the price of the debentures, which could result in a capital loss.

Mr. Moyers said he did not understand the term coupon yield. Mr. Dippe explained that the coupon yield was the interest rate that the debenture holder received when the annual interest payment, in this case, $48.75, was compared to the par or face value of the debenture, in this case $1,000. While the actual dollar interest payment in the coupon remained at the stated amount throughout the life of the bond, the bond price could fluctuate up or down, changing the relationship of the coupon to the bond price. The coupon in relation to the current market price, Mr. Dippe explained, was known as the current yield, which in this case also happened to be 4 7/8%. The return to the investment over any particular holding period would be the interest payments received during that period plus any capital gain realized at the time of sale as a percentage of the original purchase price. Mr. Dippe could not estimate this holding period return because he did not know how long Moyers intended to hold the debenture or what the selling price would be when Moyers did decide to sell.

With the other $10,000, Mr. Moyers bought 250 shares of American Telephone and Electronics at $40 a share. Mr. Dippe had explained that the stock held good prospects for growth because of the increasing use of telephones, while paying a good dividend of $2.60. The dividend, Mr. Dippe explained, would yield a nice income, far in excess of what could be gotten on other securities of the same caliber, while not exposing the investment to a large potential loss. Selling at only ten times the estimated $4.00 a share earnings, the stock seemed reasonably priced.

On December 30, 1973 after receiving the interest on the debentures and the dividend on the stocks, Mr. Moyer returned to Mr. Dippe to discuss his account. The GTT debentures were now selling at 72 points, instead of par (100 points) which Mr. Moyers had purchased them for. Mr. Dippe told Mr. Moyers not to worry because if he held the bonds to their maturity in 1989, he would get his full purchase price back. He advised Moyers to purchase more of the debentures, since their current yield was now up and their yield to maturity was very attractive. Mr. Dippe had to explain to Mr. Moyers that the yield to maturity reflected the relationship of the coupon plus the capital gain realized if the debentures were held to maturity. The yield to maturity could be read from the yield tables or approximated by the formula:

$$YTM_t = \frac{C + \dfrac{M - P_t}{n}}{\dfrac{M + P_t}{2}}$$

where YTM_t = yield to maturity

C = coupon yield in dollars
M = maturity value
n = number of years until maturity
P_t = current price

The American Telephone and Electronics stock had over the period risen to $50 a share, and although earnings per share had risen to $5.00, the dividend had not changed.

QUESTIONS

1. When Moyers returned to Mr. Dippe in 1973 what was the current yield on his GTT debentures? Why did this differ from the original current yield? In terms of his original investment, which current yield is Moyers receiving?

2. Debentures and bonds are quoted in points, how much is each point worth in dollars? As of 1973 what is the coupon yield and the face value of the GTT debentures? Compare the 1973 figures with the 1967 figures.

3. If Mr. Moyers were to sell the GTT debentures in 1973, what would be his holding period return? If he held the debentures until maturity what would be his holding period return?

4. What is the GTT debentures' yield to maturity in 1973? How does this affect Moyers' original purchase? If Moyers bought more GTT debentures in 1973 and held them to maturity, what would be his realized capital gain? What would be Moyer's capital gain on his present GTT debentures, if held to maturity?

5. What is the earnings yield for the American Telephone and Electronics stock in 1967? in 1973? What is the dividend yield in each of those two years?

6. If Moyers sold his shares in the American Telephone and Electronics Co. in 1973, what would be his holding period return?

Case 7

SCOUT PAPER COMPANY

Financial Statement Analysis

You, as a security analyst with a large brokerage firm, are responsible for keeping a constant surveillance of companies in the paper industry. Among these companies is the Scout Paper Company which is one of the largest companies in the industry. As part of your job you are required to issue a report on the status and prospects for the company from its recently issued financial statements.

As an external analyst you know that Scout is a large, integrated producer of paper and paper products, including such items as consumer papers, waste paper, and writing papers. Sixty-three percent of last year's sales were consumer oriented, such as toilet and facial tissues, napkins, and paper towels. Another 28% of the revenues were from printing and writing paper; while the remainder came from assorted related products.

The company has always had an effective marketing and advertising program. Many of its brands have a strong identification for the consumer and the firm's products have always been prominently featured on the shelves of the stores through which it is sold. The firm's products are sold both in the United States and Canada and throughout the world, with most of the international sales and production handled through 50% owned subsidiaries. The other 50% of these foreign subsidiaries generally being owned by the nationals of the country in which the subsidiary operates.

The company's plant and equipment have always been maintained and are among the most efficient in the industry. Capital expenditures for the ensuing year are estimated at approximately $80 million. The firm also has large timber reserves of approximately 3 million acres, enough to ensure a steady supply of raw material.

The paper industry in general has been expanding its capacity in recent years, despite some easing in the economy. This has caused some pressure on the industry's prices. However, it is not expected that any further weakening in the price structure will occur and that the economic environment next year will resemble that which prevailed in the year just past. Other problems also face the industry such as water pollution which has generally been associated with the disposal of the waste from the production of paper. The Scout Paper Company has taken steps to solve this problem, but the expenditures are not expected to adversely affect the company's sales and earnings performance.

17

The following financial statements are available for your analysis:

SCOUT PAPER COMPANY

COMPARATIVE CONSOLIDATED BALANCE SHEET, AS OF DECEMBER 31
(Taken from reports filed with Securities and Exchange Commission)

ASSETS	1973	1972	1971	1970
Cash	$ 21,340,000	$ 16,875,000	$ 16,979,000	$ 13,994,000
Marketable Securities, at cost	—	—	—	—
Accounts & Receivable	73,243,000	56,829,000	55,369,000	41,394,000
Inventories	107,675,000	99,018,000	96,313,000	81,328,000
Other Current Assets	5,402,000	4,600,000	4,543,000	4,864,000
Total Current Assets	$207,660,000	$177,322,000	$173,204,000	$141,580,000
Stock of Bruns. Pulp & Paper Co.	29,745,000	28,152,000	26,184,000	24,223,000
Other Investments	54,644,000	51,118,000	44,207,000	41,744,000
Standing Timber, cost less depletion	57,956,000	58,746,000	41,961,000	30,045,000
Property, Plant & Equipment	811,020,000	756,484,000	712,309,000	534,537,000
Less: depreciation & depletion reserves	353,786,000	323,163,000	291,709,000	225,274,000
Net property accounts	$457,234,000	$433,321,000	$420,600,000	$309,263,000
Patents, goodwill, etc.	—	—	—	—
Unamortized Debt Expenses	61,000	81,000	97,000	44,000
Miscellaneous assets	4,658,000	1,942,000	1,440,000,000	1,547,000
Total Assets	$811,958,000	$750,682,000	$707,693,000	$548,446,000

SCOUT PAPER COMPANY (Continued)

COMPARATIVE CONSOLIDATED BALANCE SHEET, AS OF DECEMBER 31
(Taken from reports filed with Securities and Exchange Commission)

LIABILITIES	1973	1972	1971	1970
Loans & current maturity of longterm debt	90,022,000	32,639,000	31,106,000	215,000
Accounts payable etc.	66,452,000	61,017,000	53,503,000	40,485,000
Prov. for Federal Income & State Taxes	10,556,000	9,005,000	8,070,000	10,450,000
Dividends Payable	64,000	64,000	64,000	64,000
Total Current Liabilities	$167,104,000	$102,725,000	$ 92,743,000	$ 51,214,000
Longterm Loans	74,371,000	86,327,000	79,133,000	78,684,000
3% Conv. Debentures, Due 1975	6,189,000	8,103,000	10,162,000	10,305,000
Sinking Fund Debentures	25,500,000	32,402,000	27,477,000	17,200,000
Deferred Federal Income Taxes	33,690,000	27,000,000	28,500,000	—
$4.00 Preferred Stock	2,444,000	2,444,000	2,444,000	2,444,000
$3.40 Preferred Stock	4,684,000	4,684,000	4,684,000	4,684,000
Common Stock	204,971,000	200,927,000	195,581,000	170,248,000
Paid-in Additional Capital	6,012,000	6,030,000	6,035,000	6,300,000
Retained earnings	305,539,000	281,049,000	261,943,000	207,367,000
Stockholders' equity	523,650,000	495,134,000	470,687,000	391,043,000
Less: Treas. stock	18,546,000	1,009,000	1,009,000	—
Net stockholders' equity	505,104,000	494,125,000	469,678,000	391,043,000
Total Liabilities	$811,958,000	$750,682,000	$707,693,000	$548,446,000

COMPARATIVE CONSOLIDATED INCOME ACCOUNT, YEARS ENDED DECEMBER 31

(Taken from reports to Securities and Exchange Commission)

INCOME ACCOUNTS	1973	1972	1971	1970
Sales, Less Discounts, Returns & Allow	$731,510,000	$677,408,000	$623,391,000	$490,676,000
Cost of goods sold	419,215,000	399,831,000	376,185,000	284,293,000
Selling, Administrative & General expense	159,449,000	141,670,000	123,164,000	103,212,000
Depreciation & Depletion	44,312,000	38,342,000	34,013,000	27,544,000
Operating Profit	108,534,000	97,565,000	90,029,000	75,627,000
Other Income	3,990,000	3,522,000	2,033,000	3,023,000
Income before Interest and Taxes	112,524,000	101,087,000	92,062,000	78,650,000
Interest Paid	9,032,000	7,315,000	6,536,000	2,993,000
Income before Taxes	103,492,000	93,772,000	85,526,000	75,657,000
Canadian & State Income taxes	5,690,000	2,710,000	3,055,000	2,530,000
Provision for Federal Income taxes	37,790,000	37,795,000	34,130,000	28,490,000
Net Income to Retained Earnings	60,012,000	53,267,000	48,341,000	44,637,000
Retained Earnings, Beg. of Year	282,064,000	261,943,000	207,367,000	192,027,000
Surplus Credits	2,205,000	–	39,597,000	–
Dividends, Preferred	255,000	255,000	255,000	255,000
Dividends, Common	34,077,000	33,107,000	33,107,000	29,042,000
Retained Earnings end of Year	$305,539,000	$281,049,000	$261,943,000	$207,367,000

From examining the industry as a whole, you have calculated certain key ratios which you use as a standard of comparison. For the paper industry you have compiled the following data.

	1973	1972	1971	1970
Interest Coverage	11.05	12.86	14.09	22.28
Net tangible assets per $1,000 longterm debt	$4,932	$4,566	$4,298	$4,199
Current ratio	2:1	1.9:1	2.1:1	2.2:1
Sales/Inventory	6.5	6.4	6.0	6.8
Sales/Accounts Receivable	8.8	7.8	9.8	7.9
Sales/Assets	82.5	83.5	84.5	83.2
Net Income/Assets	6.5	6.7	6.7	6.4
Net Income/Net Worth	10.5	10.2	9.5	10.0
Capital structure:				
% longterm debt	25%	27%	23%	17.5%
% Preferred Stock	3.0%	4.0%	2.5%	2.5%
% Common Stock & Surplus	72%	69%	74.5%	80%

Common size income statement for the paper industry:

Sales	100%	100%	100%	100%
Cost of Sales	58.7	58.9	60.4	59.8
Selling & Administrative Expenses	22.0	23.1	22.4	21.5
Depreciation	6.0	5.9	5.8	5.9
Operating Income	13.3	12.1	11.4	12.8
Interest expenses	1.0	1.1	1.1	1.0
Net Income before Taxes	12.3	11.0	10.3	11.8
Income Tax	6.0	5.4	5.0	5.1
Net Income	6.3	5.6	5.3	6.7

QUESTIONS

1. Compute the key financial and operating ratios and a common size income statements for 1972 and 1973 for the Scout Paper Company and compare your results with the prevailing industry average. From your comparison evaluate the status of Scout Paper Company.

2. Compute the trends in the income accounts for Scout Paper Company from 1970 through 1973. From your trend analysis, evaluate the status of the company. Compare the advantages and disadvantages of the common size analysis and the trend analysis.

3. From your calculations and the general comments contained in the case give your opinion for the prospects for the Scout Paper Company. Make a crude estimate of next year's earnings. How did you derive your estimate?

4. Comment on the problems encountered when using ratio analysis as an analytical tool.

Case 8

JAMES AND CARL MORRISON

Depreciation and Amortization

In late 1971, Paul Morrison, the founder and guiding force of Morrison Oil, Inc. died, leaving his two sons, Carl and James, to run the firm. Carl and James, although brothers, had never really gotten along and had worked together, despite their mutual dislike, only because it was the wish of their father. Now, with his death, the feud broke into the open and neither brother would even speak to the other. The feud was very distressing to the family since both boys had been brought up and trained by the father with the intent that they would some day take over the business, which he had labored so long and hard to build.

Starting from one wild cat oil well drilled in Houston, Texas in 1936, Paul Morrison had struggled to build the Morrison Oil Co., into a well established producer, refiner, and retailer of oil in the five Texas counties surrounding El Paso. Sales had grown to $60,000,000 by the end of 1971. The main revenues and profits came from the 100 discount, retail gasoline stations that the firm owned and operated. The 100 producing oil wells which were wholly owned by the company provided all the oil production that the retail outlets sold and had sufficient proven reserves to supply the retail needs of the firm for at least the next 10 years. All the refining of the crude oil was done at one of the two refineries located in the suburbs of El Paso and San Angelo, Texas. All property, plant, and equipment used in the business was owned by the firm, since Paul Morrison did not believe in tying himself into long term leases.

In consultation with the family lawyers and accountants, the brothers decided to create two separate companies, which on January 1, 1972 would absorb the equally divided assets and liabilities of the Morrison Oil Co. The two companies were to be known as the Carl Oil Co. and the James Oil Co. and each was to absorb exactly half of the retail outlets, half of the producing wells and reserves, and one of the refineries. Each company would also assume half of the Morrison Oil Co.'s liabilities and stockholders' equity. And so it was, that on January 1, 1972, the Carl Oil Co. received the assets listed in Schedule 1 and assumed $15,000,000 in 10% long term debt repayable at maturity, $15,000,000 in capital stock and $5,000,000 in retained earnings. The James Oil Co. received the assets listed in Schedule 2 and an equal amount of liabilities and stockholders' equity as Carl Oil.

After one year in operation, both firms had their accountants render a balance sheet and income statement as of December 31, 1972. The two different accounting firms both certified that the balance sheets and income statements (Exhibits 1–4) were made in accordance with generally acceptable accounting principles. However, despite that certification, Carl had decided when he started his firm to capitalize his drilling and exploration expenses for the year and then amortize the amount at 10% annually for the next 10 years, starting in the following year. James had decided to expense his drilling and exploration outlays as his father had done before him. The two also differed in their approaches to depreciation. Carl decided to use the straight-line method of depreciation, while James had decided to use the double declining balance method. Both had been satisfied with their accounting procedures and had decided to continue with the same procedures in force during 1973.

During 1973, the two firms experienced a stable period, wherein little changed from the year before. Both firms viewed the period as one of consolidation. Sales for 1973 remained at $30 million for each company, the same as 1972. Current assets rose, but liabilities remained constant. Both the firms spent $1 million on drilling and exploration, but neither firm undertook any capital expansion. Expenses stabilized at the same proportion of sales as they had done in 1972.

EXHIBIT 1
CARL OIL CO.
Balance Sheet, 12/31/72

ASSETS

Current Assets		$ 7,750,000
Plant, Property, & Equipment	$36,000,000	
less accumulated depreciation	3,000,000	
Net Plant, Property, & Equipment		33,000,000
Drilling & Exploration Investment		1,000,000
Total Assets		41,750,000

LIABILITIES

Current Liabilities	5,000,000
Long Term Debt (10% deb '99)	15,000,000
Stockholders Equity	
Capital Stock ($15 par)	15,000,000
Retained Earnings	6,750,000
Total Liabilities	41,750,000

EXHIBIT 2
CARL OIL CO.
Income Statement, 12/31/72

Sales		$30,000,000
Cost of Goods Sold	$15,000,000	
General selling and Administrative expenses	7,000,000	
Depreciation	3,000,000	
		25,000,000
Operating profit		5,000,000
Interest		1,500,000
Net income before taxes		3,500,000
Taxes (50%)		1,750,000
Net Income		1,750,000

EXHIBIT 3

JAMES OIL COMPANY
Balance Sheet, 12/31/72

ASSETS		
Current Assets		$ 9, 500,000
Plant, Property, & Equipment	36,000,000	
less accumulated depreciation	6,000,000	
Net Plant, Property, & Equipment		30,000,000
Total Assets		39,500,000
LIABILITIES		
Current Liabilities		5,000,000
Long Term Debt (10% deb'99)		15,000,000
Stockholders' Equity		
Capital Stock ($15 par)		15,000,000
Retained Earnings		4,500,000
Total Liabilities		39,500,000

EXHIBIT 4

JAMES OIL COMPANY
Income Statement, 12/31/72

Sales		$30,000,000
Cost of Goods Sold	15,000,000	
General Selling & Administrative Expenses	7,000,000	
Depreciation	6,000,000	
Drilling Expense	1,000,000	
		29,000,000
Operating profit		1,000,000
Interest		1,500,000
Net before taxes (50%)		(500,000)
Taxes		—
Net Income (loss)		(500,000)

SCHEDULE 1

CARL OIL COMPANY

Schedule of Assets, 12/31/71

BUILDINGS	COST	DATE ACQUIRED	EXPECTED LIFE	SALVAGE VALUE
Main Office	$10,000,000	1972	20 years	$1,000,000
Field Offices	1,000,000	1972	20 years	0
Retail Stations	6,000,000	1972	20 years	0
PLANT & EQUIPMENT				
Refinery No. 2	10,000,000	1972	10 years	0
Storage Tanks	3,000,000	1972	10 years	0
Other Equipment	6,000,000	1972	6 2/3 years	0

SCHEDULE 2

JAMES OIL COMPANY

Schedule of Assets, 12/31/72

BUILDINGS	COST	DATE ACQUIRED	EXPECTED LIFE	SALVAGE VALUE
Main Office	$10,000,000	1972	20 years	$1,000,000
Field Offices	4,000,000	1972	20 years	0
Retail Stations	6,000,000	1972	20 years	0
PLANT & EQUIPMENT				
Refinery No. 1	10,000,000	1972	10 years	0
Other Equipment	6,000,000	1972	6 years	0

QUESTIONS

1. Explain the differences in the income statements and balance sheets of the two firms as of 1972.

2. Calculate the depreciation for each firm in 1973.

3. Construct the 1973 income statement for each firm. (For simplicity, pattern your answer after the 1972 statement and ignore tax loss.)

4. Construct the 1973 balance sheet for each firm. (For simplicity, pattern your answer after the 1972 statement and assume current assets rose and no dividends paid).

5. In projecting earnings for 1974, for each of the companies, how would you account for the differences in accounting methods. Which firm is more likely to have the higher price earnings ratio based on reported earnings for 1973? How do different accounting procedures hinder ratio analysis of the firms?

Case 9

THE NAT CO.

Liquidity Analysis

The Nat Co. was founded in 1960 by Nathaniel Nast and his two sons, Seth and Steven, to hand tailor men's high quality dress shirts on order from custom-made clothes departments of several large department stores in the area. Most of these stores already had a few tailors who did most of the work, but during the peak season around Christmas they turned to Nat Co. for additional production. In addition, the number of tailors available to the store was declining, and the Nat Co. thought they could fill the demand through some of their assembly line techniques. The firm had been a mild success and had always provided a reasonable salary to the family plus a little profit, but prospects for any rapid growth appeared dim, and the two sons were getting restless. In all of 1967, the firm had sales of $500,000 and a profit after taxes of only $10,000.

In late 1967, Seth approached his father and brother with the idea of producing customized shirts for the bowling industry which was just beginning to show signs of rapid growth, as it was becoming the "in sport." Seth proposed that Nat Co. offer a line of brightly colored sports shirts in a limited number of styles, which the company would embroider with the bowlers first name across the breast pocket and with the emblem and name of the team's sponsor on the back. Late in 1967, Nat Co. embarked on its bowling shirt line.

Just as Seth had predicted, the bowling craze took hold in force in 1968 and the sales of Nat Co. skyrocketed. Sales rose to $2 million in 1968, to $4 million in 1969, to $10 million in 1970, and to $12 million in 1971. Sales were recorded upon the receipt of the order although the billing was not sent until the shirt was shipped. Normally the delay between the order and the shipping was 6 weeks, but in the sudden rush the delay stretched to 6 months. During the delay several customers would cancel their orders for such reasons as switching sponsors, dropping from the team, or otherwise not needing the shirt. Since Nat Co. had not requested a deposit upon order or had otherwise prepared for this, the company reversed the sale, did not bill the customer, and put the finished shirt into inventory, hoping to sell it later. Although, this was very unlikely as the shirt was usually embroidered by that time. As a consequence, despite the sales growth, inventories rose substantially, as reported in Exhibit 1. All during this increase in the inventory, operating efficiencies remained the same, and profits rose from $200,000 in 1968 to $600,000 in 1971.

EXHIBIT 1
NAT CO.
Selected Balance Sheet Items

	CURRENT ASSETS	CURRENT LIABILITIES	INVENTORY
1967	.125 (mil)	.05 (mil)	.1 (mil)
1968	1.0	.7	.5
1969	2.0	1.5	1.5
1970	5.0	4.0	4.5
1971	8.7	8.3	8.6

Selected Income Statement Items

	SALES	COST OF GOODS SOLD	EARNINGS
1967	.5	.4 (mil)	$ 10,000
1968	2.0	1.8	200,000
1969	4.0	3.2	400,000
1970	10.0	8.0	500,000
1971	12.0	10.0	600,000

As shown in Exhibit 1, the Nat Co. inventory rose quite sharply as the delay between orders and shipping increased causing an accompanying increase in the number of cancellations. In an effort to finance this ever growing inventory, the Nat Co. first turned to reducing its cash position, speeding up the collection of its accounts receivable, and delaying payment to its creditors. These actions had worked well until 1970 when the company was forced to resort to a short term bank loan to finance the sharp rise in inventories and a plant expansion to meet the increased sales. The firm arranged with the Local Bank and Trust Co. to borrow $8 million, secured by the firm's inventory. The Nat Co. agreed to repay the entire loan at the end of 1972.

During the course of 1972, it became obvious that the craze in bowling was beginning to wane. Sales began to taper off, and Nat Co. expected a loss by the end of the year, the first in its history. In consultation with the bank, the company was unable to get an extension of the loan or further financing to see it through what it interpreted as a temporary set back in the bowling shirt market. By the end of 1972, sales had dropped to $10 million and earnings had become a loss of $2.0 million, as reported in Exhibit 2. The company's balance sheet, Exhibit 3, showed the firm's policy of accumulating dead inventory. The bank's note was due, and the firm's creditors were pressing for payment, while the firm's major asset was its inventory. The Nat Co. filed for bankruptcy.

EXHIBIT 2

NAT CO.

Income Statement, 1972

Sales		$10,000,000
Cost of Goods Sold	9,000,000	
Selling and General		
Administrative Expenses	1,000,000	
Depreciation	1,000,000	
		11,000,000
Operating Income (loss)		(1,000,000)
Interest		1,000,000
Profit before taxes (loss)		(2,000,000)
Taxes		0
Profit after taxes (loss)		(2,000,000)

EXHIBIT 3

NAT CO.

Balance Sheet, 1972

ASSETS

Current Assets		
Cash		$ 100,000
Accounts Receivable		1,000,000
Inventory		12,400,000
		13,500,000
Plant, Property, Equipment	13,500,000	
accumulated depreciation	7,500,000	
Net plant, property and equipment		6,000,000
Total Assets		19,500,000

LIABILITIES

Current Liabilities		
Notes payable		$ 8,000,000
Accounts Payable		5,000,000
Accrued Taxes		400,000
Others		100,000
		13,500,000
Capital Stock Stock	1,000,000	
Capital Additional Paid-in	2,000,000	
Retained Earnings	3,000,000	
		6,000,000
Total Liabilities		19,500,000

QUESTIONS

1. Compute the current and quick ratios for the Nat Co. in each of the years 1967 through 1972. Examine the trend in these ratios.
2. Comment on the inventory situation. What had happened? Could you have foreseen the possibility of impending difficulty from your examination of the inventory accumulation and inventory policy?
3. Comment on the firm's ability to meet its debt obligations?

Case 10

TYPICAL COMPANIES

Financial Statement Analysis

When John Garrisson first came to work for Irving Archer, vice-president in the investment trust department of First National Town Bank, he had been warned to expect a substantial amount of statistical work as part of his training. Each morning Irving would drop recently received annual financial reports of various companies on John's desk for John to examine and prepare a financial analysis. This morning Irving dropped four reports on the desk. These reports were from Typical Bank, Inc., Typical Airline, Inc., Typical Electrical Power Co., Inc., and Typical Industrial, Inc. The reports are reproduced on the following pages:

Typical Bank, Inc.
Consolidated Statement of Condition

Assets	December 31, 1972
Cash and Due from Banks	$ 6,220,255,436
Investment Securities:	
U. S. Government Obligations, Direct and Guaranteed	770,146,717
Obligations of States and Political Subdivisions	1,591,107,501
Other Securities	270,646,156
Total Investment Securities	2,631,900,374
Trading Account Securities	547,549,475
Investment in Subsidiaries not Consolidated	55,837,015
Mortgages	1,423,278,536
Loans	12,505,720,544
Premises and Equipment	196,669,837
Customers' Liability on Acceptances	496,476,944
Other Assets	448,015,079
	$24,525,703,240

Liabilities	
Deposits:	
Demand	$ 9,695,170,348
Savings and Other Time	4,645,626,840
Overseas Offices	6,886,597,547
Total Deposits	21,227,394,735
Federal Funds Purchased and Securities Sold Under Repurchase Agreements	540,450,000
Other Liabilities for Borrowed Money	166,092,040
Acceptances Outstanding	505,214,852
Accrued Taxes and Other Expenses	166,629,076
Other Liabilities	189,788,250
Reserve for Loan Losses	301,192,004
Capital Funds:	
Capital Notes (4.60% Due 1990)	194,575,000
Convertible Capital Notes (4-7/8% Due 1993)	149,501,900
Total Capital Notes	344,076,900
Stockholders' Equity:	
Common Stock (Par value $12.50 per share)	
(Authorized shares 40,000,000; outstanding shares 1972, 31,881,236; 1971, 31,879,115)	398,515,450
Surplus	500,121,894
Undivided Profits	186,228,039
Reserve for Contingencies	—
Total Stockholders' Equity	1,084,865,383
Total Capital Funds	1,428,942,283
	$24,525,703,240

Typical Bank, Inc. (Continued)
Consolidated Statement of Income

	1972
Operating Income:	
Interest and Other Fees on Loans	$ 836,377,736
Interest and Dividends on Investment Securities:	
U. S. Government Obligations, Direct and Guaranteed	40,396,071
Obligations of States and Political Subdivisions	60,977,363
Other Securities	4,690,737
	106,064,171
Trading Account Income	27,609,567
Trust and Fiduciary Investment Income	48,631,337
Other Income	76,108,338
	1,094,791,149
Operating Expenses:	
Staff	
Salaries	171,747,016
Provision for Thrift-Incentive Contribution	16,021,126
Pension, Social Security and Other Employee Benefits	20,785,224
	208,553,366
Interest Paid on:	
Capital Notes	16,512,875
Federal Funds Purchased and Securities Sold Under Repurchase Agreements	56,050,732
Other Borrowed Money	54,490,593
Deposits	411,673,270
	538,727,470
Net Occupancy Expense	40,041,481
Provision for Loan Losses	20,914,000
Other Expenses	92,511,428
	900,747,745
Income Before Taxes and Securities Gains (Losses)	194,043,404
Less: Applicable Income Taxes	61,033,000
Income Before Securities Gains (Losses)	133,010,404
Securities Gains (Losses), after Applicable Taxes of $21,959,000 and $29,326,180, Respectively	(18,663,760)
Gain on Sale of Investments in Associated Companies, after Applicable Taxes of $1,497,591	2,990,476
Net Income	$ 117,337,120
Per Share, Based on Average Shares Outstanding of 31,881,112 and 31,878,666, Respectively:	
Income Before Securities Gains (Losses)	$4.17
Net Income	3.68
Net Income, Assuming Full Conversion of Convertible Capital Notes	3.49

Typical Airline, Inc.
Consolidated Statement of Operations (thousands)

	Year Ended December 31, 1972
Revenues	
Passenger	$1,014,668
Freight	86,564
Mail	22,433
Express	6,349
Other	2,765
	1,132,779
Expenses	
Flying Operations	340,577
Maintenance	175,610
Passenger Service	122,519
Aircraft and Traffic Servicing	217,374
Promotion	123,778
General and Administrative	54,718
Depreciation and Obsolescence	106,068
	1,140,644
Operating Income (Loss)	(7,865)
Interest and Miscellaneous	
Interest on long-term debt	34,231
Interest income	(4,487)
Interest capitalized	(14,060)
Loss from RW (Note 11)	3,176
Miscellaneous—net (Note 10)	10,386
	29,246
	(37,111)
Federal Income Tax (Credit) (including deferred tax: 1972— ($476; 1971—$11,031) (Note 5)	(10,350)
	(26,761)
Other Income (Loss)	
Net earnings of SC, Inc. (Note 1)	804
Profit (loss) on disposal of property and equipment, net of Federal Income tax effect: 1972—$(180); 1971—$315	(441)
	363
Net Earnings (Loss) for the Year	$ (26,398)
Earnings (Loss) Per Share (Note 7)	
Earnings (loss) per share of common stock	$(1.30)
Earnings per share assuming full dilution	—

Typical Airline, Inc. (Continued)
Consolidated Balance Sheet (in Thousands)

	Year Ended December 31, 1972
Assets	
Current Assets	
Cash	$ 33,236
Marketable securities, at cost	2,800
Receivables	203,856
Spare parts, materials and supplies, at average cost less	
obsolescence reserve (1972—$7,036; 1971—$9,820)	40,315
Prepaid expenses	4,231
Total Current Assets	284,438
Operating Equipment and Property (Notes 2 and 3)	
Flight equipment, at cost	1,276,639
Less: Accumulated depreciation and obsolescence	465,855
	810,784
Cash deposits with manufacturers for purchase of flight	
equipment	184,632
	995,416
Land, buildings and other equipment, at cost	231,183
Less: Accumulated depreciation	65,473
Operating Equipment and Property—Net	1,161,126
Investments and Other Assets	
Investment in and advances to SC, Inc. (Note 1)	27,312
Receivable on sale of aircraft and other equipment (net of	
deferred income and reserve for doubtful accounts:	
1972—$21,392; 1971—$16,238) (Note 4)	27,786
Miscellaneous Investments	7,606
Deferred charges	16,678
Total Investments and Other Assets	79,382
Total Assets	$1,524,946

Typical Airline, Inc. (Continued)
Consolidated Balance Sheet (in Thousands)

	Year Ended December 31, 1972
Liabilities and Stockholders' Equity	
Current Liabilities	
Accounts payable	$ 151,606
Accrued salaries and wages	46,383
Other accrued liabilities	25,284
Long term debt maturing within one year	19,171
Air travel plan subscribers' deposits	9,781
Unearned transportation revenue	25,386
Total Current Liabilities	277,611
Long-Term Debt (Note 4)	
Senior	430,200
Subordinated convertible debentures	282,870
Total Long-Term Debt	713,070
Other Credits	
Deferred federal income tax (Note 5)	146,266
Self-insurance	18,344
Employee stock purchase plan (Note 8)	8,977
Total Other Credits	173,587
Stockholders' Equity (Notes 4, 6, 8, 12 and 13)	
Preferred stock—no par value	
5,000 shares authorized; none issued	
Common stock—$1 par value	
40,000 shares authorized; 20,281 shares issued	
and outstanding	20,281
Additional paid-in capital	96,576
Retained earnings	243,821
Total Stockholders' Equity	360,678
Total Liabilities and Stockholders' Equity	$1,524,946

Typical Airline, Inc. (Continued)
Operating Statistics

	Year Ended December 31, 1972
Revenues, Expenses, Earnings (in thousands)	
Revenues	
Passenger	$1,014,668
Freight	86,564
Mail	22,433
Express	6,349
Other	2,765
Total	1,132,779
Expenses	
Wages, Salaries and Employee Benefits	518,299
Depreciation and Obsolescence	106,068
Other Operating Expenses	516,277
Interest and Miscellaneous	29,246
Federal Income Tax:	
Current	(9,874)
Deferred	(476)
Total	1,159,540
Other Income	
Net earnings of SC, Inc.	$804
Profit (loss) on disposal of property and equipment (net)	(441)
Net earnings (loss)	(26,398)
Common Stock Per Share Information	
Shares outstanding at year end	20,281,000
Book value per share	$17.78
Earnings (loss) per share	(1.30)
Dividends paid per share	.80

Typical Airline, Inc. (Continued)
Operating Statistics

	Year Ended December 31, 1972
Capital Expenditures (in thousands)	
Flight	$118,215
Ground	70,671
Deposits (net change)	(13,182)
Total	175,704
Financial Position at End of Year (in thousands)	
Net Working Capital	$6,827
Operating equipment and property (net)	1,161,126
Long-term debt	
Senior	430,200
Subordinated	282,870
Deferred Federal Income Tax	146,266
Retained earnings at end of year	243,821
Stockholders' Equity	360,678
Number of stockholders	66
Operating Statistics	
Revenue per revenue passenger mile (yield)	5.92¢
Operating expense	
Per available ton mile	20.28¢
Per revenue ton mile	47.42¢
Available passenger seat miles (millions)	34,259
Revenue passenger miles (millions)	18,170
Passenger load factor	50.9%
Revenue plane miles flown (millions)	302
Revenue passenger carried (thousands)	19,438
Ton miles (millions)	
Available	5,623
Revenue (all classes of traffic)	2,405
Freight	463
Mail	105
Express	20

Typical Electrical Power Co., Inc.
Consolidating Statement of Income, Year Ended December 31, 1972

	CONSOLIDATED (after inter-co. eliminations)
OPERATING REVENUES, ELECTRIC	$ 665,667
Income from Subsidiaries Consolidated:	
Dividends on Common Stocks	—
Totals	665,667
OPERATING EXPENSES:	
Operation	278,528
Maintenance	55,951
Depreciation	83,031
Taxes, Other Than Income Taxes	55,907
State Income Taxes	182
Federal Income Taxes	18,051(a)
Provision for Deferred Income Taxes—	
Liberalized Depreciation	5,473(a)
Income Taxes Deferred in Prior Years (Credit):	
Accelerated Amortization	−7,031(a)
Liberalized Depreciation (Amortization of Prior Years' Provisions)	− 984(a)
Total Operating Expenses	489,108
OPERATING INCOME	176,559
OTHER INCOME AND DEDUCTIONS:	
Allowance for Funds Used During Construction	43,810(f)
Miscellaneous Nonoperating Income less Deductions	7,688(f)
Total Other Income and Deductions	51,498
INCOME BEFORE INTEREST CHARGES	228,057
INTEREST CHARGES:	
Long-Term Debt	90,372
Short-Term Debt and Miscellaneous	16,532
Total Interest Charges	106,904
Net Income, Before Preferred Stock Dividend Requirements of Subsidiaries	121,153
Deduct Preferred Stock Dividend Requirements of Subsidiaries	4,267
NET INCOME, APPLICABLE TO COMMON STOCK OF ELECTRIC POWER COMPANY, INC.	116,886
Cash Dividends Paid on Common Stock	84,450
Current Year's Earnings Undistributed	$ 32,436

Typical Electrical Power Co., Inc. (Continued)
Consolidating Balance Sheet, December 31, 1972

	CONSOLIDATED (after inter-co. elimination)
Assets and Other Debits	
UTILITY PLANT (at original cost):	
Production	$1,267,161
Transmission	803,105
Distribution	758,298
General and Miscellaneous	157,856
Construction Work in Progress	784,596
Total Utility Plant	3,771,016(b)
Less Accumulated Provisions for Depreciation and Depletion	879,192(c)
Utility Plant, less Provisions	2,891,824
EXCESS OF COST OF INVESTMENTS in Subsidiaries Consolidated	
Over Book Value at Dates of Acquisition	31,906
OTHER PROPERTY AND INVESTMENTS (less provisions)	107,579(f)
CURRENT ASSETS:	
Cash	43,287
Special Deposits and Working Funds	1,943
Temporary Cash Investments (at cost)	9,652
Accounts Receivable—largely from customers (less provisions)	58,697
Materials and Supplies, including Fuel	76,010
Prepayments and Other Current Assets	7,647
Total Current Assets	197,236
DEFERRED DEBITS	13,343
Totals	$3,241,888

Typical Electrical Power Co., Inc. (Continued)
Consolidating Balance Sheet, December 31, 1972

	CONSOLIDATED (after inter-co. elimination)
Liabilities and Other Credits	
LONG-TERM DEBT	$1,638,493
PREFERRED STOCKS OF SUBSIDIARIES (including premiums)	100,180
COMMON STOCK:	
Electric Power Company, Inc.:	
Shares of $6.50 Par Value: Authorized —65,000,000 Outstanding—54,000,000	351,000(d)
Premium on Common Stock	249,312(d)
Subsidiaries Consolidated	—
OTHER PAID-IN CAPITAL	234
RETAINED EARNINGS	292,642(a)(e)
ACCUMULATED DEFERRED INCOME TAXES	147,312(a)

(Amounts recorded in this account, derived from reductions in Federal income taxes resulting from accelerated amortization and liberalized depreciation, are invested in the business and recorded, in accounts maintained pursuant to various State regulatory requirements, in part as restricted earned surplus and in part as unrestricted earned surplus)) (See* footnote below)

CURRENT LIABILITIES:	
Notes Payable to Banks	30,645
Commercial Paper	207,215
Accounts Payable	84,473
Taxes Accrued	72,494
Other Current Liabilities	54,471
Total Current Liabilities	449,298
DEFERRED CREDITS AND OPERATING RESERVES	6,785
CONTRIBUTIONS IN AID OF CONSTRUCTION	6,632
Totals	$3,241,888(f)
* Restricted Earned Surplus	$ 142,987
Unrestricted Earned Surplus	4,325

Typical Electrical Power Co., Inc. (Continued)
Comparative Consolidated Operating Statistics

	1972
Operating Data	
System capability (in thousands of kw)	$ 12,000(b)
Net system peak load	10,201
Load factor (%)	72.4
Heat rate (Btu per kwh of net generation)	9,689
Tons of fuel used (in thousands)	24,254
Miles of line (pole miles)	87,980
Total Load	
Net generation (in millions of kwh)	56,924
Purchased	6,636
Net interchange	1,105
Total	64,665
Energy Sales	
Residential. . .(in millions of kwh)	11,200
Commercial(c)	6,305
Industrial	30,625
All others(c)	11,996
Total	60,126
Customers—Year-End	
Residential	1,451,284
Commercial(c)	171,054
Industrial	8,852
All others(c)	7,162
Total	1,638,352
Operating Revenues	
Residential (in thousands)	$ 203,044
Commercial(c) (in thousands)	115,764
Industrial (in thousands)	241,789
All other from kwh sales(c) (in thousands)	98,318
Other operating revenues (in thousands)	6,752
Total (in thousands)	$ 665,667

Typical Electrical Power Co., Inc. (Continued)
Comparative Consolidated Operating Statistics

	1972
Residential Customers with Electric Heating	
Customers (Year-End)	138,255
Total kwh used (in millions)	2,981
Revenue from all uses (in thousands)	$ 40,233
Average Use, Bill and Price Per Customer	
Residential Customers with Electric Heating:	
Annual kwh use	23,224
Annual bill	$ 313.39
Price per kwh (cents)	1.35
All Residential Customers:	
Annual kwh use: EP System	7,808
All investor-owned utilities	6,720(P)
Annual bill: EP System	$ 141.55
All investor-owned utilities	$ 149.18(P)
Price per kwh (cents): EP System	1.81
All investor-owned utilities	2.22(P)
All Customers:	
Price per kwh (cents): EP System	1.10
All investor-owned utilities	1.68(P)
Utility Plant[a]—Additions and Retirements	
Gross Additions (less nuclear fuel) (in thousands)	$ 497,532
Gross Additions to nuclear fuel (in thousands)	$ 10,192
Retirements (in thousands)	31,462
Other Changes (in thousands)	−87
Net additions (in thousands)	$ 476,175

[a]Net Utility Plant—based on original cost less accumulated provision for depreciation—was $2,879,056,000 at December 31, 1970. This compares with a net amount of $4,090,278,000 that would be obtained by converting the book balances at December 31, 1939, and subsequent annual changes into terms of 1970 dollars of equivalent purchasing power on the basis of the U. S. Bureau of Labor Statistics Index for the purchasing power of the dollar as measured by consumer prices.

Typical Electrical Power Co., Inc. (Continued)
Statistics of Subsidiary Companies—1972

	Consolidated Subsidiaries (after inter-co. eliminations)
Territory Served	
Communities (population 100 or over)	$ 2,236
Population (in thousands)	5,644
Miles of Line	
23 kv and higher (pole miles)	13,151
Less than 23 kv	74,829
Total	87,980
Total Load	
Net Generation:	
Steam (in millions of kwh)	56,286
Hydro & Pumped Storage (in millions of kwh)	589
Other (in millions of kwh)	49
Total Net Generation (in millions of kwh)	56,924
Purchased (in millions of kwh)	6,636
Net Interchange (in millions of kwh)	1,105
Total Load (in millions of kwh)	64,665
Energy Sales	
Residential (in millions of kwh)	11,200
Commercial (in millions of kwh)	6,305
Industrial (in millions of kwh)	30,625
All others (in millions of kwh)	11,996
Total (in millions of kwh)	60,126

Typical Electrical Power Co., Inc. (Continued)
Statistics of Subsidiary Companies—1972

	Consolidated Subsidiaries (after inter-co. eliminations)
Customers—Year-End	
Residential	1,451,284
Commercial	171,054
Industrial	8,852
All Others	7,162
Total	1,638,352
Operating Revenues	
Residential (in thousands)	$ 203,044
Commercial (in thousands)	115,764
Industrial (in thousands)	241,789
All Other from kwh sales (in thousands)	98,318
Other Operating Revenues (in thousands)	6,752
Total (in thousands)	$ 665,667
Residential Customers with Electric Heating	
Customers (Year-End)	138,255
Total kwh used (in millions)	2,981
Revenue from all uses (in thousands)	$ 40,233
Average Use, Bill and Price	
Residential Customers with Electric Heating:	
Kwh used per customer	23,224
Annual bill	$ 313.39
Price per kwh (cents)	1.35
All Residential Customers:	
Kwh use per customer	7,808
Annual bill	$ 141.55
Price per kwh (cents)	1.81
All Customers:	
Price per kwh (cents)	1.10

Typical Industrial, Inc.
Consolidated Operations

(thousands of dollars)

	1972
Sales	$755,710
Costs and expenses	
Product costs	478,006
Marketing and distribution	147,482
Research, administration and general	43,059
Interest	14,032
	682,579
Income from operations before taxes	73,131
Taxes on income	
Current	
Federal	22,799
State and foreign	3,617
Deferred	3,174
	29,590
Net Income from operations	43,541
Share of the earnings of international affiliates	5,611
Net Income	$ 49,152
Amount earned per common share	$1.42
Dividends per common share	$1.00

Typical Industrial, Inc. (Continued)
Consolidated Balance Sheets

(thousands of dollars)

			December 31 1972
Assets			
Current Assets			
Cash			$ 11,441
Receivable from			
Customers, less reserves for discounts and			
doubtful items of $2,656–1972; $2,595–1971			62,403
Others			9,250
Inventories, at lower of cost (principally latest			
production or purchase cost) or market	**1972**	**1971**	
Finished products	$ 53,837	$ 40,196	
Work in process	17,705	15,231	
Pulp, logs and pulpwood	29,762	22,412	
Other materials and supplies	31,616	29,836	132,920
Prepaid items			7,692
			223,706
Plant Assets, at cost			
Land	9,844	9,455	
Buildings	147,713	133,599	
Machinery and equipment	710,871	667,966	
	868,428	811,020	
Accumulated depreciation	(384,672)	(353,786)	483,756
Timber Resources, at cost less depletion			57,665
Investments in Affiliates, at cost ($56,157–1972;			
$50,387–1971) plus equity in undistributed			
earnings			
International	62,585	52,769	
Domestic	32,343	30,075	94,928
Other Investments, at cost			1,434
Patents, Trademarks and Goodwill			
Other Assets			5,329
Total Assets			$866,818

Typical Industrial, Inc. (Continued)
Consolidated Balance Sheets

(thousands of dollars)

			December 31 1972
Liabilities and Shareholders' Investment			
Current Liabilities			
Payable to suppliers and others			$ 65,966
Loans and current maturities of long term debt			54,020
Dividend declared on preferred shares			64
Estimated taxes on income			8,362
			128,412
Long Term Debt			180,781
Deferred Income Taxes			36,864
Shareholders' Investment			
Cumulative preferred shares without par value			
Authorized—110,640 shares			
Outstanding	**1970**	**1969**	
$3.40 series—46,205 shares	$ 4,684	$ 4,684	
$4.00 series—24,435 shares	2,444	2,444	
Investment of preferred shareholders			7,128
Voting preferred shares			
Authorized—1,000,000 shares			
Issued—none			
Common shares without par value			
Authorized—80,000,000 shares			
Issued—35,102,062 shares—1972;			
35,044,750 shares—1971	212,493	210,983	
Reinvested earnings	320,104	305,539	
	532,597	516,522	
Common shares in treasury, at cost			
630,038 shares—1972;			
616,750 shares—1971	(18,964)	(18,546)	
Investment of common shareholders			513,633
Total Liabilities and Shareholders' Investment			$866,818

QUESTIONS

1. Compute the following financial ratios for each company: current ratio, net profit margin, operating profit margin, times interest earned, debt/equity ratio, return on total assets, return on equity, book value per share.
2. Explain the differences in the ratios in terms of the operating characteristics of each firm. Why are some of the ratios applicable to some of the firms and not to others?
3. Analyze the operating statistics presented in the reports of Typical Airlines and Typical Electrical Power Co. What do they tell you? What other operating characteristics of these firms would be helpful in analyzing the firm?
4. What other information would you need to make a valid interpretation of these financial and operating ratios?

Case 11

THE BETA CO.

Earnings Forecasting

As a security analyst for Harried Up and Co., members of the New York Stock Exchange, you are responsible for covering the pollution control stocks. You are to keep abreast of developments in the pollution field and in individual companies that operate in the field. Each year at this time you are required to estimate the earnings of the companies in the field for next year.

You have decided to start your forecasts with the Beta Co., an old line producer of pollution control chemicals. Beta Co. has been located in the industrial southeast section of Pennsylvania since 1922, when Mr. George Beta first started producing chemicals for the treatment of waste disposal. For years, until the beginning of World War II, the company's main product was carbontryelthene acid, a powerful disinfectant used by several of the chemical companies for cleaning their distillation tanks. During World War II, production shifted to war chemicals, but returned to the cleaning compounds after the war. Sales remained relatively constant until about 1963, when the company developed chemicals for the treatment of chemical plant effluent and sewage disposal wastes. These products met with a growing demand as the nation became more aware of the pollution situation and more assertive in its demands that anti-pollution measures, such as chemical treatment of wastes, be undertaken. Finally, in 1969, the Congress passed an anti-pollution law which required chemical treatment of many wastes.

The control of the Beta Co. remained in the hands of the Beta family, despite a public stock offering in 1955, and the management had remained conservative in its current operations and in its financing of capital expansion. The firm's capital structure never had debt and the firm's liquidity was always kept strong. All expansion was financed through internally generated funds. The firm's 1972 balance sheet, Exhibit 1, reveals that the current ratio is 4 to 1 and that the company's production facilities are relatively new.

EXHIBIT 1

BETA CO.

Balance Sheet, December 31, 1972

ASSETS (000)		
Current Assets		
Cash	$15,000	
Accounts Receivable	2,500	
Inventory	2,500	
Total Current Assets		20,000
Plant, Property and Equipment	30,000	
Accumulated Depreciation	10,000	
Net Plant, Property and Equipment		20,000
Other Assets		5,000
Total Assets		45,000
LIABILITIES (000)		
Current Liabilities		
Accounts Payable	3,400	
Accrued Expenses	500	
Other Current liabilities	100	
Total Current Liabilities		5,000
Stockholder's Equity		
Capital Stock $10 par outstanding		
1972–1 million shares)		10,000
Capital in excess of par		10,000
Retained Earnings		20,000
Total Liabilities		45,000

An examination of the firm's historical earnings record for the past ten years, Exhibit 2, shows that earnings have grown steadily from year to year, although during the recession of 1965 the growth was not as rapid. A large jump in earnings occurred in 1969 when the anti-pollution act became law. In 1969 earnings doubled from $600,000 to $1.2 million.

EXHIBIT 2

BETA CO.

Net Earnings and Dividends Per Share

1963-1972

	NET EARNINGS (000)	DIVIDENDS PER SHARE
1963	$ 100	$.02
1964	300	.02
1965	350	.04
1966	400	.05
1967	500	.05
1968	600	.10
1969	1,200	.15
1970	1,400	.20
1971	1,700	.25
1972	2,100	.30

In speaking to the management of Beta, you learn that they are very optimistic and expect to grow at approximately the same rate as they have done in the last ten years, barring any unforeseen slowdown in the economy or change in the anti-pollution movement. Since neither one of these is anticipated, the firm should be operating in an environment similar to that which prevailed in 1972, which is about average for the last decade.

The firm is presently operating at 90% of capacity which management claims is their desired operating level. But in the expectation of increased sales, the firm plans to double its capacity over the next ten years. A new $10 million complex is already nearing completion and should be on stream at the beginning of 1973. The complex is expected to operate at about the same efficiency as the other plants and is designed to expand production capacity by 90% of its rated capacity in 1973, not to replace the existing facilities. In your discussions, management has told you they have a target rate of return of 10% on net plant, property and equipment. Further, they plan no new equity or debt financing in the coming year, despite the new plant, because of their currently strong cash position and the future earnings they expect to generate. All in all, management expects earning to increase again to another record level.

With the data you have gathered, you return to your office to estimate next year's earnings for Beta. Several methods of estimation are available. Your firm requires that you estimate earnings at least several different ways and reconcile the differences in your report. Your report requires you to calculate Beta's growth rate and to extrapolate your earnings projections under the various methods of graphic analysis, moving average, and trendline analysis as well as what your firm calls the return on investment method. This last method requires that you project Beta's net plant, property and equipment figure for the coming year, apply an appropriate rate of return, and make your projection from that.

QUESTIONS

1. Calculate the simple and the compound growth rate in net earnings for Beta from 1963 to 1972, inclusive. Project 1973 net earnings using your compound growth rate.

2. Using semilogarithmic graph paper, plot the net earnings in the last ten years and extrapolate to derive your 1973 projection. Using arithmetic graph paper, plot the net earnings of Beta for the past ten years and extrapolate your 1973 projection. What is your estimate of earnings per share in each case? Explain the difference between your two estimates?

3. Using a three year moving average of Beta's net earnings growth, project 1973 net earnings.

4. Fit a trendline to Beta's net earnings for the last ten years and extrapolate your estimate for Beta's 1973 net earnings. Compare the pre 1969 and the post 1969 periods and explain any differences. Would your comparison lead you to make any adjustments to your trendline fit? Explain.

5. Using the return on investment approach, estimate Beta's net earnings for 1973 (for simplicity ignore 1973 depreciation expense).

6. Compare the estimates you have obtained in your answers to 1-5 and reconcile any differences.

Case 12

GENERAL AUTOS

Earnings Forecasting

General Autos is the largest automobile manufactuer in the nation with sales of over $30 billion in 1972. The firm produces a complete line of passenger cars ranging from small compact models to luxurious limousines, covering the entire spectrum of prices from $2,000 to $15,000. In addition, the firm has interests in trucks, home appliances, and heavy industrial equipment, although these account for a relatively small portion of total sales and earnings. Over the years, the firm has managed to maintain a high return on its investment, averaging over 15% annually, but because of the nature of the automobile market, its sales and earnings have been cyclical. Almost without exception during the period after World War II until the present, the company's sales and earnings have fluctuated almost in unison with the national economy. All efforts by management to smooth this cyclical pattern have failed for one reason or another, and the decision has been made to just live with the business cycle by keeping a large cushion of liquid reserves to meet sudden downturns in the economy and to improve the company's economic forecasting as much as possible.

The firm's major competitors also offer full lines in the passenger car, almost in direct price and product competition. On several occasions, competitors have tried to capture a larger share of the passenger car market by biting into General Autos commanding position in the field. But despite all their efforts, General Autos still maintains a 50% shrae of the market. In the last ten years, General AM Autos' share of the domestically produced passenger car market has never shrunk below 50% and on rare occasions has actually risen to 56%, although management intentionally tries to avoid capturing too large a share of the market for fear of government anti-trust action. The really threatening competition for the firm and the industry in general comes from the importation of foreign produced automobiles, particularly in the less expensive compact end of the line. Foreign autos have captured close to 10% of the domestic U.S. market, but General Autos and the industry have introduced their own less expensive compacts and believe they have stabilized the imports at 10% of the market for at least the next few years.

In the last ten years, General Autos has developed sophisticated models for economic forecasting which has allowed it to maintain a reasonably stable net profit margin on sales, despite fluctuations in the economy and in sales. On average, net profit margins have been 10%, although in recessions they have shrunk to 9% and in unexpected boom periods they have risen to 11%. Management has been most innovative in this area and has developed a system of dealer discounts and production schedulings which allows a quick and rapid adjustment to changes in sales and so assures a constant profit margin.

As a new, young statistically-oriented financial analyst for the stock brokerage firm of Wilton & Company, Jerry Grimes, has been asked to project General Autos' earnings for the coming year. He has fully grasped the fact that General Autos' sales are cyclical and highly correlated with the general economy and has gathered data on both the Gross National Product (GNP) and the auto industry's sales for the last 10 years, Exhibit 1. He has also talked with Wilton & Company's economist, Abe Hooper. Abe predicts that the economy will grow about 3.9% in current dollar terms in the coming year with GNP rising from its present level of $866 billion to $900 billion. Abe has compiled a survey of all the GNP estimates among the economists at the Business Economist's local chapter which shows estimates of GNP ranging from $890 billion to $910 billion, with the most commonly mentioned figure being $900 billion.

EXHIBIT 1

	GNP (bil)	AUTO INDUSTRY SALES (bil)
1963	$483	$36.9
1964	503	37.0
1965	519	34.4
1966	556	40.1
1967	591	43.4
1968	632	45.8
1969	684	53.2
1970	750	53.9
1971	794	53.7
1972	866	60.7

QUESTIONS

1. Using the accompanying worksheets, calculate by regression analysis the relationship between the GNP and the auto industry's sales.
2. Estimate General Auto sales for next year, assuming the firm maintains its historical share of the market. If its share of the market is expected to rise to 55% next year what would your estimate be then?
3. Estimate General Auto's net earnings for next year, assuming it maintains its average net profit margin. If you expect the net profit margin to rise to 12% what would your net earnings estimate be?

$$\text{formula for slope: } b = \frac{\Sigma XY - \Sigma X\, \Sigma Y/n}{\Sigma X^2 - (\Sigma X)^2/n}$$

$$\text{formula for intercept: } a = \frac{1}{n}[\Sigma Y - b\Sigma X]$$

1973 projection of auto industry sales = a + b(est. 1973 GNP)

WORKSHEET

Regression GNP and Auto Industry Sales

YEAR	X(GNP)	Y (AUTO SALES)	XY	x^2
1963				
1964				
1965				
1966				
1967				
1968				
1969				
1970				
1971				
1972				
Total				

Case 13

THE P & D TOOTHPASTE CO.

Market Penetration

Marshall Jones is a security analyst with the Wall St. investment banking firm of Red, Welding and Co., an old line firm with many large financial institutions as clients. Marshall's job since he joined the firm in 1969, after several years with other firms in the industry, has been to investigate and to report to the large institutional clients the information he has gathered on potential special situations (which, in his opinion, may be profitable) and to relate the conclusions he has drawn from that information. Among the many signs that Marshall constantly looks for is the shift in market share among established firms within a large, well defined but growing market. Towards this aim, he is in contact with the management of all the firms within such industries as the automobile manufacturers, the toothpaste manufacturers, the soap producers, and the cereal companies, each of which is dominated by a few large firms, with well defined shares of the total market, who are always trying to capture a larger share through the introduction of new products and advertising campaigns.

Marshall has heard a rumor that the P & D toothpaste company, one of the major manufacturers of toothpaste in the country has begun test marketing a new toothpaste called Nadir which is reported to be the most effective advance to date in the prevention of tooth decay—one of the major reasons people buy toothpaste. If this is true, it could very well increase P & D's share of the market, boost its earnings, and increase the price of P & D's stock.

The toothpaste market, as Marshall discovered from his preliminary research before approaching the P & D management for an interview, had $100 million sales in 1972, up from $95.2 million in 1971, $90.7 in 1970, and $86.4 in 1969. The national market for the product was expected to increase at about the same 5% compound annual growth it had experienced over the last decade. This growth in sales revenues had come mainly from the increase in the population, particularly in the under 18 year old category which used almost 60% of all the toothpaste and by price increases which were slightly less than the rate of inflation for the general economy.

Marshall also learned that the general marketing strategy revolved around three basic points: (1) decay prevention, (2) cosmetic whiteness, and (3) clean breath. The Cosmetic and Drug Report, the trade journal of the industry, reported that 75% of all toothpaste bought was purchased on the consumer's belief it would fight tooth decay. The other 25% of toothpaste purchases were for cosmetic reasons and breath reasons. As a consequence, most industry advertisement was directed at these themes. Another interesting point which Marshall discovered in his preparation was that although 60% of all toothpaste was consumed by those under the age of 18 years, almost all toothpaste was purchased by the wife in the family with the thought that she was doing the right thing for her children by preventing decay. As a result, the family dentist usually played a large part in guiding the family's choice of brands, since he was the recognized expert in the field to which the family turned for advice.

The toothpaste industry itself consisted of 10 major producers, who had held almost constant shares of the market for years. The undisputed leader was the C & P Toothpaste Company with a steady 30% of the market. Its major brand, Colplate, had been a standard for years and had remained almost unchanged except for the package and some of the advertising, because the management did not want to tamper with success. The other producers fell in behind C & P with P & D having 10%, Pepipaste having 10% and the others with their fragmented but steady shares of 2% to almost 10%.

The industry had remained in this relative competitive position among the companies for years, despite large advertising campaigns by each of the firms to carve out a bigger share of the market. The competitive strategy dictated that large amounts of advertising, as much as 20% of sales revenues would be devoted to direct public advertising such as television and magazines as well as to promotional advertising such as personal calls by the firm's representatives on dentists. The other selling expenses, including the cost of maintaining a sales force, was another major expense. The cost of the product itself was only about 20% of each sales dollar. On average, firms in the industry experienced a 15% net profit margin after taxes. It was very unlikely that this would increase for any spurt in profit was usually plowed back into the advertising budget in an attempt to increase market penetration.

P & D was no exception to the industry average. Its annual report, Exhibit 1, revealed that its sales were $10 million in 1972 and its advertising expense was 20% of its sales revenues.

EXHIBIT 1

P & D TOOTHPASTE CO.
Income Statement, 1972

Net Sales		$10,000,000
Cost of Goods Sold	2,000,000	
Advertising Expense	2,000,000	
Selling and General Admin. Expenses	2,000,000	
Depreciation	1,000,000	7,000,000
Operating Income		3,000,000
Net Before Taxes & Interest		3,000,000
Taxes (50%)		1,500,000
Net Income		1,500,000

P & D's 10% of the toothpaste market came from its two brands, NO-D-K, an anti-decay toothpaste and Klean, a cosmetic toothpaste. These two brands were the only products in the P & D line and accounted for 100% of the firm's sales. This made P & D much more dependent on the toothpaste market than several of the other firms that had interests in such diversified areas as soap detergent, household cleaners, and chemicals.

Late in 1969, the firm's chemists had, after years of experimentation, discovered that a small amount of flouride in the toothpaste appeared to prevent decay. This conformed with the Federal Government's studies on the use of flouride in the drinking water of certain cities. P & D undertook much more extensive testing of the new toothpaste with flouride added, which they branded Nadir. In an effort to insure the reliability of the study and to give it more impact, the firm asked for and got the cooperation of the U.S. Dental Association (USDA) in supervising the testing procedures. The results of the test and a possible USDA endorsement of Nadir as an effective decay prevention aid within a proper program of oral hygiene were, according to rumor, imminent. With this background information Marshall arranged for a short interview with the management of P & D.

Marshall learned from the management that it was true they were conducting the rumored tests but that any further results would have to wait a formal announcement from the USDA team conducting the experiment. However, on the initial results of the company's own chemists and a local test market for Nadir with advertising based on those results, the firm's share of that local test market had increased to 40% and was still doing well. Management estimates that if the USDA report is favorable and an endorsement is forthcoming, they could probably capture as much as 50% of the national market. Half of this increase should, management figures, come at the expense of C & P's market share, which could shrink to as low as 10% if the Nadir brand is very successful. In response to Marshall's question as to the effect on profit margins of a Nadir success, the management responded that they did not plan to change their pattern of operation and would continue to spend 20% on advertising and another 20% on other selling and general administrative expenses. Their goal would still be 15% net profit on each sales dollar. In addition, Marshall surmised from the discussion, although he was not directly told, that the cost of producing the Nadir brand with its added ingredient would be no more expensive than the other brands and that Nadir's price would be about the same which prevailed for other toothpastes. Other than that, P & D management was very guarded in its discussions, not wishing to violate any disclosure guidelines of the Securities and Exchange Commission.

When Marshall returned to his office, he examined the stock market information on P & D and on C & P. P & D was presently selling at $7.50 a share or ten times its 1972 earnings per share of $.75. In the last week the stock had risen in response to the rumors about Nadir from 5 1/4 on relatively large volume, despite the reluctance of P & D to confirm or deny the rumor or to release any further information other than that which they had given Marshall. Before the rumors started about a week ago, C & P stock sold for $45 a share or 15 times reported 1972 earnings per share. Since the rumor, C & P stock had fallen slightly to $44 a share. Other toothpaste manufacturers which prior to the rumor, had sold at about seven times reported earnings had also experienced a slight drop in their stock prices.

QUESTIONS

1. Assuming Nadir receives the USDA endorsement, project the firm's 1973 sales and profits if its market penetration increases to 30%, 40%, or 50%? Assuming half of all P & D's increased market penetration comes at the expense of C & P's brands, what would be the effect on C & P's 1973 toothpaste sales and profits if P & D captured 30% of the national market, 40%, 50%?

2. What effect would any USDA endorsement have on the price-earnings ratios of C & P and of P & D? What would be the effect on their respective growth rates? What would be the probable effect on their stock prices? If the USDA did not give its endorsement to the Nadir brand, what would be the immediate possible effect on the stock prices of each firm? Assuming the USDA withheld its endorsement but did not refute the results of P & D's chemist, what do you think would happen if the local test market results were indicative of the nation?

3. If Marshall had decided the following probabilities were indicative of P & D's market share after any USDA announcement, what would be his expected sales and expected profits for P & D in 1973?

1973 share of market	probability
10%	15%
20	15
30	20
40	20
50	30

4. Comment on Marshall's emphasis on P & D's marketing ability and strategy and his almost total disregard for P & D's financing or production capability. Do you think a good analyst can afford to ignore these latter two areas of a firm's operations, particularly in this case? How could the financing and production areas offset any successful marketing strategy?

Case 14

FAST DOG, INC.

Market Saturation

Jim Swing, a security analyst with a New York Stock Exchange member firm, is responsible for retailing stocks. Among the industries which he has followed successfully has been the fast food retailers. In 1965, when the fast food franchises were just beginning to become recognized among the larger financial institutions, Jim had been among the first to recommend the purchase of Fast Chicken and Fast Dog, both of which had since that time shown a very outstanding growth performance and had performed well. The stock of Fast Dog had risen over 700% since Jim's original recommendation from a low of $10 a share adjusted for the 3 for 1 stock split in 1968 and the 100% stock dividend in 1970 to its present price of $75 a share. Jim, being one of the first analysts to recommend the stock, naturally had a good relationship with the management of Fast Dog and a good working knowledge of the industry and of that particular company.

Jim had seen the industry grow from a small base of only $20 million in annual sales to its $850 million in 1972. The industry had started in the Southeastern U.S., where under the guidance of a local restauranteur, a small cafe featuring chicken as a specialty had begun to do a thriving business in outgoing orders of its specially prepared chicken. Several interested parties from outside the area who had happened to stop at the restaurant noticed this and asked the owner for his secret recipe. He had refused but he did offer to go into partnership with several of the people. He would supply the recipe for a fee, and they would establish the business. Several of these restaurants were established, when a certain Charles Hughes decided to apply the cooking technique of high pressure to speed up the process. In conjunction with the owner of the chicken recipe he decided to establish a chain of these restaurants, but the lack of financing forced them to take in partners on a franchise basis, and the idea of selling franchises in the fast food business was born.

From there the idea grew. It was formally established that the Fast Chicken franchises would be uniform in operation, including appearance and menu and could be purchased from the parent company at a set figure plus a fee of 5% of the franchise's gross sales. The Fast Chicken franchise was an immediate success. This success enouraged the competition, among the first of which was Fast Dog.

The fast food franchise industry grew rapidly. The number of franchisers in the industry belonging to the Fast Food Franchisers Association formed in late 1967 totaled 350 by the end of 1972, up from the original 2, Fast Chicken and Fast Dog.

Not only had the number of franchisers increased, but also, as a direct result, the number of franchised outlets offering the same type of fast food and the variety of types of outlets increased rapidly. It was no uncommon for Jim to see several franchise outlets offering a wide variety of foods ranging from chicken and hot dogs to tacos and pizzas along his drive home from work where previously only a Fast Chicken outlet had stood by itself.

TABLE 1

FAST FOOD FRANCHISE INDUSTRY

	SALES (000)	NO. OF FRANCHISERS
1965	$ 20,000	2
1966	40,000	10
1967	80,000	15
1968	150,000	30
1969	300,000	80
1970	600,000	160
1971	750,000	200
1972	850,000	350

Jim began to wonder about the degree to which this proliferation in the number of franchisers and of outlets could continue before the competition began to take its toll on the large, growing profits which almost all the firms in the industry were reporting. According to the Fast Food Franchiser, trade journal of the industry association, sales for the industry were expected to continue their almost uninterrupted climb into 1973 and beyond. To satisfy his curiousity and resolve his concern, Jim took the annual reports of a 10 firm sample from among the industry leaders and constructed his own indicators of the industry's progress. In Table 2, Jim traced the average net profit margins, the average rate of return on total capital, and the average sales per outlet for his 10 firm sample from 1965 to 1972. His results were disquieting. While the industry had boomed and profits for all the firms had continued to grow, some of the other measures of profitability within the industry had declined. Jim, therefore, decided to undertake a review of his entire position on the industry's prospects.

TABLE 2

AVERAGE INDUSTRY FIGURES
(adjusted for inflation)

	NET PROFIT MARGINS	RETURN ON CAPITAL	OUTLET SALES/OUTLET
1965	25%	30%	$200,000
1966	25	25	175,000
1967	25	25	175,000
1968	20	18	150,000
1969	15	17	135,000
1970	10	15	130,000
1971	5	13	115,000
1972	3	8	90,000

In a recent interview, the president of the industry trade association predicted with great confidence that sales for the industry would surpass the $1,000 million mark in 1973. He cited the tremendous continuing growth in the number of outlets under construction and the increased frequency with which people were going out to eat as definite signs of improvement in the industry's prospects. He predicted that there would not be a place in the entire country within a few years that would not have a variety of fast food franchise outlets "to provide the consumer with what he wants."

The president of the trade association also commented on the impending investigation of the industry by the U.S.Congress in response to what some columnists had called the shady practices of some fast food franchisers. It had been reported that several companies within the field were offering franchises on promises of profit and performance that could not reasonably be reached.Several people who had purchased these franchise outlets had either never seen the franchiser again after placing a downpayment or had been so long delayed by excuses that they lost interest and forfeited their deposits. The Federal Trade Commission and the Congress now planned an investigation into these allegations.

The president simply stated that he expected the investigation to reveal that only a few instances of this had occurred among franchisers who were not members of his association. He assured everyone that this could not happen within the association and suggested that any potential franchise purchaser write to his organization for references on the franchiser before placing a deposit. He reiterated his oft uttered statement that franchising was making capitalism available to the people and that soon through the modern method of franchising everyone could be his own boss and run his own business.

Jim had noticed that when the investigation was first announced the stocks of most of the fast food franchisers had declined but had recovered after a few days and were now again hitting new highs. He also noticed that the president of the association had discounted fears of any impending shakeout in the industry, saying it was as strong as ever and that its future growth was assured by the millions of people who had come to accept the fast food franchise outlet as a way of life.

Knowing that his clients were very heavily invested in Fast Dog, Inc. at his suggestion, Jim turned to a review of the company and its operations. Fast Dog had started in the same geographical area as had Fast Chicken, but instead of specializing in chicken, it sold hot dogs boiled in beer. It, too, had experienced a great success from the start and owned none of the outlets. The number of franchised Fast Dog outlets rose rapidly from only 12 in 1965 to 200 by the end of 1972, as revealed in Jim's Table 3. Net earnings for the firm had grown equally as rapidly from only $1.2 million in 1965 to over $5.16 million in 1972 According to the 1972 annual report of the company, 2/3 of its net income in 1972 was derived from the 5% franchise fee which the parent company collected

TABLE 3

FAST DOG

	NET EARNINGS (000)	NO. OF OUTLETS
1965	$1,200	12
1966	1,440	20
1967	1,730	28
1968	2,007	45
1969	2,480	90
1970	2,990	130
1971	3,580	160
1972	5,160	200

from every dollar of sales at each of the franchised outlets. The other third of 1972 net income came from the sale of franchises. It was the policy of Fast Dog, Inc. to sell to the individual owner the right to operate as a Fast Dog outlet for an initial fee ranging from $20,000 to $50,000, depending on the site selected and on the prospects for the individual outlet. The parent company required at least a 10% payment on this fee from the purchaser of the outlet and would arrange to have the remainder financed for 10 years through a local bank in the area for the purchaser under the guarantee of the parent company. When the advance was paid and the remainder financed, the total amount of the sale price would be recorded as revenue to the parent company under the accounting policy of Fast Dog, Inc.

In an interview with the president of Fast Dog, Inc., Mr. Joe Shimk, Jim learned that the firm expected to franchise only 20 new outlets in 1973, at an average price about equal to that which prevailed in 1972. Mr. Shimk credited the decline in the number of new units to a tight money situation which prevented the financing of new outlets. Jim also learned that in some areas of the firm's territory, there was some price cutting. Because of price competition, some of the outlets had to lower prices to 29¢ for a hot dog from the regular 49¢. While Mr. Shimk was not pleased with this, he did not say it would not affect the parent firm's earnings because the number of outlets having to do this was still very few. In addition, even with the price cutting, almost all of the outlets were still profitable. In the overall picture, Mr. Shimk thought 1973 would be a banner year for Fast Dog, Inc. In total, sales at outlets were going to set a new record, which should help the parent company's earnings since it gets 5% of the total. Only ten outlets were losing money and in danger of going out of business, thus causing the parent company to pay off the remainder of the bank loan which it had guaranteed. However, Mr. Shimk thought Fast Dog had set aside a sufficient reserve to handle any such situation.

QUESTIONS

1. What signs are there of saturation in the fast food franchise industry? If saturation does occur, what is the probable effect on the sales, profits, and selling prices of the firms within the industry? Give reasons for your answers. What might specifically happen to Fast Dog's earnings from its sales of franchises and its commission on sales if saturation occurs? What effect might the failure to pay their bank loans of many of Fast Dog's franchises have on the profits and cash position of the parent company?

2. What does the president of the trade association mean by an "industry shake-out"? How does this fit the concept of the industrial life cycle?

3. What effects would you normally expect from a situation of saturation in any industry on the stock prices, growth prospects, and the price-earnings ratios of companies within that industry? Give reasons for your answers? Is Fast Dog more likely to suffer in an industry shakeout than for example, a relatively new firm with a marginal position in the industry? Give reasons for your answer.

4. Reconcile the trade association president's prediction of a new record in total industry sales with the indication of an impending industry shakeout. How is it possible to have both at the same time? Why does no one but Jim seem to be worried about an industry shakeout?

5. The stock of Fast dog, Inc. was split 3 for 1 and also had 100% stock dividend, what was the original price at which Jim first recommeded the stock? What might cause the prices of stocks in the industry to dip in response to the announcement of a Congressional investigation? State your answer in terms of earnings prospects and business risk.

Case 15

POULTRY PACKERS, INC.

Earnings Forecasting

When Alex Gore had first started working as a security analyst for Ira Heap & Co. about ten years ago, he had hoped to receive the responsibility for investigating and reporting on the then glamorous and rapidly growing aerospace stocks. However, he was charged with the food companies, instead. This meant he had to keep track of the events in all the companies engaged in the growing, processing, and distributing of foodstuffs. Taking his disappointment in stride, he had set out to familiarize himself with the operating procedures of the industries and companies involved.

Among the first companies Alex encountered was Poultry Packers, Inc., a newly formed firm started by two mid-western farmers with the idea of raising frying and broiling chickens on a large-scale, automated basis. Up until then, most chickens were raised on small farms, which usually devoted only part of their time to chicken raising. As a result, the cost of producing chickens was quite high. Poultry Packers hoped to lower that cost considerably by the more economical purchases of feed in large quantities, better feed mixtures which encouraged faster growth in the chickens, and other scientific and automated procedures which produced a consistently meatier, healthier, and tastier chicken for lower labor and production costs per chicken.

The fryer and broiler chickens which the firm sold were dressed and frozen in the firm's own, nearby plant and then shipped at the prevailing wholesale price to large customers, mostly supermarket chains and fast food operations specializing in chickens.

For several years after its inception, the firm had done well and sales and profits had grown. Then, in the second half of the 1960's, other firms began to use the automated, large scale chicken raising techniques and soon the industry was plagued by overcapacity, which caused the wholesale price of chickens to fall. The wholesale price fell, until, in 1972, it was only $.15 a pound, or half of what it was in 1965. At the present price, chicken was one of the least expensive meats in the family food budget, and it was estimated by the Department of Agriculture that per capita consumption had doubled from 1965 to almost 6 pounds per person in 1972, because of the price decline. Based on that information, Alex figured that for every 5¢ per pound change in the price, the per capita consumption would change 1 pound, or approximately 200 million pounds for the industry.

While the price decline had increased the industry's sales volume, it had adversely affected the profit margins and profits of companies within the industry. Many of the firms were operating at substantial losses, and it was rumored that one large producer, a subsidiary of a major food processing firm, with sales of 100 million pounds of chicken a year was planning on leaving the industry. Poultry Packers might have been able to capture as much as 25% of the other firm's annual sales in the event it did leave the industry. This could have been a significant increase in Poultry Packers' sales, which in 1972, amounted to 200 million pounds, almost 16% of the market, for a sales revenue of $30 million. Poultry Packers' management also expected that in 1973, the supply-demand situation should be more in balance and that some firming in the price could be expected. But, the management was not as optimistic on the industry's attempts to get Federal government support for prices.

Alex also learned from management that they expected the price of beef, the chief competition chicken raisers faced in their fight for the consumers' food spending, to rise. According to the latest Department of Agriculture's report, the supply of beef cattle in the feeding farms of the United States had dwindled in the face of increased, less expensive imports of beef from Australia and New Zealand. But, with the recent devaluation of the U.S. Dollar, the price of the imported beef was now comparable to domestic beef, although it would take at least two years for the domestic beef raising industry to bring production back to the level of prior years. Poultry Packers' chief economist estimates that the price of beef should rise to $1.30 a pound in 1973 from its present $1.20 a pound. This ten cents a pound increase in beef could mean additional sales of 1 million pounds of chicken to the firm.

Poultry Packers' economist had also recently completed a study for the company on the demographic factors which affect chicken consumption in the United States. He showed this report to Alex. Based on the last ten years, the study showed that meat and poultry consumption per capita averaged 30 pounds a year, with chicken being 20% of the total. The study showed that according to Department of Agriculture figures, almost all the chicken consumed was by people over 15 and under 60. The Census Bureau estimated that 3 million people would enter and that another 1 million would leave that age span in 1973.

Further, in his discussions with management, Alex learned that the business of automated poultry raising was one of the relatively high fixed costs. Fixed costs were $5,000,000 in 1972 for poultry packers. Most of the equipment was expensive, but, once in place, it did most of the work. The only major variable cost was the feed which management estimated costs $.21 a chicken over the one year raising cycle. All other variable expenses including the labor, administrative, and selling expenses Alex figured were 9¢ a chicken. The average weight of a chicken Alex was told was about 3 pounds, for at this weight, the chicken generally had the most flavor and the highest meat to waste ratio. If the chicken was allowed to grow any larger, it lost some of its consumer appeal and had to be sold as a soup chicken at a lower price.

Alex also learned that the firm was evaluating the possibility of installing a new computer which through its servo-mechanical peripheral equipment would control the preparation of the feed and the entire feeding process, as well as automate the firm's bookkeeping and accounting operations and allow greater cost control. Alex estimated that the new computer would double the firm's fixed costs but bring the variable costs per chicken down to about 8¢ a pound. Alex expected that the firm would lease the new computer, as it did the other machinery, if it decided to replace the old machinery, because the firm had not borrowed money since it paid off its bank loans in 1965 and now had a reasonably comfortable cash position.

QUESTIONS

1. Compute Poultry Packers' present breakeven point and operating profit. Recompute Poultry Packers' operating profit if the wholesale price of chicken rose to $.20 a pound. What is the effect on the firm's operation profit margin if the price goes to $.20 a pound? Explain this effect in terms of the relationship between the firm's fixed costs and the variable costs. What do you conclude about the effect of the price of chicken on the firm's profits?

2. Assuming the price of beef rose $.10 a pound, what would be the effect on Poultry Packers' operating earnings? Why?

3. Compute the firm's operating earnings if the 2 million 1973 population increase forecasted by the Census Bureau is correct (assume the other factors used in your answers to questions 1 and 2 are constant at their 1972 levels and the price per pound is $.15).

4. If the Food and Drug Administration suddenly announced it had discovered that chickens contained mercury, what would be the effect on the firm's earnings prospects and its share price? Give specific reasons for your answer.

5. If the large producer which is rumored to drop out did so at the beginning of 1972, what effect, in specific figures, would this have had on Poultry Packers' 1972 operating profits?

6. Assuming the firm leases the new computer, what would be the effect on its breakeven point and on operating profits? Recompute your answer in question number 1 assuming the new computer is leased and the price is $.15 a pound. Is the firm better off with the new computer in terms of profits?

Case 16

McCLAIN INDUSTRIES

Earnings Forecasting under Risk

Towards the end of 1972, John Axle, a security analyst with Merrill, Link and Co., made a routine field trip to speak to the management of McClain Industries, a producer of heavy industrial equipment. He met with Paul McClain, the founder and president of McClain Industries, who talked of the company's prospects for the coming year.

Much of McClain's production was sold to the cyclically-prone automobile industry or to the sheet metal working industry. Both industries made extensive use of the firm's stamping and milling machines which were the mainstays of the McClain line. All of the company's products were made to order, with a lead time of approximately two months from the time of order to shipment. As is common among the heavy machinery producers, their orders fluctuated substantially over the business cycle. They were among the first to feel a pick up or a slackening in the economy. As a consequence, it was most important that John consistently be alert to the present state and the prospects for the economy when trying to forecast McClain Industries' earnings.

During the interview, McClain told John he expected McClain Industries could earn at least $1.00 a share in 1973, equal to the $1.00 in 1972 on the 10 million shares outstanding, and could earn up to $1.50 a share if the economy picked up and if the new sales campaign and the new electronically controlled milling and stamping machines scheduled for introduction to the market in January, 1973 were successful. Paul McClain explained that despite estimated sales of only $100 million in 1972 with a cpacity of $130 million, the company was building a new plant to go on stream in 1973 to replace what McClain considered inefficient plant and to produce the new electronically automated machinery which the competition already had on the market. He realized that this would place a burden on the firm's immediate earning power if the new products did not succeed, but he felt that in any event it would not jeopardize the solvency of the company since the new plant was being financed from retained earnings and the firm's comfortable cash position. According to Paul McClain, there was a 60% chance that the new machines would be an immediate commercial success, and would raise his minimum expected 1973 earnings per share by $.20. Even if the new machines were not a commercial success, Paul McClain still estimated $1.00 a share earnings for 1973.

McClain also told John of his new sales campaign designed to better the competition. The firm's marketing department had convinced him to introduce the lay-a-way plan for credit purchases, under which customers would place a down-payment on machinery without placing any specific order in return for a guarantee by McClain that when they need machinery they would receive priority in the production schedule and that the price of the machinery would not rise more rapidly than the average rate of inflation for the country as a whole from the time the deposit was first placed. McClain's marketing department estimated this had a 90% chance of adding $.10 a share to earnings in 1973 and that if it failed it would only cost $.10 a share. Thus, if the new machinery and the new sales campaign were both successes, earnings per share could rise to $1.30.

The most important effect on next year's earnings per share was the expected pick up in the economy. McClain was very confident that both the economy and his sales would improve rapidly in the coming year. Paul McClain told John that his economist estimated a 70% chance of a rapidly improving economy which could push McClain Industries' earnings per share up as much as $.20 a share over and above what the introduction of the new products and the new sales campaign might increase earnings per share. Even in the event the economy did not respond as well as anticipated, which, according to McClain, was only a 30% chance, earnings were still expected to increase $.10 a share.

John returned to his office after the interview and consulted with Abe Hoffman, Merril, Link's chief economist. Abe was optimistic about the prospects for a rising GNP in 1973, although he had a finer breakdown than McClain had given John. Abe gave John the firm's official estimate of next year's GNP which had just been released to the press. GNP was expected to rise from the $1,000 billion level of 1972 to between $1,000 and $1,040 billion in 1973. Abe's estimates with their respective probability of occurrence are reproduced below:

GNP	Probability
$1,000 bil	15%
1,010	20
1,020	30
1,030	20
1,040	15

John also studied the historical response of McClain Industries to a recovery in the economy and found that in the year immediately following a recession, the percentage increase in machinery sales was generally three times that of the increase in the GNP. John also gathered the following information on the stock performance of McClain Industries:

Year	Average price	Earnings per Share	Business cond.
1967	$20	$2.00	normal
1968	16	.50	recession
1969	14	.40	recession
1970	24	3.00	boom
1971	20	1.50	recession
1972	15	1.00	recession

QUESTIONS

1. Using Paul McClain's subjective estimates of the success or failure of the new electronically controlled machinery, the new sales campaign, and the resurgence in the economy, construct all the possible earnings per share and the probability of each occurring. Compute the mean and the standard deviation using the probability distribution you have constructed.

2. Using Abe Hoffman's forecast for the 1973 GNP and the relationship between McClain Industries sales and the GNP discovered by John, compute the probability distribution, the mean, and the standard deviation of estimated 1973 sales. If McClain's net profit margins were 10% of sales, what would your earnings per share estimate be for 1973? Reconcile the earnings per share estimate in question

2 with that made in question 1. What are you assuming about net profit margins
in your answer to question 2?

3. Compute the price-earnings ratio for McClain Industries in each year from
1967 to 1972, inclusive. Describe the cyclical pattern in the price earnings ratio.
Explain the cyclical pattern you have just described.

4. If John were reporting his 1973 earnings per share estimates to a very conservative client of the firm who wanted to be 97.5% certain that your estimate
would not be too low, how could John adjust the estimate downward to achieve
this? What would be the appropriate estimate?

Case 17

OLLIE KRINKLE

Earnings Forecasting under Risk

Ollie Krinkle has been with a capital gains oriented mutual fund since 1962,
when she started as a young trainee in the research division. Almost from the very
first day she has been directly involved with "following" the metal stocks, a job
which forces her to keep current with the prospects for the earnings and stock
price of the United States Tin Co., of Scranton, Pa. Each year the fund's portfolio managers ask her to forecast the probable stock price action of U. S. Tin for
the coming year as one point of information on which to base their investment decisions. They want Ollie to tell them what she thinks the price of U. S. Tin Stock
is likely to be in the coming year.

Ollie, like all the other analysts, uses the forecasting technique developed at the
fund. The method first requires the analyst to independently estimate the earnings
per share for the firm, using the pertinent variables which influence the firm's earnings and then, second, to estimate independently the price earnings ratio (P/E) for
the firm under the various possible market conditions which might prevail. Then,
third, the analyst is required to estimate the stock price under the various possible
combinations of price earnings ratios and earnings per share.

Ollie has learned over the years that U. S. Tin's earnings depend to a great extent on the general level of activity in the economy since so much of tin production is used in the production of other finished consumer goods, such as automobiles, and on the price of tin, which also generally varies with the economy's effect
on the industry's supply-demand conditions. Sales in the tin industry, which were

16 million tons in 1972, have historically risen in direct proportion to the Gross National Product (GNP), although tin prices usually have fluctuated at a slightly greater rate in response to changes in the level of economic activity. Ollie has received the economic forecast of the fund's economist in which he predicted that the GNP in 1973 would rise 10% above the 1972 level of $1,000 billion. The economist hedged his forecast with the usual warnings about unforeseen political and economic events which might upset his estimate, but he was 80% certain his forecast would be realized. There was only a 20% chance, in his opinion, that the economy would rise but 5% in 1973. From the tin industry trade association, Ollie gathered that there was firming in the demand for tin, and if the economy rose the forecasted 10%, which seemed to be the most commonly used figure, tin prices could be expected to average almost $12 a ton in 1973, up from $10 a ton in 1972. However, less than a 10% rise in the GNP would probably not take up all the slack in the industry's excess capacity and would leave prices unchanged from their prior year level.

Ollie also learned that the price earnings ratio for the tin industry generally fell during upswings in economic activity because interest rates would be rising and earnings would be recovering from unusually depressed levels. Since 1972 had not been an unusually depressed year, but rather average, the present price earnings ratio of ten times seemed appropriate to Ollie provided interest rates did not rise. According to the fund's economist, the prevailing triple A bond rate of 5% had about a 40% chance of remaining at that level through 1973, but, because of the expected increase in the demand for business loans to finance expansion and inventory procurement, interest rates had a 60% chance of rising to 6%.

U. S. Tin, like the industry, had a cyclical pattern in its earnings per share and profit margins, as seen in Table 1. When the rate of growth in the GNP slackened, U. S. Tin earnings and profit margins dropped off because of the volatile reaction of the firm's sales to the economic cycle and because of the high fixed cost nature of the tin manufacturing process. U. S. Tin, in particular, had been making steady strides to reduce fluctuations in its profit margins, and Ollie believed that U. S. Tin's net profit margins had an 80% chance of rising to 25% of sales from their 1972 levels of 20%.

As far as U. S. Tin expanding its share of the tin market in 1973, Ollie considered that very unlikely as the company already controls 25% of the domestic market and is very likely to encounter anti-trust action if it attempts to expand.

U. S. Tin was also exploring the idea of implementing a new tin conversion process which could substantially reduce the cost of manufacturing. However, the installation of the new process would require $200 million of long term debt financing, which would raise the proportion of debt in the firm's capital structure to 70% and could depress the price earnings ratio by 2 points, at least until the project is proven profitable, which may be more than four years away. Already the firm's average interest rate was 8%, approximately 4% above the U. S. Government rate on long term bonds and was costing the firm $.60 a share in annual interest payments. Management had told Ollie in her last field trip that there is only a 50/50 chance of them undertaking the project at this time, because the firm does not want to jeopardize the present $.50 a share dividend which is right on the 50% target payout ratio management has as a goal. Historically, U. S. Tin stock had sold at a dividend yield equal to that of the triple A bond yield, because most investors do not consider it a growth company with above average profit potential and wanted the stock to provide current income. Therefore, both management and Ollie felt that a rise in interest rates or a cut in the dividend would affect the firm's price earnings ratio.

TABLE 1

	EARNINGS/SHARE	NET PROFIT MARGINS	GNP (bil)
1972	$1.00	20%	$1,000
1971	.90	17	955
1970	1.20	19	970
1969	1.00	19	950
1968	.50	15	850

Ollie constructed the following payoff matrix outline to begin her analysis:

SALES

PROFIT MARGINS

QUESTIONS

1. Construct a payoff matrix for the 1973 earnings per share of U. S. Tin, using the information Ollie has available (hint: use the U. S. Tin's share of market and net profit margins). Assign a probability of occurrence to each possible earnings per share.
2. Construct a payoff matrix for the possible 1973 price earnings ratio for U. S. Tin, using the information available to Ollie. As in question 1, assign a probability of occurrence to each possible price earnings ratio.
3. Based on your answers to questions 1 and 2, construct a payoff matrix for U. S. Tin's 1973 share price.
4. If you were Ollie, would you recommend the stock as an attractive investment for 1973? Why or why not?
5. Why should U. S. Tin's dividend yield be approximately the same as the yield on triple A bonds? Why is the dividend yield lower than the firm's average bond yield? Why does the price earnings ratio expand in the recession and contract in the prosperity years? Explain in terms of future earnings expectations and P/E considerations. Why should U. S. Tin's price earnings ratio be affected by the prospect of new financing and the implementation of a new, untried process? Why does U. S. Tin's dividend yield move in tandem with the interest rate? Can you think of a situation when it would not?

Case 18

TOM THOMAS, Ph.D.

Interest Rate Forecasting

Tom Thomas is a trained quantitative economist with a Ph. D. in Economics from the University of Houston in charge of the economics research division at the Third National Bank of New York. One of the major tasks of the economics research division is to forecast the investment outlook for the coming year in the money and capital markets. Each year around this time Tom and his staff gather to estimate what they believe will be the conditions of the markets in the year to come, particularly as to the direction and level of interest rates and as to the conditions of ease or tightness which characterize the market. Their estimates are used extensively within the bank itself for setting general investment policy in the trust and in the investment departments as well as among the other financial institutions across the country.

The economics research division has followed the same procedure in deriving their forecasts for many years now. The staff categories the participants in the market for money and capital as demanders or as suppliers of funds. Last year, the major participants who entered the market demanding funds were the residential and commercial mortgagors who needed funds to finance their building, the corporations who sold bonds and stocks to finance their capital expansion, state and local governments whose sold municipal bonds to finance their capital projects or their deficits, an assortment of short term borrowers, and the Federal Government. The suppliers of funds were for the most part the country's financial institutions. The life insurance and casualty insurance companies invested much of the funds they received from their clients in mortgages and corporate bonds. The pension funds invested substantial funds which they received from their contributors in common stocks and corporate bonds. The various savings institutions, including savings and loan associations and the mutual savings banks invested their depositors' funds in mortgages, government securities and bonds. The mutual funds invested their shareholders funds in stocks and bonds. The commercial banks bought large quantities of government securities with their depositors' funds. Nonfinancial institutions, such as corporations with excess cash balances, bought government securities. Even the government under its contractual obligations to purchase securities for its trust funds, such as the social security trust fund, bought government securities. Foreign investors, individuals, and others accounted for the remainder of the funds supplied.

The staff's estimate for 1972, Exhibit 1, had projected a total demand for funds of $100 billion with almost 65% of that coming from the demand for mortgage money and for short term borrowing. The staff estimated that the $100 billion would be supplied with 36% coming from the commercial banks and another 22% coming from savings institutions. The staff also had estimated that it would take a 9% interest rate to equate the supply of funds with the demand for funds. At an interest rate higher than that they expected the suppliers would be willing to supply more than the demanders would be demanding. At an interest rate less than 9%, the demand for funds would exceed the supply.

EXHIBIT 1

1972 SUMMARY OF FUNDS

Supplied and Demanded

FUNDS DEMANDED (bil)	
Real Estate Mortgages	$ 30
Corporate Bonds	15
Stocks	5
State and local governments	10
Short term borrowers	35
Federal Government deficit	5
	5
Total	$100

FUNDS SUPPLIED (bil)	
Insurance Companies	$ 10
Pension funds	11
Savings institutions	22
Mutual Funds	2
Commercial banks	36
Non-financial institution	8
Federal Government	3
Others	4
Individuals	4
Total	$100

The 1972 estimate proved to be very accurate, and the staff decided to build the 1973 estimate with the same categories of demanders and suppliers. The staff using last year's results, constructed the following demand equations for each of the demander categories:

Real estate mortgage = $40 bil − 80(i)
Corporate bonds = $20 bil − 30 (i)
Stocks = $10 bil − 30(i)
State and local governments = $14 bil − 10(i)
Short term borrowers = $33 bil − 20(i)
Federal Government = revenues − expenditures
    i = interest rate in decimal form

Each of the equations represent the demand for each category which the staff expects to prevail at an interest rate, i, which will equate the demand and the supply of funds. The Federal Government's demand is equal to the spending deficits, which the staff estimates will be $10 billion, the difference between the estimated $250 billion in expenditures and $240 billion in tax revenue.

On the supply side the staff has estimated the following supply equations for each of the categories of suppliers:

Insurance companies = $5 bil + 50(i)
Pension funds = $10 bil + 20(i)
Savings institutions = $20 bil + 30(i)
Mutual funds = $1 bil + 10(i)
Commercial banks = $30 bil + 80(i)
Non-financial institutions = $8 bil + 10(i)
Federal Government = $4 bil
Others = $6 bil
Individuals = $6.0 bil

Except for the individuals, others, and Federal Government estimates which are taken from official Government publications, the staff projects that the supply of funds from each category will increase as the interest rate, i, increases and at some interest rate common to both, the supply will equate with the demand.

QUESTIONS
1. Assuming the staff's equations are correct, calculate the demand and the supply for funds if the interest rate, i, is expected to be 9%. Does the supply equate with the demand at a 9% interest rate? If not, is the interest rate likely to be higher or lower than 9%.
2. Recalculate the estimated supply and the estimated demand at an interest rate of 10%. Does the market clear at this interest rate? If so, at what amount?

Case 19

WILLIAM STOWE

Money Supply and Stock Prices

William Stowe is vice-president and senior financial analyst at a stock brokerage house. He has been examining the performance of the portfolios of the firm's clients and the accuracy of the firm's staff of analysts in making earnings forecast as well as recommending stocks which perform well. Stowe is interested in determining just how well his firm's clients fared over the last market cycle so that he may use any favorable results as a selling point to some rather large institutional clients he is trying to win over. Stowe found surprising results. During the sustained market upswing, which lasted for about two years, the brokerage house clients averaged a 15% compound annual return on their portfolios compared to a 13.5% compound annual return for the market in general. Some of the more speculative portfolios did even better, with compound annual returns of over 17%. In the sustained downtrend in the market which saw the market decline almost 20% in less than one year, the firm's clients also fared relatively well. Despite the market slide, the average of all portfolios actually rose 2%, although some of the more speculative portfolios declined in excess of 20%

While Mr. Stowe was pleasantly surprised to see that his clients fared well in the upswing and in the downswing of the market, he noticed that at the turning points in the market, when the peaks and troughs in the S & P Index Average were reached, the performance of the portfolios sadly lagged. Within the two month period immediately succeeding the peak, the portfolios, on average, fell almost twice as much as the market, indicating that the portfolio managers were not adjusting their clients' portfolios until after the turning point had been well advanced. A similar pattern could also be observed at the troughs in the market. In the period immediately succeeding the bottom of the market, the average return to the portfolios was significantly less than the return to the market. Portfolio managers were not adjusting to the new market environments fast enough and were costing the firm's clients money. Mr. Stowe's investigation lead him to believe that analytical staff was not anticipating the market turning points or adjusting their recommendations rapidly enough to profit from turns in the market. Although, he did believe that once the turns were recognized as such, the analytical staff was doing an outstanding job in selecting the better performing stocks.

In his further investigation of the analytical staff, Mr. Stowe observed that his analysts had a very high accuracy in forecasting a company's earnings for the coming year. Ninety percent of the forecasts were less than 3% off the actual figures. In addition, the analysts had consistently recommended the better performers during most of the up and down phases of the market, but, as noted before, did not do well at the turning points. Many of their recommendations in effect at the market peak were among the worst performers during the succeeding months, and many of their recommendations in effect at the trough in the market were also among the worst performers during the succeeding months.

Obviously, Mr. Stowe concluded, the analysts were very capable of selecting the right stock, provided the market environment did not change on them. If he could provide the analysts with an indication of the probable market environment in the near future, they could adjust their recommendations accordingly, and their performance would improve.

Mr. Stowe hired a monetary economist to develop leading indicators for the market. The economist explained that he believed the best leading indicator of the market is the rate of growth in the money supply. He explained that as the money supply growth rate slowed it was likely to lead to a contraction in liquidity which forced the liquidation of stocks and lower stock prices. As the money supply grew rapidly it increased liquidity which encouraged the purchase of stocks and lead to rising stock prices. Mr. Stowe asked the economist to support his thesis from the monthly data gathered in Table 1.

TABLE 1

MONEY SUPPLY (bil) (seasonally adjusted)	S & P INDEX
203.3	104.62
204.0	99.14
204.3	94.71
204.0	94.18
204.0	94.51
204.1	95.52
204.3	96.21
204.6	91.11
206.1	90.31
204.3	87.16
206.5	88.65
208.3	85.95
209.0	76.06
209.6	75.59
210.6	75.72
211.8	77.92
212.8	82.58
213.0	84.37
213.0	84.28
214.6	90.05
214.8	93.49
217.3	97.11
219.4	99.60
221.1	103.04

QUESTIONS

1. Explain how a financial analyst can be accurate in forecasting the earnings and prospects for a particular firm and still have the price of the company's stock not perform according to his forecast. What factors in the analysis of the company's stock performance might the analyst overlook if he just concentrates on the factors affecting only the company?

2. Compute an annualized six month moving average for the percentage rate.

3. Plot the six month moving average you calculated in question 2 and the Standard and Poor's Index in Table 1 on arithmetic graph paper. Use the left vertical axis for the rate of change in the money supply scale and the right vertical axis for the S & P scale. Compare the two series, particularly at turning points, and evaluate the significance of the rate of change in the money supply as an indicator of general market performance.

4. Suggest other factors which you might want to consider besides just the rate of growth in the money supply if you were attempting to forecast general market performance.

Case 20

MARY SACKOFF

Money Market Conditions

Mary Sackoff is the leading financial analyst with the government bond dealer, Saloma and Co. As such, it is her job to keep abreast of conditions in the money and capital markets. One of her major functions in that area is to analyze the weekly statements of the Federal Reserve System to detect any noticeable shifts in monetary policy which may have implications for interest rates. Each week she receives the Fed's reports and looks to see what the Fed did in the way of buying or selling money and capital market securities such as U. S. Government bills and bonds and Federal Agency obligations and to see how the Fed responded to the demands of the banking system in making discounts and advances to those banks which requested them. Reproduced on the following pages are the weekly reports that Mary received from December 9 through December 22, 1971.

FEDERAL RESERVE STATISTICS
Weekly Average of Daily Figures
(in millions of dollars)

	Wk. ending Dec. 8, 1971	Averages of daily figures Chng. from wk. ending Dec. 1, 1971	Chng. from wk. ending Dec. 9, 1970	Wednesday Dec. 8, 1971
Reserve Bank credit:				
U. S. Government securities:				
Bought outright—System Account	68,482	+ 249	+7,584	*68,542
Held under repurchase agreement	88	− 322	− 162	219
Federal agency obligations:				
Bought outright	340	+ 92	+ 340	340
Held under repurchase agreement	31	− 48	− 24	93
Acceptances:				
Bought outright	56	+ 1	+ 16	56
Held under repurchase agreement	10	− 43	− 69	26
Discounts and advances:				
Member bank borrowings	60	− 641	− 230	85
Other	−	−	−	−
Float	3,079	+ 64	+ 66	3,005
Other Federal Reserve assets	892	+ 33	− 86	921
Total Reserve Bank credit	73,036	− 617	+7,432	73,287
Gold stock	10,132	−	− 985	10,132
S. D. R. certificates	400	−	−	400
Treasury currency outstanding	7,594	+ 3	+ 479	7,592
	91,162	− 614	+6,927	91,411
Currency in circulation	60,563	+ 137	+3,907	60,964
Treasury cash holding	456	− 3	+ 14	463
Treasury deposits with F. R. Banks	1,749	− 145	+1,115	936
Foreign deposits with F. R. Banks	133	− 36	− 5	187
Other deposits with F. R. Banks	717	− 15	−	779
Other F. R. liabilities and capital	2,398	+ 70	+ 35	2,428
	66,016	+ 7	+5,155	65,757
Member bank reserves:				
With F. R. Banks	25,146	− 621	+1,771	25,654
Currency and coin	5,586	+ 114	+ 243	5,586
Total reserves held	30,732	− 507	+2,014	31,240
Required reserves	30,618	− 63	+2,036	30,618
Excess reserves	114	− 444	− 22	622

Note: Data do not include $306 million daily average excess reserves eligible for carry-over into the statement week ended Dec. 8 from the week ended Dec. 1 and $34 million daily average deficiencies carried into the statement week ended Dec. 8.

*Includes $79 million securities loaned—fully secured by U. S. Govt. securities pledged with Federal Reserve Banks.

On December 8, 1971 marketable U. S. Government securities held in custody by the Federal Reserve Banks for foreign and international accounts were $25,866 million, an increase of $1,266 million for the week and an increase of $14,648 million from the comparable date a year ago.

Week 1

FEDERAL RESERVE STATISTICS (Continued)
(in millions of dollars)

	Wk. ending Dec. 15, 1971	Averages of daily figures Chng. from wk. ending Dec. 8, 1971	Dec. 16, 1970	Wednesday Dec. 15, 1971
Reserve Bank credit:				
U. S. Government securities:				
Bought outright—System Account	68,421	− 61	+7,195	*67,692
Held under repurchase agreement	−	− 88	− 508	−
Federal agency obligations:				
Bought outright	340	−	+ 340	340
Held under repurchase agreement	−	− 61	− 79	−
Acceptances:				
Bought outright	59	+ 3	+ 13	66
Held under repurchase agreement	−	− 10	− 51	−
Discounts and advances:				
Member bank borrowings	27	− 33	− 372	29
Other	−	−	−	−
Float	3,350	+ 266	+ 423	3,820
Other Federal Reserve assets	927	+ 34	− 79	983
Total Reserve Bank credit	73,124	+ 82	+6,881	72,930
Gold stock	10,132	−	− 985	10,132
S. D. R. certificates	400	−	−	400
Treasury currency outstanding	7,602	− 8	478	7,614
	91,257	+ 89	+6,373	91,076
Currency in circulation	61,040	+ 472	+4,076	61,271
Treasury cash holdings	457	+ 1	+ 28	462
Treasury deposits with F. R. Banks	1,563	− 186	+ 800	2,127
Foreign deposits with F. R. Banks	143	+ 10	+ 8	173
Other deposits with F. R. Banks	710	− 7	− 24	709
Other F. R. liabilities and capital	2,219	− 179	− 80	2,198
	66,132	+ 110	+4,808	66,940
Member bank reserves:				
With F. R. Banks	25,125	− 21	+1,565	24,136
Currency and coin	5,896	+ 310	+ 418	5,896
Total reserves held	31,021	+ 289	+1,983	30,032
Required reserves	30,946	+ 328	+2,028	30,946
Excess reserves	75	− 39	− 45	− 914

Note: Data do not include $207 million daily average excess reserves eligible for carry-over into the statement week ended Dec. 15 from the week ended Dec. 8 and $40 million daily average deficiencies carried into the statement week ended Dec. 15.

*Excludes $850 million of securities sold and scheduled to be bought back under matured sale-purchase transactions. Includes $29 million securities loaned—fully secured to U. S. Govt. securities pledged with Federal Reserve Banks.

On Dec. 15, 1971, marketable U. S. Govt. securities held in custody by the Federal Reserve Banks for foreign and international accounts were $26,740 million, an increase of $874 million for the week and an increase of $15,663 million from the comparable date a year ago.

Week 2

FEDERAL RESERVE STATISTICS (Continued)
(in millions of dollars)

	Wk. ending Dec. 22, 1971	Averages of daily figures Chng. from wk. ending Dec. 15, 1971	Dec. 23, 1970	Wednesday Dec. 22, 1971
Reserve Bank credit:				
U. S. Government securities:				
Bought outright—System Account	68,398	− 23	+6,886	*68,155
Held under repurchase agreement	88	+ 88	− 99	12
Federal agency obligations:				
Bought outright	465	+ 125	+ 445	435
Held under repurchase agreement	7	+ 7	− 65	−
Acceptances:				
Bought outright	67	+ 8	+ 13	77
Held under repurchase agreement	22	+ 22	− 15	3
Discounts and advances:				
Member bank borrowings	144	+ 117	− 181	828
Other	−	−	−	−
Float	4,471	+1,006	+ 672	3,996
Other Federal Reserve assets	988	+ 61	− 63	1,018
Total Reserve Bank credit	74,651	+1,412	+7,615	74,572
Gold stock	10,132	−	− 985	10,132
S. D. R. certificates	400	−	−	400
Treasury currency outstanding	7,615	+ 13	+ 437	7,622
	92,768	+1,426	+7,066	92,726
Currency in circulation	61,242	+ 202	+4,008	61,620
Treasury cash holdings	450	− 7	+ 33	452
Treasury deposits with F. R. Banks	1,895	+ 332	+1,067	2,031
Foreign deposits with F. R. Banks	426	+ 283	+ 283	473
Other deposits with F. R. Banks	736	+ 26	+ 40	725
Other F. R. liabilities and capital	2,234	+ 15	+ 58	2,250
	66,983	+ 851	+5,490	67,551
Member bank reserves:				
With F. R. Banks	25,815	+ 575	+1,577	25,175
Currency and coin	5,377	− 519	+ 317	5,377
Total reserves held	31,192	+ 56	+1,894	30,552
Required reserves	31,180	+ 234	+2,092	31,180
Excess reserves	12	− 178	− 198	− 628

Note: Data do not include $212 million daily average excess reserves eligible for carry-over into the statement week ended Dec. 22 from the week ended Dec. 15 and $61 million daily average deficiencies carried into the statement week ended Dec. 22.

*Includes $23 million securities loaned—fully secured by U. S. Govt. securities pledged with Federal Reserve Banks.

On December 22, 1971 marketable U. S. Government securities held in custody by the Federal Reserve Banks for foreign and international accounts were $27,697 million, an increase of $957 million for the week and an increase of $16,648 million from the comparable date a year ago.

Week 3

QUESTIONS

1. What is meant by Reserve Bank credit? What comprises reserve bank credit?
2. Distinguish between the data reported as of Wednesday, December 8, 1971 and as of the week ending December 8, 1971.
3. In the week 3, December 22, 1971, there is a large increase in the float account. Can you explain this in terms of seasonality and the Christmas selling season?
4. From the data you have before you does the Fed appear to be conducting a policy of actively entering the market by selling or purchasing large quantities of securities or does it appear to be merely stabilizing the markets with relatively little buying or selling? Support your answer with data from the Fed's reports. If the Fed were trying to ease the money market conditions what action would it take? Where would this show up in the weekly report?
5. Given your interpretation of Fed policy, what are the implications for money market conditions?
6. Calculate free reserves in each week?

Case 21

C. J. HEAVENLY & CO.

Yield Structures

C. J. Heavenly and Co. is a Wall Street bond dealer engaged in the purchase and sale of all types of government and industrial bonds and debt securities for its own account and profit. Every day it transacts over $500 million in bonds, varying the prices at which it sells securities and at which it buys in response to supply and demand conditions.

Among the most common debt securities traded are those of the U. S. Government, including the short term Treasury bills and the longer term bonds and notes. On a typical day in 1972, the closing prices quoted by the firm for the government securities were:

Decimals in bid-and-asked and bid changes represent 32nds (101.1 means 101 1-32).
a—Plus 1-64. b-Yield to call date. d-Minus 1-64.

TREASURY BONDS			Bid	Asked	Bid Chg.	Yld.
4s,	1972	Feb	100.4	100.6	−.3	0.42
2-1/2s,	1967-72	Jun	99.20	99.24	−.1	3.19
4s,	1972	Aug	100.4	100.8	-	3.52
2-1/2s,	1967-72	Sep	99.4	99.8	−.2	3.75
2-1/2s,	1967-72	Dec	98.24	98.28	−.1	3.84
4s,	1973	Aug	98.24	98.4	−.6	4.60
4-1/8s,	1973	Nov	98.26	99.2	−.2	4.68
4-1/8s,	1974	Feb	98.15	98.23	−.2	4.79
4-1/4s,	1974	May	98.14	98.22	−.1	4.86
3-7/8s,	1974	Nov	96.24	97.0	−.6	5.04
4s,	1980	Feb	86.22	87.6	+.2	6.04
3-1/2s,	1980	Nov	83.2	83.18	+.2	5.93
7s,	1981	Aug	106.16	107.0	−.2	6.02
6-3/8s,	1982	Feb	100.0	100.3	-	6.37
3-1/4s,	1978-83	Jun	76.16	77.16	−2.	6.01
3-1/4s,	1985	May	76.6	77.6	−.2	5.73
4-1/4s,	1975-85	May	81.10	82.10	−.2	6.23
6-1/8s,	1986	Nov	98.2	98.10	−.2	6.31
3-1/2s,	1990	Feb	76.4	77.4	−.2	5.52
4-1/4s,	1987-92	Aug	78.2	79.2	−.6	6.05
4s,	1988-93	Feb	77.4	78.4	-	5.82
4-1/8s,	1989-94	May	77.2	78.2	−.2	5.91
3s,	1995	Feb	76.6	77.6	−.2	4.62
3-1/2s,	1998	Nov	76.22	77.22	−.2	5.03

U. S. TREAS. NOTES				
Rate	Mat	Bid	Asked	Yld
4-3/4	2-72	100.5	100.7	0.49
7-1/2	2-72	100.8	100.10	0.68
4-3/4	5-72	100.11	100.15	3.03
6-3/4	5-72	100.29	101.1	3.00
5	8-72	100.21	100.25	3.51
6	11-72	101.14	101.18	3.95
4-7/8	2-73	100.12	100.14	4.44
6-1/2	2-73	102.1	102.5	4.34
7-3/4	5-73	103.26	104.2	4.45
8-1/8	8-73	104.29	105.5	4.60
7-3/4	2-74	105.14	105.20	4.81
7-1/4	5-74	104.26	105.2	4.88
5-5/8	8-74	100.26	101.2	5.19
5-3/4	11-74	100.31	101.7	5.27
5-3/4	2-75	100.26	101.2	5.37
5-7/8	2-75	101.3	101.9	5.41
6	5-75	101.18	101.26	5.39
5-7/8	8-75	101.0	101.8	5.48
7	11-75	104.25	105.1	5.52
6-1/4	2-76	102.14	102.22	5.50
5-3/4	5-76	100.6	100.8	5.68
6-1/2	5-76	103.2	103.10	5.62
7-1/2	8-76	107.0	107.8	5.66
6-1/4	11-76	102.11	102.19	5.62
8	2-77	109.12	109.28	5.72
7-3/4	8-77	108.25	109.9	5.77
6-1/4	2-78	101.2	101.18	5.94
6	11-78	99.28	100.0	6.00

U. S. TREAS. BILLS					
Mat	Bid	Ask	Mat	Bid	Ask
	Discount			Discount	
2- 3	3.40	2.74	5-31	3.49	3.27
2-10	3.27	2.73	6- 1	3.55	3.37
2-17	3.22	2.74	6- 8	3.58	3.40
2-24	3.20	2.74	6-15	3.64	3.48
2-29	320	2.74	6-21	3.66	3.52
3- 2	3.22	2.92	6-22	3.68	3.54
3- 9	3.25	2.97	6-29	3.68	3.54
3-16	3.27	2.98	6-30	3.67	3.47
3-23	3.30	3.06	7- 6	3.81	3.69
3-30	3.31	3.07	7-13	3.81	3.69
3-31	3.32	3.08	7-20	3.82	3.70
4- 6	3.32	3.18	7-27	3.82	3.70
4-13	3.37	3.23	7-31	3.78	3.64
4-20	3.37	3.23	8- 3	-	-
4-21	3.39	3.29	8-31	3.82	3.71
4-27	3.40	3.28	9-30	3.97	3.85
4-30	3.42	3.22	10-31	4.01	3.91
5- 4	3.43	3.33	11-30	3.94	3.80
5-11	3.48	3.30	12-31	3.90	3.74
5-18	3.48	3.28	1-31	4.12	4.02
5-25	3.47	3.27			

C. J. Heavenly & Co. also trades in all of the other government securities including Federal Land Bank, Federal National Mortgage Association, World Bank, Foreign Government, Federal Home Loan Bank Board, and State and Municipal bonds.

The firm also actively trades in the debt securities of private, corporate borrowers. These include all qualities of public utility, industrial corporation, and railroad bonds as well as most of the shorter term debt instruments such as commercial paper, bankers' acceptance, negotiable certificates of deposit, and Eurodollars.

The firm maintains an index of yields for the various qualities of bonds by issuers, which on the same day as the Treasury security yields were:

Yield To Maturity (%)

Issuer	Public Utility				Industrial				Railroad				Municipal
Quality	AAA	AA	A	BBB	AAA	AA	A	BBB	AAA	AA	A	BBB	
	7.65	7.84	8.37	8.73	7.31	7.44	7.72	8.60	7.64	8.29	8.20	8.94	5.78

The firm does not deal in bonds which rate lower than BBB, what the rating service defines as medium grade with some speculative elements beginning to appear. The AAA bonds were the highest grade, while the AA were considered by the rating agency to differ only in a small degree from the AAA obligations. The A bonds were regarded as upper medium grade quality.

At the time of these prices, the general economy was just beginning to recover from a relatively serious recession with unemployment still hovering around 6% of the labor force, although most economic forecasts, both government and private, foresaw a large growth from the $1,000 billion GNP of this year. Inflation expectations had been curtailed at the time of these prices, with the present annual target of 3% within the realm of possibility by the end of the coming year. Already, because of the surpressed expectations on inflation, a rapidly expanding money supply, and a slack demand for loanable funds on the part of the recession affected industries, interest rates have fallen substantially, with the major commercial banks following the trend in the government securities market and lowering the prime commercial lending rate from 7% to 4½% in less than six months. It was also commonly anticipated that the Federal Government would require relatively light deficit financing of $15 billion in the coming year in comparison of the $40 billion it had borrowed in the present year. The Treasury was expected to refinance about $50 billion of intermediate term debt (1980-85).

Many of the financial institutions that commonly participated in the money and capital markets were also becoming very liquid as the flow of money into the insurance companies and the savings and loan associations, as well as the banks, pick up momentum. Further, since it was a presidential election year, it was commonly assumed that there would be a concerted effort on the part of the administration to keep these institutions supplied with funds and to keep interest rates low.

In the international sector, the country's balance of payments had remained reasonably steady and almost in balance after a currency revaluation earlier in the present year.

QUESTIONS

1. Graph the yield curve for the Treasury bonds. Interpret your graph in terms of the bond market's expectations and the current and future prospects for the economy. Why is the yield curve not a completely straight line, explain in terms of the participants' supply and demand.

2. Distinguish among the various types of short term and long term securities in which C. J. Heavenly and Co. trades. Describe the main features of each security in terms of its issuer, maturity, trading basis, marketability, and obligation.

3. If the yield curve were downward sloping, such that the longer term maturities were yielding less than the shorter term maturities, would that change your answer to question 1? If so, how?

4. Compute the yield spread between the Treasury 4¼'s of 87-92 and the AAA industrial bonds. What usually happens to this spread during prosperity? Why? How should this affect your investment strategy? Why are the yields for the industrial bonds generally lower than those for either the public utility bonds or the railroad bonds?

5. If you were the manager of a large life insurance company investment portfolio, which bonds would you favor?

6. If you were investing in only stocks, how might the yield curve and the yield spread be useful in your investment strategy?

Case 22

JOHN SILBER

Bond Prices and Yields

John Silber received his MBA from New York University in 1967 and immediately started in the training program of one of the largest banks in New York City. He worked his way through the entire training program, gathering all he could about the various departments and how they worked. At the end of his training he was assigned to the personal loan department as a loan officer. John stayed there, despite the fact that his real interest lay in managing the bank's bond investment department. When the opportunity arose for John to become assistant to the vice president in charge of the investment group at the 2nd National Bank of New York, a smaller, recently chartered institution in the area, he grabbed it.

The Second National had been in existence for only five years, during which time it had been most successful through aggressive advertising and marketing campaigns in attracting new depositors and deposits. The bank was now in a reasonably strong financial position. However, despite its success in attracting funds, the bank had a very disappointing record in its bond portfolio. Like most banks in the area, the Second National maintained a portfolio of U. S. Government securities, including all maturities ranging from short term Treasury Bills due within a few months to long term bonds due to mature in 20 years. Funds, which had been deposited at the bank, were given to the bond department to invest. One of the purposes of the investment was to earn a return from the funds, which otherwise would have been uninvested and idle, until they could be loaned out at higher interest rates to the bank's customers. When the funds could be loaned out, the bond department was expected to liquidate some of its bond holdings and to return the money to the loan department. The other major purpose of the bond portfolio was to be a safe, interest earning haven for the bank's liquid reserves, which were put aside to meet unforeseen deposit withdrawals.

Unfortunately for the bond department and the bank, the bond portfolio had taken substantial capital losses in the performance of its job. When called upon to provide funds to the loan department, the bond department always had to sell its holdings at usually much lower prices than it had paid for these holdings and so showed a loss. These losses occurred mostly in the liquidation of the long term bonds, which made up a large portion of the bond portfolio. What usually happened is that when the bank made the funds available to the bond department for investment, the highest interest rates prevailing at that time were among the longer term bonds. Attracted by these higher rates in an effort to show a good performance, the bond department would put most of its holdings in these longer term issues. Usually, later, when the loan department wanted its funds back and the bond department had to liquidate its holdings, the market price of the bonds had shrunk, and the bonds were sold at a loss.

John's boss finally decided he had to stop these large capital losses and asked John to prepare an analysis of bond prices and yields over the cycle to see if they could discern some pattern which would help them in their bond investments. John first had to find some indicators of the money and capital market environment which would help explain bond price and yield movements in general. Once he could do this with some confidence, John figured he could make a sensible judgment on how to adjust the bond portfolio's holding among the long term, short term, and intermediate bonds. Thus, if John could get some indication of the direction bond yields were likely to take, he could arrange the portfolio's holdings to minimize the capital loss potential. His problem was to determine how the various segments in the maturity range reacted to the change in general interest rates.

John, therefore, gathered data on what he considered to be possible factors affecting interest rates. These were the Consumer Price Index (CPI), as a measure of the rate of inflation, the money supply, and the Federal Reserve's index of industrial production. John felt these might influence interest rates. He also compiled data for the same period on prices and yields for short term, intermediate term, and long term bonds.

TABLE 1

CPI	MONEY SUPPLY (bil) (seasonally adj.)	FRB INDUST. PROD. INDEX
109.0	$203.3	172.5
109.7	204.0	173.7
110.2	204.3	174.6
110.7	204.0	174.3
111.3	204.0	173.9
111.8	204.1	173.1
112.5	204.3	171.4
113.3	204.6	171.1
113.8	206.1	170.4
114.3	204.3	170.5
114.9	206.5	171.1
115.2	208.3	170.4
115.7	209.0	169.0
116.3	209.6	168.8
116.7	210.6	169.2
116.9	211.8	168.8
117.5	212.8	165.8
118.1	213.0	162.3
118.5	213.5	161.5
119.1	214.6	164.4
119.2	214.8	165.6
119.4	217.3	165.2
119.8	219.4	165.5
120.2	221.1	166.2

TABLE 2

BOND YIELDS

LONG TERM	INTERMEDIATE TERM	SHORT TERM
5.99%	6.39%	5.76%
6.22	6.56	6.09
6.21	6.69	6.52
6.12	6.71	6.68
6.38	7.16	7.07
6.38	7.21	7.12
6.61	7.04	7.25
6.86	7.47	7.85
6.91	7.79	8.02
6.59	7.63	7.87
6.61	7.01	7.14
6.71	7.34	7.20
7.11	7.84	7.59
7.17	7.77	7.74
6.77	7.56	7.51
6.93	7.37	7.46
6.79	7.26	7.09
6.77	7.07	6.82
6.51	6.52	6.22
6.18	5.98	5.61
6.06	5.90	5.48
5.96	5.53	4.78
5.63	4.98	4.07
5.79	5.55	4.64

TABLE 3
BOND PRICES
(IN POINTS, 1 POINT = $10)

LONG TERM	INTERMEDIATE TERM	SHORT TERM
70.70	80.03	91.37
68.89	79.20	90.38
68.93	78.49	89.13
69.70	78.40	88.67
67.72	76.19	87.58
67.68	75.95	87.44
66.00	76.77	87.01
64.21	74.71	85.39
63.88	73.20	84.95
66.15	73.95	85.34
66.02	76.95	87.39
65.30	75.31	87.22
62.47	72.94	86.15
62.07	73.28	85.70
64.86	74.24	86.43
64.12	75.16	86.67
64.70	75.71	87.51
64.85	76.65	88.28
66.70	79.39	90.01
69.23	82.21	91.80
70.16	82.63	92.21
70.94	84.64	94.32
73.60	87.74	96.54
72.31	84.57	94.78

QUESTIONS
1. Using arithmetic graph paper, plot the movements in long term bond prices, the CPI, the money supply, and the index of industrial production over time. Compare the fluctuations in the bond prices to the fluctuations in the other series. Draw conclusions on what you believe John should learn from analyzing your graphs.
2. Plot the prices of short term, intermediate term, and long term bonds over time. What conclusions can you draw from your plot as to the effect of a general change in interest rates on each of the three segments of the maturity range? Specifically compare the degree to which the prices fluctuate.
3. Plot the short term, intermediate term, and the long term bond yields over time. What conclusions can you draw from your plot as to the degree which each segment's yield fluctuates in response to general interest rate shifts?
4. Put forth an investment strategy which John might follow in order to minimize his capital losses.

Case 23

RICHARD SINGLETON

Purchasing Power Risk

In 1969, after four years of trying to save for a house, Richard Singleton and his wife, Mary, were beginning to be discouraged. When they first started to save, their dream house on the edge of town was selling for $29,500 with a $3,000 down payment and $500 in closing expenses and fees. They had decided to put $700 a year into a savings account for the next five years so that in 1970 they could afford the downpayment and closing expenses. However, by 1969, after four years of savings, their accumulated total with interest totaled $3,100, but the cost of their dream house had risen to $35,000 and the downpayment had jumped, beyond their reach, to over $4,000. Mary was almost in tears when she realized she was not going to have her house, and Dick decided to do something about it.

For years he had heard that inflation destroyed savings and purchasing power, and he had just had his most vivid first hand experience. But, he had also heard that investing in the stock market was a way of combating the erosion of purchasing power by inflation. Responding to the advertisement of a brokerage house in the local newspaper, Dick went to listen to one of their representatives give a lecture on the benefits of investing in common stocks as a method of avoiding inflation. The representative talked about studies done at the University of Chicago which showed that from 1929 to 1960, an investment in stocks would have grown at a compound rate of almost 9% a year, far in excess of the 5% inflation during the same period. This meant that the stock investor would have beaten the inflation and have come out ahead. Dick was very impressed with the idea of "beating inflation."

After the lecture Dick approached the representative and wanted to know if he too could still beat inflation in this day. The representative, Jack Yeager, assured him he could if he would just open an account with the firm. Jack convinced Dick that investing in stocks was the only method of beating inflation. He pointed to the savings accounts in the last few years which paid 5%, but because of the inflation of almost 7% a year actually lost 2% in value in real dollar terms. Jack stated that any investment which offered a fixed interest rate suffered during inflation because of the purchasing power erosion. Jack went on to say the only investments which enabled one to beat inflation were variable income securities such as stocks, which were able to increase their earnings and dividends during inflations and so offset the purchasing power erosion.

Convinced by the arguments, Dick opened an account with Jack and put his entire savings, which he and Mary had accumulated for the downpayment, into the stock market. In May of 1969, when the Standard and Poor's Index (S&P) was 104.62, Dick bought his stocks. At that time the Consumer Price Index (CPI) stood at 109.0. The Consumer Price Index measure of inflation continued to climb steadily and rapidly throughout the remainder of the year and into May of 1970, when it stood at 115.7, a jump of over 6%. During the same period the downpayment on Dick and Mary's dream house had jumped another $100. Dick had been busy with his work and with their new child so he really had not paid much attention to his investments, giving them the same attention as he would have given his savings and loan account. However, with the new baby, he decided it was time to withdraw his funds from the market for the downpayment on the house. To his surprise the stock market had declined during the period to 76.06 on the S&P index, a drop of over 25% in his investment. Dick was furious and confused because he could not understand how during all this inflation when stocks are supposed to beat inflation by rising in value, his investments had declined by 25%.

In desperation he turned to Kim Havoc, a close high school friend, who after going to the Wanton School of Finance, was now an accountant with a financial consulting firm. She relayed his desperation to one of the firm's consultants who explained that the historical performance of inflation of common stock returns showed that while it was true one would have beaten inflation in the long run with stock investments, that in the shorter runs, especially in periods of a year or less, as in Dick's case, rapid inflation usually accompanied a decline in stock values. The consultant provided Kim with Exhibit 1, to show that in the short run inflation depressed both bond (raised yields) and stock prices. From Exhibit 1, the consultant drew the conclusion that as the rate of inflation increased interest rates would rise and stock prices would drop. As the rate of inflation showed signs of tapering off, as it did in the Exhibit from May, 1970 to April, 1971, interest rates and stock prices tended to rise.

EXHIBIT 1

DATE	CPI	BOND YIELDS	S&P INDEX
May, 1969	109.0	6.33%	104.62
June, 1969	109.7	6.64	99.14
July, 1969	110.2	7.02	94.71
August, 1969	110.7	7.08	94.18
September, 1969	111.3	7.58	94.51
October, 1969	111.8	7.47	95.52
November, 1969	112.5	7.57	96.21
December, 1969	113.3	7.98	91.11
January, 1970	113.8	8.14	90.31
February, 1970	114.3	7.80	87.16
March, 1970	114.9	7.20	88.65
April, 1970	115.2	7.49	85.95
May, 1970	115.7	7.97	76.06
June, 1970	116.3	7.86	75.59
July, 1970	116.7	7.58	75.72
August, 1970	116.9	7.56	77.92
September, 1970	117.5	7.24	82.58
October, 1970	118.1	7.06	84.37
November, 1970	118.5	6.37	84.28
December, 1970	119.1	5.86	90.05
January, 1971	119.2	5.72	93.49
February, 1971	119.4	5.31	97.11
March, 1971	119.8	4.74	99.60
April, 1971	120.2	5.42	103.04

QUESTIONS

1. Using arithmetic graph paper plot the Consumer Price Index, the interest rate series, and the Standard and Poor's Index presented in Exhibit 1 over time. Interpret your graph. Does it support the contention of the consultant that an accelerating rate of inflation is usually associated with depressed bond and stock prices in the short run?
2. Give a logical explanation of why an accelerating rate of inflation should depress bond prices and stock prices. If the rate of inflation where expected to remain constant, what do you think would be its effect on bond prices?
3. What do you think of Jack Yeager's, the stockbroker, argument that stocks are the best method of beating inflation? In the longer run, would he have been correct?

Case 24

HIVERSIDE ELECTRIC LIGHT AND POWER

Inflation and Earnings

The Hiverside Electric Light and Power Co. (HELP) provides electricity to a relatively small but growing rural community in Southwest Wisconsin. The population of the area served has been growing at a steady rate over the years, and, as a result, HELP's unit sales of electricity have also grown. In 1972, sales were up 10% over 1971. Sales in 1973 are expected to grow another 10%. This growth has necessitated an expansion of the firm's generating capacity. In 1972, the firm added $13 million of plant and equipment to its rate base under the previously obtained authorization of the Wisconsin Public Utility Commission (PUC). Yet, despite this increase in generating capacity, sales averaged 84% of capacity in 1972, up from 80% in 1971. During the peak operating periods, when demands on the system were at their highest, sales were dangerously close to capacity, and the PUC had granted HELP temporary emergency authorization to expand the rate base by $7 million in 1973, although depreciation is to remain unchanged. Exhibit 1 shows the firm's average rate base for 1971 and 1972.

EXHIBIT 1
AVERAGE NET INVESTMENT RATE BASE
HIVERSIDE ELECTRIC LIGHT & POWER
12 months ending December 31

	1971 (mil)	1972 (mil)
Utility Plant in Service	$200	$210
Deduct: Reserve for Depreciation	118	123
Retirement Work in Progress	—	—
Contributions in aid of Construction	2	3
Total	$120	$126
Net Utility Plant Inservice	80	84
Add: Materials & Supplies	5	6
Prepayments	—	1
Cash Working Capital Requirement	12	15
Construction Work in Progress	23	27
Net Investment Rate Base	$120	$133

The big disappointment to HELP's management and its stockholders had been the first decline in the annual earnings of the firm since its inception. As Exhibit 2 shows, the total operating income for the firm fell from $14 million in 1971 to $10 million in 1972, despite the increase in capacity utilization and sales. Management blamed the decline on the very expensive labor contract which they signed with their employees in 1972. Under that contract, the firm's wage expense rose 12% in 1972 and is to rise another 10% in 1973. In addition, the price of fuel oil and coal, the two basic fossil fuels the firm uses in generating its electricity, had jumped sharply in 1972. The effect was to increase operating expenses 16% in 1972. Management foresees no immediate let up in the rising costs and forecasts a 10% overall increase in operating costs in 1973. Under these circumstances, management has asked the PUC for permission to increase the rate charged to its customers. Management claimed that if they do not get the rate increase, net operating income will again decline.

EXHIBIT 2

HIVERSIDE ELECTRIC LIGHT & POWER

Earnings Statement December 31

	1971 (mil)	1972 (mil)
Operating Revenue	$100	$110
Operating Expenses		
Operating & Maintenance	75	91
Depreciation	5	5
Taxes, Other than Income Taxes	1	1
Federal Income Taxes	4	3.5
State Income Taxes	1	.5
Total	$ 86	$100
Operating Income	$ 14	$ 10

Under Wisconsin law, the PUC is charged with regulating all utility rates and rate bases within the state. The intent of the law is to encourage better service by creating a natural monopoly, with only one company serving a specific area, while regulating the price to see that customers were not overcharged and that the utility itself received a "fair" return on its investment. To do this the PUC must first determine the rate base upon which the return is to be earned and then, second, the fair rate and charges necessary to bring about that fair return. Under court decision, the rate must be high enough to "maintain the financial integrity of the firm" and allow it to raise capital for expansion.

In the particular case of HELP and similar utilities in Wisconsin, the PUC had decided that, approximately, a 12% return of operating income to the rate base was appropriate. Since HELP's management did not earn 12% on their rate base in 1972 and were not expected to earn that rate in 1973, they petitioned the PUC, as they were required to do under the state statutes, for an increase in rates.

And, as it was required to do by law, the PUC promised a public hearing on the matter and scheduled a rate hearing for the end of 1975, the first free date on the commission's calendar. A hearing could not be scheduled sooner since almost all the utilities in the state were simultaneously petitioning for rate increases. Any HELP rate increase would have to wait at least until the hearing.

At the same time HELP was finding its earnings pinched by inflation, General Autos (GA) was also facing the same problem. Although no regulatory body controlled its prices, GA had a target rate of return of 12% net income on its net investment. In 1972, General Autos had experienced labor difficulties and had settled, without a strike, for a wage increase of 15% with an additional increase of 10% in 1973. In 1972, total operating expenses had increased 13% over the previous year, and they were expected to increase 10% in 1973. Because of the increased operating costs and despite a 10% increase in dollar sales in 1972, General Autos (GA) suffered a decline in operating income as shown in Exhibit 3, of $20 million.

EXHIBIT 3
GENERAL AUTOS
Earnings Statement December 31

	1971 (mil)	1972 (mil)
Sales	$1,000	$1,100
Cost of Goods Sold	800	900
Selling and General Administrative Expenses	100	120
Total Operating Expenses	$ 900	$1,020
Operating Income	100	80
Interest	10	10
Taxes	42	35
Net Income	48	35

In response to the profit decline, GA raised the price of its automobiles 13% in late 1972 and has just announced another 10% hike for 1973. Despite the price hike, the firm believes that unit sales will remain constant from 1972 because of the relative price inelasticity for automobiles, the expected slight increase in the nation's general economic activity, particularly consumer's disposable income, and the population growth in the driver age brackets, which should offset any decreased demand because of the increased prices. In addition, the company feels the Federal government has sufficiently blunted the thrust of the imported cars with its new safety regulations, and that at least in 1973, the number of imports sold in the country should remain the same as in 1972. With unit sales expected to remain the same, the firm is not planning to expand its plant and 1973 net investment sould be the same $400 million as in 1972.

QUESTIONS

1. Estimate the 1973 net operating income for HELP and for GA, taking into consideration the effects of inflation and price hikes.

2. Compute the return on investment for HELP in 1971 and in 1972. Why did the utility experience a decline in 1972 operating income in face of increased revenues? If the PUC grants the utility a sufficient increase in 1973, which is unlikely because of the commission's backlog, to bring HELP's return back up to 12%, what would be the likely effect on HELP's 1973 earnings? Why?

3. Assuming that HELP's stock sells at 20 times operating income and the firm has 10 million shares outstanding, what is HELP's average stock price likely to be in 1973? If the firm had been given an immediate rate increase by the PUC to bring the return on the invested rate base up to 12%, what would be the average 1973 stock price? Explain why your two answers are different.

4. What effect should the price hike of cars have on the stock price of GA shares in 1973? Compare the effect of the auto price increases on GA stock price to the effect of a 1975 PUC authorized rate increase on the stock price of HELP shares in 1973.

5. Assuming the inflation raised interests rates and caused stockholders to seek a higher rate of return on their investments, what would be the effect on the share price of each company? Why?

6. If the PUC announced it was accelerating the regulatory review process by allowing the utilities to automatically raise rates to compensate for increased costs instead of requiring a hearing, what would be the effect on the stock price of HELP shares? Why?

Case 25

SOUTH AMERICAN COPPER CORPORATION

Business Risk

South American Copper Corporation is a small, U.S. owned operator of an open pit copper mine in the mountains of the South American country of Quepasa. Ever since 1919, when the mine was first opened by the company, South American Copper Corp. has enjoyed a profitable operating history, never experiencing a loss, even during the world depression of the 1930 decade. The mine has always produced a high grade, easily mined and refined ore, and its proven reserves have been estimated to last at least until the turn of the century, seemingly assuring the company a continuing source of profit.

In 1972, the company earned $1.50 a share, of which 80% was directly attributable to the Quepasa mine, a proportion that in recent years has remained the same. The other 20% of earnings came from the firm's investments in the securities of domestic mining companies. These investments were carried at cost on the firm's balance sheet as marketable securities.

Historically, the firm's earnings have fluctuated in response to the price of copper ore on the world markets. The most profitable year the firm had was when the copper mines in the Congo closed because of the raging Civil War there. This sent world copper prices soaring and, since the firm's production was not interrupted, its earnings to record levels. However, since then the situation has returned to normal, and the firm's recent earnings per share were:

	EARNINGS	AVERAGE STOCK PRICE
1972	$1.50	$15.00
1971	1.75	17.50
1970	1.60	16.00
1969	1.50	15.00
1968	1.25	12.50
1967	1.35	13.50

Since the price of copper has firmed and should stay higher during the rest of 1973, the firm expects to earn $2.00 a share in 1973. Almost all the security analysts who follow the firm agree with this estimate.

The firm's stock price has moved in a relatively narrow range, always selling about 10 times earnings per share. The firm is not considered by most to be a growth firm as it pays out each year a regular $1.00 per share dividend plus a year-end dividend of approximately 50% of all earnings above $1.00 and reinvests the rest in its portfolio of marketable securities. The firm has no debt. However, despite the expected increase in earnings per share, the stock is selling at $12 a share, 6 times expected earnings.

Since late 1972, the political climate in Quepasa has been upset by the strong showing of Marxist candidates in the Quepasa congress. In the last national election, the Marxists almost won a majority of the congress and are now trying to form an alliance with a leftist leaning party to vote out the present government and to install their candidate who promises to nationalize the mining and industrial operations in the country. Since he is the first Marxist candidate to come close to being elected, he has received wide publicity in the U.S. papers.

Throughout the country's entire history, it has had a firm policy of welcoming foreign capital to spur development and has always provided a stable, climate in which to do business. South American Copper Corporation has always had extremely friendly relationships with the government, but this is very likely to end if the Marxist is elected to head the government. For the first time in years the miners have threatened to strike and, in what was otherwise a peaceful country, armed guerilla bands have assassinated some army officials.

South American Copper Corporation has issued statements that they are aware of the situation and are maintaining a close watch on the situation, although they have not taken any active move to negotiate the sale of the mine or to counter the threat of nationalization with diversification efforts or similar possibilities. Management has consistently maintained that the firm's current liquidity position was strong enough to withstand any temoprary disruption in operation. The firms balance sheet for 1972 revealed a current ratio of 3:1.

EXHIBIT 1

SOUTH AMERICAN COPPER CORP.

Balance Sheet, 1972

(000)

CURRENT ASSETS		
Cash & Marketable Securities	$10,000	
Accounts Receivable	1,000	
Inventory	1,000	
Total Current Assets		12,000
Fixed Assets (Net of Depreciation) all located in Quepasa		4,000
Total Assets		16,000
CURRENT LIABILITIES		
Accounts Payable	3,000	
Other Current Liabilities	1,000	
Total Current Liabilities		4,000
Net Worth (1 million shares)		12,000
Total Liabilities		16,000

QUESTIONS

1. Despite the expected increase in earnings per share to $2.00 in 1973, why has the stock price dropped? What has happened to expected earnings after 1973? What has happened to the company's operating environment? Even if Quepasa does not nationalize the firm's Quepasa properties, what is the effect on the firm's business risk?

2. What has happened to the firm's price-earnings ratio? Give specific reasons for your answer.

3. Compute the variance in the firm's earnings per share from 1968 to 1972 inclusive. Can you use this figure to evaluate the firm's business risk after 1973?

4. Compute the book value per share. Assuming the Quepasa government expropriated the firm's foreign properties, recompute the book value. If the Quepasa government nationalized the firm's mine in exchange for $10 million worth of 30 year, 10% Quepasa government notes which were presently selling at their par value on the New York Stock Exchange, what would be the book value? If the bonds were not negotiable, would this change your answer? Would it force you to readjust your estimate of the worth of the exchange? Why?

Case 26

HARVARD HOE CO.

Horizontal Diversification

The Harvard Hoe Co. (HH) of Terre Haute, Indiana, is a manufacturer of small, hand gardening implements and tools for the rapidly growing amateur gardening market. The firm's major products include hoes, rakes, and most of the other commonly used tools. All are relatively small items and are priced to appeal to the mass market and the replacement market. The increase in leisure time and the desire for hobbies among consumers has lead to a steady growth in the firm's sales and earning over the past ten years, as shown in Exhibit 1.

EXHIBIT 1

HARVARD HOE CO.

Statement of Income, December 31, 1972

Sales	$10,000,000
Cost of Golds Sold	5,000,000
Selling & Gen'l. Admin. Expenses	3,000,000
Depreciation	100,000
Total	8,100,000
Operating Income	1,900,000
Interest	—
Taxes	900,000
Net Income	1,000,000

Balance Sheet, December 31, 1972

Cash		$ 1,000,000
Accounts Receivables		500,000
Inventory		500,000
Total Current Assets		2,000,000
Fixed Assets	4,000,000	
Depreciation	2,000,000	
Net Fixed Assets		2,000,000
Total Assets		4,000,000
Accounts Payable		1,000,000
Other		500,000
Total Current Liabilities		1,500,000
Stockholder's Equity (1 million shares)		2,500,000
Total Liabilities		4,000,000

Despite the success of the operation, however, the management began to explore ways in which it might improve efficiency. One of the biggest problems was the seasonal pattern of the firm's sales and manufacturing process. Six months of the year, the firm operated at full capacity, employing 20 full time people in the plant and office and ten full time salesmen in the field. However, during the remaining six months of the year, the firm employed only five full time personnel. This seasonality was rather expensive for the firm, because the periodical lay off of workers had kept its unemployment insurance premiums to the U. S. Government $300,000 a year above what they otherwise would have been. Retraining and start up expenditures ran $100,000 a year above what they would have been if the firm had an annual operating basis. In addition, the firm's new warehouse, costing $500,000 a year, was only used half of the year.

In order to solve this seasonality problem and to eliminate these expenses, HH entered into merger discussions with the Fast Sled Co. (FS) of Terre Haute, Indiana. Fast Sled's only product was childrens' snow sleds. The firm usually did well in periods of prosperity when parents' could afford to buy their children a

new sled. However, profits usually suffered during recessions when consumer in-
comes were down. This was in contrast to the steady and uninterrupted climb in
HH's earnings.

The firms were very similar in other areas. Both had severe seasonality problems. Fast Sled's only product sold well during the winter season, while HH's
products sold well only during the summer season. In fact, FS all but closed
down for six months of the year. It, too, had to lay off its personnel and this
was costing FS $100,000 in additional unemployment insurance premiums and
$50,000 in start up and retraining expenses. In addition, its warehouse, which
it rented for $300,000 a year, was only fully utilized half of the time. Both firms
used the same production and machinery techniques. Both used forged iron and
treated wood for their raw materials and the same type of drop forges and stamping machines for the manufacturing process. HH's management estimated that it
would cost $50,000 a year in retooling expense if the firms merged.

The managements of both companies also agreed that if they merged it would
totally eliminate the extra unemployment insurance premiums because they
could keep a steady work force employed all year round. In addition, retraining
and start up expenses could be eliminated, and FS could use the HH warehouse.
The firms agreed to merge on the basis of one share Harvard Hoe stock for each
share of Fast Sled stock.

EXHIBIT 2

HARVARD HOE CO.

Earnings Record

	EARNINGS (000)
1972	$1,000
1971	950
1970	900
1969	850
1968	825
1967	800
1966	750
1965	700
1964	675
1963	650

EXHIBIT 3

FAST SLED CO.
December 31, 1972

Sales	$11,000,000
Cost of Goods Sold	5,000,000
Selling and Gen'l. Admin. Expenses	2,500,000
Depreciation	500,000
Total	8,000,000
Operating Income	3,000,000
Interest	100,000
Taxes	1,400,000
Net Income	1,500,000

Balance Sheet, December 31, 1972

Cash		$1,500,000
Accounts Receivable		500,000
Inventory		500,000
Total Current Assets		2,500,000
Fixed Assets	5,000,000	
Depreciation	2,000,000	
Net Fixed Assets		3,000,000
Total Assets		5,500,000
Accounts Payable		1,500,000
Other		500,000
Total Current Liabilities		2,000,000
Long-Term Debt (10%)		1,000,000
Stockholder's Equity (1 million shares)		2,500,000
Total Liabilities		5,500,000

EXHIBIT 4

FAST SLED CO.

	EARNINGS (000)
1972	$1,500
1971	1,300
1970	1,000
1969	700
1968	1,000
1967	200
1966	1,300
1965	1,000
1964	500
1963	700

QUESTIONS

1. Construct a pro forma balance sheet and statement of income for the merged company (assume all assets are carried at market value on a pooling of interests basis).
2. Taking into consideration all the possible savings which could be derived from the merger, estimate the earnings for the merged company. How much does the merged company save in operating expenses? What are the synergistic effects?
3. What has happened to the seasonality in the merged firm's operations?
4. Compute the statistical variance in the past earnings for each of the firms. Assuming the merger had taken place in 1962, recompute the variance in the earnings and compare the result with the previous variances. What has happened to the merged firm's business risk?

Case 27

MAGNESON COPPER TUBING CO.

Vertical Diversification

Merlin C. Bloch, III, is a security analyst with an investment banking firm. Ever since joining the firm in late 1962, Merlin has been in charge of the corporate merger and acquisition department, and it is his job to initiate merger discussions between firms which, in his opinion, would benefit all concerned, especially his firm which gets a 5% commission on the total value of the transaction if the merger is consummated. Therefore, Merlin is constantly seeking possible mergers and trying to point out the advantages of merging to each firm involved in the negotiations.

Merlin's latest effort involves the Magneson Copper Tubing Co. (MCT) of of Mesa, Arizona. MCT is a relatively large producer of copper tubing for the residential home construction market. The firm is only one of the many suppliers of copper tubing to this cyclically prone industry, and especially during recessions, price competition among the copper tubing fabricators is usually quite sharp. Since none of the firms in the industry is recognized as a price leader or commands any position of price control, none of the firms, including MCT, is capable of influencing the market.

MCT buys all of its raw copper ore in the world commodities exchanges at prices which prevail there, since the firm, unlike some others, is not affiliated or does not control a copper ore mining operation. After purchasing the raw copper, MCT refines it in its own refinery, extrudes it into the appropriate shapes for the housing market and, finally, markets the finished product through its own sales force and marketing organization. The erratic price of raw copper and the cyclical nature of the residential home construction industry have together caused MCT's sales and operating earnings to fluctuate widely, as shown in Exhibit 1. Often, when housing starts are off, the firm's sales and operating earnings decline, and sometimes, even in the face of rising housing starts, operating earnings are held down because of a rise in the price of raw copper, which the firm is unable to pass along to the consumer.

EXHIBIT 1

MAGNESON COPPER TUBING CO.

	SALES (mil)	OPERATING EARNINGS (000)	COPPER ORE PRICE (¢/lb.)	HOUSING STARTS (mil)
1972	$50.0	$1,000	$.35	2.0
1971	46.0	900	.39	1.8
1970	56.0	1,500	.30	2.3
1969	46.0	1,000	.33	1.9
1968	42.0	800	.42	1.7
1967	40.0	700	.40	1.6
1966	40.0	800	.39	1.5
1965	44.0	1,000	.36	1.8
1964	36.0	600	.45	1.2
1963	38.0	500	.46	1.3

In 1972, MCT had operating income of $1 million on sales of $50 million. This was a good year for the firm because both housing starts were up and the price of raw copper was down in the same year. In 1972, MCT used 5 million pounds of raw copper; in 1973, the firm expects to use the same amount since it anticipates housing starts to level off. It also expects the same operating expenses in 1973 as it had in 1972.

Merlin has approached MCT with the idea of merging the Arizona Desert Rose Copper Mining Corp., a copper mine located 50 miles into the desert from Mesa, with MCT. Merlin has explained to MCT management that if they acquired this mining operation it would be a steady source of raw copper for the firm's refinery and extrusion operations and that, with good management, the firm could keep the price of copper ore from the mine at a steady level. This would help to stabilize earnings. Merlin's consulting geologist has appraised the mine's ore at the same quality which MCT is presently buying on the market and confirmed that proven reserves were enough to supply MCT's anticipated needs for at least the next 20 years. The geologist estimates that MCT could mine this copper and deliver it to the Mesa refinery for $.40 a pound, $.05 a pound more than the going market price, because of the strict Arizona strip mining laws and transportation costs.

QUESTIONS

1. Compute the variance in MCT's operating income from 1963 to 1972, inclusive.
2. Assuming it takes one pound of copper ore to produce $10.00 in final revenues, what would have been the effect on the firm's operating earnings for each year 1963 through 1972, if the firm had purchased the Arizona Desert Rose Copper mine on January 1, 1963 (assume mining costs were constant at $.40 a pound).
3. Recompute the variance in the operating income on the basis of your answer to question 2, i.e., if the mine had been purchased in 1963. What would this have done for the firm's business risk?
4. What is the most likely effect on the firm's earnings prospects, price-earnings ratio, and stock price, if the merger is consummated? Why? (Assume the merger is without the issuance of additional common stock or an increase in MCT's debt service obligation.)

Case 28

BASE INDUSTRIES INC.

Management Evaluation

James C. Baul, a security analyst with a New York Stock Exchange firm is taking his first field trip to Base Industries, Inc., a producer of heavy industrial machinery which has just changed management. Baul wants to talk to the new management and to discuss its plans for Base Industries.

Baul's first question of George Abel, head of the new management team was to confirm that the estimate of $2.00 a share in earnings and $1.00 in dividends for the coming year was in the ball park. The firm had paid this $1.00 a year dividend for some time now and with the stock selling at $20 a share, the yield of 5% had attracted some of Baul's clients. The new management agreed with Baul's earnings estimate but was much more interested in detailing the firm's plans for future growth which they targeted at 30% year. They pointed to the relatively static and cyclical earnings record of Base Industries from 1963 to 1972 when earnings per share ranged from $1.00 to $3.00, and averaged $2.00 a share.

Management's first major thrust was to try to smooth the cyclical earnings through planned diversification. According to Abel, Base was going to diversify over a wide range of areas, with emphasis on consumer and leisure products and on high technology electronic instrumentation. To reflect this diversification and to project the firm's new image, management planned to change the company name to Leisdyne General, Inc. at the next annual stockholders meeting.

The management, as a team, had no previous record and only limited experience in corporate management. Most of the team were MBA's from the State University, and all were indoctrinated with the total management concept, which preached that uniform management practice could solve any problem and the delegation of responsibility and authority. The team believed strongly in this latter point and planned to operate their acquisitions as autonomous subsidiaries. They believed in giving young, capable men complete control and letting them "sink or swim on their abilities." Some of the team did have experience as engineers or lawyers and all had been among the top in their graduating class. The team also comprised the entire board of directors of the firm, although they promised to elect some outside public directors soon.

Baul also met with Marc Rosen, the head of marketing, and Ben Otis, the head of production. Marc had been a brilliant and aggressive marketing major at State U. specializing in mathematical modeling. He, alone, was charged with the responsibility of handling all of the firm's marketing and inventory policies, which he intended to do through his large, computerized models of demand based on early 1960's data. Ben Otis, like Marc, was a brilliant and aggressive individual, who after receiving his engineering degree went on for his MBA. While his personality was rather high strung and domineering he, nevertheless, had the respect of his whole department because of his ability in the use of sophisticated computerized models. Both men stressed their use of such techniques as discounted cash flow for evaluating potential investments.

The whole team was highly motivated toward success. The head man, George Abel, wanted to put his company into the top 40 firms in total sales within five years, and expected earnings to grow at a 30% compounded annual rate over that time. The team was also moving the firm's headquarters from Moline, Ill. to New York City where they had leased the top three floors of a major skyscraper in anticipation of their expansion and had purchased a company jet.

The entire team agreed that the "modern approach" to management was to pay young executives well and demand that they do well. With this in mind most of the team had been granted large stock options, although few owned large amounts of the stock, as incentives to perform. The corporate headquarters staff was doubled in anticipation of the new larger organization.

As a first step in diversification, the new management was acquiring a manufacturer of private label televisions in exchange for $50 million of the firm's 10% convertible subordinated debentures due 1990 and talking to a real estate developer located in the San Andreas Fault, California. Baul asked if the interest rate was not a little high since the market yield for bonds of this type was about 7%. Management avoided the question, but did stress that these acquisitions were at arms length even though the companies were being acquired from two relatives of the new management team. The firm's plans called for turning the San Andreas Development into a self-contained community, using 90% financing borrowed from local insurance companies. Baul questioned the use of such a high proportion of debt, but management assured him that it was typical of the real estate industry, in general. In addition, the firm was presently in merger discussions with about 30 firms.

To finance their plans, the team planned to use a significant amount of debt, because they believed in the power of leverage. Since Base Industries had no debt, they planned to use this untapped borrowing power and already plans were underway to borrow $100 million from local banks. After the debt issue and the acquisition, the firm's capital structure would be 60% debt, but the new team considered that "cheap money" with which to implement their plans, since it did not dilute the equity, although they planned to discontinue the dividend in order to finance their acquisitions.

QUESTIONS

1. How has the new management team changed the business and financial risk of Base industries? Give specific references to statements in the interview to support your answer. If you were a stockholder of Base Industries, would the new management philosophy be compatible with your investment objectives? Why or why not?

2. Comment on the new management's diversification plans. Do they appear to be well thought out? Have the markets chosen for expansion been carefully selected and studied, or does the choice appear disoriented? What are the problems with the proposed mergers of the TV manufacturer and the real estate developer in terms of business and financial risk? Are the two mergers likely to smooth the cyclical earnings pattern as claimed by management?

3. Comment on the new management team's record and on their management philosophy of complete independent control. Comment on the composition of the board of directors and on the depth of management.

4. How is the new management's philosophy affecting the firm's prospects? Is their use of 60% debt in the capital structure appropriate with their objectives of growth and stability in the earnings? Is it possible to expand as rapidly as they seem to intend without diluting the equity?

5. Comment on possible friction in the firm's organization structure. Could this be a potential source of trouble for the firm?

6. Comment on possible conflicts among management's goals. Are the goals clearly defined? Do you feel that management is trying to maximize its own power, even at the expense of the stockholders? Do you think management used modern management techniques, such as discounted cash flow, in evaluating the purchase of the company jet or the move to its new offices? What signs of potential unnecessary expense do you see in the firm's new management structure?

Case 29

McCLAREN INDUSTRIES

Financial Risk

Paula Parker, a security analyst, has been asked by several of the firm's account executives for her opinion on the recently announced merger plan of McClaren Industries and Whitcomb Electronics. In examining the terms of the merger, Paula became concerned over the increase in financial risk which would result if the merger were consummated. McClaren Industries on June 1, 1973 was offering to exchange $40 million of its newly created 5% subordinated debentures due to mature June 1, 1977 in exchange for all the stock of Whitcomb. Since neither firm previously had any debt in its capital structure, Paula was worried about the impact of this proposed sudden increase in the use of debt.

Paula decided she would use several methods to determine if the proposed merger would substantially increase the financial risk as measured by the variability in the firms earnings per share. She decided on the mean absolute deviation (MAD) in earnings per share, which is the sum of the absolute differences between each earnings figure and the average earnings figure divided by the number of years:

$$\text{MAD} = \frac{\sum_{i=1}^{n} |\overline{X} - X_i|}{n}$$

She also intended to compute the standard deviation (σ) in earnings per share and the coefficient of variation of earnings per share.

Both McClaren and Whitcomb were successful manufacturers of burglar alarms and other crime prevention equipment. In 1972, McClaren reported earnings of $2 million on sales of $50 million, while Whitcomb reported earnings of $1 million, after taxes, on sales of $25 million. The 1972 Statements of Income and Balance Sheets are reproduced below:

EXHIBIT 1

McCLAREN INDUSTRIES

Statement of Income ($000), December 31, 1972

Sales		$50,000
Cost of Goods Sold	$30,000	
Selling and Gen'l. Admin. Expenses	11,000	
Depreciation	5,000	46,000
Operating Income		4,000
Net Before Taxes		4,000
Taxes		2,000
Net Income		2,000

Balance Sheet ($000), December 31, 1972

Cash	$ 1,000	
Accounts Receivable	2,000	
Inventory	2,000	
Total Current Assets		5,000
Net Property		20,000
Total Assets		25,000
Accounts Payable	2,000	
Total Current Liabilities		2,000
Stockholder Equity		
Common Stock (1 million shares)	$ 5,000	
Capital Surplus	5,000	
Retained Earnings	13,000	23,000
Total Liabilities		25,000

EXHIBIT 2

WHITCOMB ELECTRONICS

Statement of Income ($000), December 31, 1972

Sales		$25,000
Cost of Goods Sold	$12,500	
Selling and General Admin. Exp.	7,500	
Depreciation	3,000	23,000
Operating Income		2,000
Net Income before taxes		2,000
Taxes		1,000
Net Income		1,000

Balance Sheet ($000), December 31, 1972

Cash	$ 1,000	
Accounts Receivable	2,000	
Inventory	1,000	
Total Current Assets		4,000
Net Property		15,000
Total Assets		19,000
Accounts Payable	2,000	
Total Current Liabilities		2,000
Stockholders equity		
Common Stock (1 million shares)	2,000	
Capital Surplus	3,000	
Retained Earnings	13,000	17,000
Total Liabilities		19,000

EXHIBIT 3

NET EARNINGS HISTORY ($000)

	McCLAREN	WHITCOMB
1972	$2,000	$1,000
1971	1,800	900
1970	1,200	600
1969	1,600	800
1968	1,400	700
1967	1,200	600
1966	1,400	700
1965	1,800	900
1964	1,300	650
1963	1,100	550

The 5% subordinated debenture which McClaren offered in exchange for the stock of Whitcomb contained provisions which provided for repayment of the entire issue in equal annual installments from 1973 through maturity. If in any year the net earnings before taxes were less than 50% of the total repayment scheduled for that year, the bondholders had the option to declare the total remaining amount due.

QUESTIONS

1. Combine the two balance sheets and statements of income as if the firms were merged on a purchase basis, assuming Whitcomb carried its assets at a book value which approximated market and that McClaren intends to amortize any goodwill over a period of 40 years. What are the debt/equity ratio, earnings before interest and taxes, and earnings per share of the merged firms? Has the leverage effect been unfavorable or favorable from a stockholder's point of view?

2. Compute the variance in the earnings per share of each company for the last ten years. Assuming the merger was consummated on a purchase basis, recompute the pro forma earning per share, including interest and amortization changes, for the last ten years and then recompute the variance. What has been the effect of the merger on the variance?

3. Recompute the variability in the actual and the pro forma earnings per share using the mean absolute deviation, the coefficient of variation, and the standard deviation. Compare the results among all three and the variance computed in question 2. Do they all indicate the same effect of the merger?

4. How much does the merged firm have to repay each year on its debentures? Are they likely to meet the 1973 payment, assuming net earnings and depreciation do not change from 1972? Are they likely to repay the entire debenture by 1977? If the firm could refinance the 5% subordinated debenture of 1977 with 9% first mortgage bonds due 1995, would it be better off?

Case 30

MARGARET FARRELL

Bond Analysis

Margaret Farrell, a bond analyst for Last of Arkansas Securities Corporation, has undertaken a complete review of all the Houtex Lighting and Power Co. (HL&P) bonds and has found a wide variety of types and indenture provisions with which to cope. Over the years, the HL&P Co. has frequently gone to the bond market to raise funds to support its rapidly growing electrical generating capacity. HL&P has found it necessary to tailor the provisions of each bond to suit the desire of the particular purchasers and to meet the conditions demanded by the market at the time of issue. Margaret has therefore, to examine the terms of each bond, which are contained in the bond indenture.

Margaret found she could classify most of the provisions into three broad categories. First, all indentures identified the bond by type, interest rate, and maturity date. For example, the first indenture she looked at was headed HL&P 4 3/4% 1st Mortgage bonds of 1990.

The second general category of indenture provisions defined the ability of the firm to call the bond for redemption. Many of the HL&P bonds were callable for sinking fund requirements or had deferred call clauses. Margaret usually computed a yield to average life in the case of a sinking fund call provision, which measured the yield as if a pro rata part of the bonds held in any portfolio was called for redemption at each sinking fund date. In the case of a simple call provision, Margaret always computed the yield to first call which, including any call premium, measured the yield as if the bond were called as soon as possible. She also compared both these yields to the yield to maturity, where appropriate.

The third general category contained all the security provisions on which the lenders had insisted in an effort to increase the degree of safety. Among the most common were the restrictions on the firm's ability to pay dividends or reduce its working capital below a specified dollar amount, in the hopes of forcing the issuer to avoid a liquidity crisis. Also commonly found in this category were provisions which provided the bondholder with additional specific security, such as liens on particular pieces of HL&P's property and equipment or restrictions on the firm's ability to sell assets. Margaret also found provisions which allowed the trustee of the indenture, who is responsible for its enforcement, to declare the entire amount of that particular issue immediately due, instead of at maturity, in the event an issuer defaulted on any debt. She also found that HL&P had guaranteed the debt of an affliated firm.

All of HL&P bonds had been rated triple A by both leading rating services, although not all the bonds had identical provisions. In the course of its expansion, HL&P had issued the following bonds which were still outstanding:

TABLE 1

AMOUNT OUTSTANDING (mil)	TYPE	YIELD TO MATURITY
$25	1st Mortgage 4-7/8's 1990	7.55%
25	1st Mortgage 4-1/2's 1990	7.50
40	1st Mortgage 4-3/4's 1990	7.60
50	Sinking Fund Debentures 4-3/4's 1990	7.75
50	Subordinated Debentures 7-1/2's 1990	7.50
50	2nd Mortgage 4-3/4's 1990	7.75
50	Subordinated Debentures 7-3/4's 1990	7.75
50	Subordinated Debentures 4-1/2's 1990	7.65
50	Sinking Fund Guaranteed Debentures South Texas L&P 4-1/2's 1990	7.80
25	Equipment Trust Certificates 4-5/8's 1990	7.48

The first mortgage 4-7/8's of 1990 were callable at par in equal annual installments which would retire the remaining amount of the issue by maturity and were secured by a lien on the major generating station and equipment in the utility's system. The 1st mortgage 4½'s of 1990 were callable for the sinking fund at par in equal annual installments which would retire the bonds by maturity and were secured by the highly valuable downtown office building which was the headquarters of the firm. The 1st mortgage 4-3/4's of 1990 were an open end mortgage on the generating equipment not elsewhere pledged. Since the original sale the firm had borrowed regularly under the terms of the indenture, always increasing the amount of this bond outstanding. The sinking fund(S.F) debentures 4-3/4's of 1990 were callable at 105 in equal serial installments designed to retire the issue by maturity. The debenture also contained dividend restrictions which prohibited the firm from paying any dividends if the retained earning fell below $75 million or if working capital fell below $14 million. The subordinated debentures 7½'s of 1990 were only callable at 105 starting four years from now. The 2nd Mortgage 4-3/4's of 1990 were also open ended. The subordinated debentures 7-3/4's of 1990 were callable at any time for 105. The subordinated debentures 4½'s 1990 were callable at any time at 105. The South Texas L&P bonds were guaranteed as to payment of interest and principal by HL&P. The equipment trust certificates were chattel mortgages on the transportation equipment owned by the company.

In her most recent interview with HL&P management, Margaret asked about the firm's philosophy in issuing debt. Specifically, she wondered why the variety in the identure terms. Management replied that they tailored each bond to meet the demands of the buyer, the public utility commission, and the general prevailing market conditions. Their objective was to keep the interest as low as possible through this tailoring. Margaret still wondered: if all the bonds could be declared in default by the trustee if any one went into default, why did the bondholders insist on these provisions? Generally, the interest coverage to any one bond was figured on the overall basis such that all interest payments had to be met, not just the interest on any particular bond. However, some investors still used the cumulative deduction interest coverage in which only the interest of bonds with prior claims on the earnings available for interest were considered in computing the interest coverage of that particular bond, despite the fact this had been misleading in many instances of default. Further, several investors still, despite the triple A rating, worried about bankruptcy and were willing to take a lower interest rate for some protection if the firm had to be reorganized or liquidated. In either case, the more senior rated securities stood a better chance of preserving their investment than the less senior securities, although management seriously doubted either situation would arise.

QUESTIONS

1. Comment on the purpose, value, and effect of the various indenture provisions contained in the bonds. Give the reasoning behind each and tell how each might be of value to the bondholder.

2. Compute the yield to first call on the subordinated debenture 7½'s of 1990. Compare this to the yield to maturity. Comment on the usefulness and purpose of the yield to first call.

3. Compute the value of the deferred call on the subordinated debentures 7½'s of 1990, assuming interest rates are now 7½% and were expected to drop to 5% one year from now (use 5% as the reinvestment rate).

4. Compute the yield to average life on the S.F. debentures 4-3/4's of 1990, assuming 18 years until maturity and a current price of $710.

5. Why should the open ended 1st mortgage bonds yield more than other first mortgage bonds? Why should the 1st mortgage 4½'s of 1990 yield less than the 1st mortgage 4-7/8's of 1990?

6. Comment on the value of the 1st morgage liens if any of the firm's bonds or debentures defaulted. What would be the effect on the other bonds and debentures in the event of default on any of the securities. What does this tell you about lien provisions?

7. Why does the subordinated debenture 4½'s of 1990 yield less than the subordinated debenture 7-3/4's of 1990 in what is obviously a period of higher than previous interest rates?

8. In the event of reorganization, which bond would have the best chance of preserving its investment? In the event of liquidation, which bond gets first claim on the liquidation proceeds?

Case 31

CAROL MINCE

Convertible Bonds

Carol Mince is a successful career woman who, in her leisure time, dabbles in the stock and bond market. Her investment objective is capital gain, leading to a growth in the value of her portfolio. On January 7, 1972, Carol held three convertible bonds in her portfolio. She felt the interest payment would provide some income for her, but more importantly, she believed these bonds offered opportunities for capital gains while limiting her downside risk.

Two of the bonds were Major Industries convertible debentures. One bond was Major Industries' 4¼ convertible subordinated debenture of 1985. This bond was convertible into 32.5 common shares of Major Industries at a price of $30.78 a share until maturity. The bond was currently selling at 83, with a current yield of 5.12%. Similarly rated bonds without conversion features were presently selling to yield 8% on a current basis. Carol had paid 55 for ten of the bonds one year prior. At the time she bought the 4¼'s, she also purchased ten Major Industries 5% convertible subordinated debentures of December, 1992 for 50. These latter debentures were convertible into 14.93 shares of Major Industries common stock at $67.00 a share until maturity, with a current yield of 8.20%, based on the current selling price of 61. Similarly rated bonds of this maturity were selling in the market to yield 10% to maturity.

Major Industries is a diversified company engaged in the electronics field. The firm had a commanding position in several areas such as electronic betting equipment and color TV tuners, but over the years has not compiled a respectable earnings record. In fact, despite the good growth prospects for several of its products, such as community antenna TV equipment and minature electronic circuitry, earnings have been erratic and lower in the last several years, as can be seen from Exhibit 1. In view of this performance the firm pays no cash dividend, although it has annually paid a 3% stock dividend, which is not protected by an anti-dilution clause in the convertible debentures. The stock's performance has similarly reflected this earnings pattern. In the mid- 1960's when the firm was experiencing rapid growth from the TV tuner market, the stock reached a high of 83. Since then, the stock has drifted downward until it is now 20½, at the lower end of its 1972 price range.

The other convertible bonds holding in Carol's portfolio are ten BB rated Fortune Stores 5's of 1993, convertible into 50 shares of Fortune Stores common at $20 a share through maturity. The bond is selling at 186, reflecting the advance over the years in Fortune's stock price to its present $37 a share. At 186, the current yield is only 2.67%. According to the latest bond analysis from the investment advisory firm of Jovial and Co., the stock value of the bond is 185, and its investment value as straight debt is only 62. One year ago Carol paid 100 for the bond.

Fortune Stores is a well established food retailer on the West Coast. It has grown with the population and through its aggressive marketing policies, has established itself as a leading regional food retailer. Earnings and dividends have risen through the years, as can be seen from Exhibit 2, and are expected to continue in their upward trend.

EXHIBIT 1

MAJOR INDUSTRIES

	EARNINGS PER SHARE	STOCK PRICE RANGE
1972	$ .44	$20-30
1971	.65	30-40
1970	.50	30-35
1969	.45	25-30
1968	1.40	44-67
1967	1.87	60-83
1966	1.50	60-70
1965	1.40	53-72
1964	1.20	48-50
1963	1.10	22-32

EXHIBIT 2

FORTUNE STORES

	EARNINGS PER SHARE	DIVIDENDS
1972	$1.80	$1.00
1971	1.79	1.00
1970	1.78	1.00
1969	1.58	1.00
1968	1.48	.90
1967	1.50	.90
1966	1.43	.90
1965	1.42	.90
1964	1.30	.80
1963	1.25	.80

QUESTIONS

1. Compute the investment value (conversion value) for each of Major Industries debentures. Compare the investment value to the selling price. Explain the difference between the two. Estimate the straight bond value of each debenture. Why have both bonds risen in selling price when the stock has fallen in price? If Major Industries common stock price had risen instead of fallen, which of the two debentures do you think would have increased in price faster? Why?

2. In the case of Fortune Stores 5's of 1993, compare the current debnture income with the current dividend income, which Carol could receive if she converted the bond into common stock. If the former was less than the later what should Carol do? Why? What is the effect on Carol's capital gain objective if she continues to hold the debentures instead of converting to Fortune Stores common stock? If the debentures were called at 105, what should Carol do? Why?

3. If Carol had borrowed an additional 70% of her original investment to increase the number of debentures she could purchase, what would have been her paper profit at today's prices? What is her total profit now, assuming she paid cash for the bonds? What has the effect of the borrowing been on her potential profit and the variability in her account?

4. Assuming stock prices remained unchanged but interest rates rose, what is the likely effect on the price of all three convertible debentures? If Fortune Stores common fell to 30 a share, what would be the effect on the 5% convertible debenture's investment value and on its market value, assuming a 1% premium over conversion value? Compare the percentage-fall in the price of the common stock and the price of the convertible. Draw conclusions.

Case 32

JOHN BLANK

Municipal Bonds

John Blank, a municipal bond analyst with a Wall St. Firm, has been requested by one of the firm's wealthiest and largest municipal bond investors to give his opinion on two bonds of Horse Co., Montana.

The investor owns $100,000 of Horse County Electrical Authority 4% revenue bonds due 2000. The issue is presently selling at $1,000 a bond. In 1970, $32-million of the bond was issued to refinance the existing debt which was rapidly approaching maturity and to provide funds for expansion. Under the terms of the underwriting, the bond was to be retired in equal annual installments until, at maturity, the entire issue would be retired. In accordance with the terms, $1 million of the issue was retired at the end of 1971 and 1972. Other terms of the issue called for the net income before debt service of the Electrical Authority to be at least 110% of the debt service in any calender year.

The Horse County Electrical Authority is the franchised agent in the county for distribution of all electrical power in the area. Long before the population had grown to its present size, the area had been without electrical service because it was unprofitable for a commercially owned utility to operate in so sparsely populated an area. So, the local citizens had banded together to form the Authority, which they empowered to purchase electricity from the High Falls Federal Generating Station and retail to the local residents. On the basis of this business, the Authority sold revenue bonds which were guaranteed as to interest and principal by the operating revenues and income of the electrical distribution system. The area had grown, and in 1970, the authority had refinanced the old debt at a more favorable interest rate. Reproduced below are the 1971 and 1972 statements of operations for the Horse Co. Electrical Authority.

The other Horse County issue which the investor asked John to evaluate was the county's 3 1/2% General Obligation bonds due 2000. These were the only bonds backed by the county's pledge to use its full faith and taxing power. There remained $100 million of the debt outstanding as of 1972, but, starting in 1973, the county was required to retire at least 3% of the outstanding amount in each of the remaining years in the life of the issue. The county has a $200 million debt ceiling and a 5% tax rate on assessed value limitation in its present charter.

Horse County had grown in recent years to a population estimated to be 82,000, up from 80,000 just two years ago. The county's property values had also increased, as well as its tax revenues. However, the residents' demand for services had strained the budget and the county had operated at a small deficit

EXHIBIT 1

HORSE CO. ELECTRICAL AUTHORITY
Statement of Operations ($000)

	1971	1972
Operating Revenues		
Residential	$ 6,000	$ 6,100
Commercial	1,000	1,200
Industrial	750	600
Pipe Line Pumping	1,250	1,200
Total	9,000	9,100

EXHIBIT 1(Continued)

HORSE CO. ELECTRICAL AUTHORITY

Statement of Operations ($000)

	1971	1972
Operating Expenses		
Purchased Power	4,100	4,200
Other	300	300
Maintenance	600	700
Depreciation	1,000	1,000
Total	6,000	6,200
Operating Income	3,000	2,900
Interest charges	1,280	1,240
Income before debt amortization	1,720	1,660
Operating Statistics		
Utility Plant In Service	$ 22,205	$ 23,534
Depreciable Reserve	4,994	5,442
Utility Plant Per $ Revenue	$3.15	$3.10
Total KWH Sold	361,942	386,644
Annual Ave KWH/Residential Customer	5,943	5,558

of $500,000 a year for several years now. This deficit had been covered from re-
serves which had been specifically put aside for the purpose in an earlier period,
but the reserve was rapidly dwindling and would shortly be expended if the deficits continue. In all respects, one might say that Horse County was a typical growing American county.

In addition to the county administration, there was a local school district
which ran the Horse County schools. The citizens had just recently authorized a
$50 million school bond issue to modernize and expand the system. This would
be in addition to the district's already outstanding $20 million bond issue. The
local county water district had $10 million in revenue bonds outstanding and the
local sewage district had $20 million in revenue bonds outstanding. The county
mosquito control district had $5 million in debt outstanding which was guaran-
teed by the mosquito levy placed on all property owners.

HORSE COUNTY STATISTICS

	1960	1970	1972 (est)
Population	60,000	80,000	82,000
Assessed Property Value	$200 (mil)	$300 (mil)	$320 (mil)
Taxes collected	$ 30 (mil)	$ 30 (mil)	$ 32 (mil)
Tax rate	1.5%	1.0%	1.0%
Assessment	100%	100%	100%
Moodys Rating	Baa	Baa	Baa
Income per capital	$1,000	$1,500	$1,500

QUESTIONS

1. Compute the debt service on the Electrical Authority revenue bonds. Do you
believe there is sufficient coverage? Assuming you are familiar with the appro-

priate standards of comparison, what are the indicators of the quality of the debt service coverage based on the data presented? Be sure to discuss such things as operating efficiency, quality of equipment, expansion prospects, customer type and quality, population, and other pertinent indicators. Under what circumstances would the Authority probably default on its bonds? What would be the investor's recourse if the bonds defaulted?

2. Compute the debt service coverage on the general obligation bonds. Is it sufficient? Assuming you are familiar with the appropriate standards of comparison, what are the indicators of the quality of that coverage based on the data presented. Be sure to discuss such indicators as the bond rating, the tax collection rate, the implications of the tax rate and the assessment rate, debt per capita, and other pertinent indicators. Under what possible circumstance would the county default on its bonds? What recourse does the bondholder have if the county defaults? Compare your answer to your answer in question 1.

Case 33

ROBERT SAWS

Mergers

Robert Saws, a security analyst with a large brokerage firm, has been asked by one of his clients to review the effect of the proposed merger of Ajax Electrical Co. with the Omega Electrical Co. The client specifically wants to know the operations and financial condition of the companies after the merger.

In response Robert Saws went to the management of both companies to ask about the merger. However, neither company would give out any statement, except to say a definite agreement to merge Omega into Ajax on a share for share basis had been reached. They were still working out the details and no announcement or discussion would be appropriate at this time.

Saws returned to his office to study the financial statements of the two firms, reproduced below, to determine if he could construct what the merged firm would look like.

EXHIBIT 1

AJAX ELECTRIC CO.

Statement of Income, December 31, 1972

Sales ($000)		$100,000
Cost of Goods Sold	$ 50,000	
Selling & Gen'l. Admin. Expense	30,000	
Depreciation	10,000	90,000
Operating Income		10,000
Interest		5,000
Net before taxes		5,000
Taxes		2,500
Net Income		2,500

Balance Sheet, December 31, 1972

Cash ($000)	$ 10,000	
Accounts Receivable	20,000	
Inventory	25,000	
Total Current Assets		55,000
Plant, Property & Equipment	100,000	
Accumulated depreciation	40,000	
Net Fixed Assets		60,000
Other Assets		5,000
		$120,000
Accounts Payable	20,000	
Acrued Taxes & Wages	5,000	
Other current liabilities	5,000	
Total Current Liabilities		30,000
Long Term Debt (10% interest)		50,000
Stockholders equity		
Capital Stock (1 million shares)		10,000
Paid-in capital		10,000
Retained Earnings		20,000
		$120,000

EXHIBIT 2

OMEGA ELECTRIC CO.

Statement of Income, December 31, 1972

Sales		$50,000
Cost of Goods Sold	$20,000	
Selling & General Admin. Exp.	15,000	
Depreciation	5,000	40,000
Operating Income		10,000
Interest		—
Net before Taxes		10,000
Taxes		5,000
Net Income		5,000

EXHIBIT 2 (Continued)
Balance Sheet, December 31, 1972

Cash ($000)	$ 5,000	
Accounts Receivable	7,000	
Inventory	8,000	
Total Current Assets		20,000
Fixed Assets	80,000	
Accumulated depreciation	60,000	
Net Fixed Assets		20,000
Other Assets		2,000
Total Assets		42,000
Accounts Payable	10,000	
Accrued Taxes & Wages	—	
Other current liabilities	1,000	
Total Current Liabilities		11,000
Stockholders equity		
Common Stock (1 million shares)		5,000
Paid-in capital		5,000
Retained Earnings		21,000
Total Liabilities		42,000

QUESTIONS

1. Construct a pro forma statement of income and balance sheet as of the end of
1972 for the merged company using the pooling of interests method. Assuming
an appraised fair market value of $80 million for the net fixed assets of Omega
and $100 share price for Ajax, construct a pro forma balance sheet for the merged
company using the purchase method.

2. Discuss the differences between the two methods, particularly examining the
strengths and weaknesses of both. Compare the two methods to the concept of an
cept of an on going firm.

Case 34

FAQUA HORSERY CO.

Subscription Rights

Since its founding in 1950 by the Faqua brothers, Bert and Harry, as a land development firm, Faqua Horsery Co. has had a very rapid growth in sales and earnings. Earning had gone from nil to $28.8 million or $2.88 a share in 1972. The company owns large tracts of grazing land in the Northeast corner of Virginia, which it is gradually developing into second home communities for families from the surrounding metropolitan areas who want to escape to the country on holidays and who are particularly interested in raising horses for pleasure. Faqua not only sells the land and builds the house, but also maintains community stable and training facilities, which the residents support through their annual maintenance fee.

Sales have accelerated rapidly since the mid-sixties, doubling almost every year for the last four years. The Faqua brothers credit this rapid growth to the rise in personal disposable income, the increase in the working man's leisure time, the deteriorated environment of the city, the desire to escape to the clean air of the Faqua "estates," and the development of better roads from the city to their lands.

In 1968, the firm started to finance the purchase of its customers' "estates". Raising money for these mortgages has put a heavy strain on the firm's finances, and, several times in the past years, the firm has borrowed large amounts of long term financing from insurance companies.

Now, in 1973, with no sign of any abatement in the firm's growth, almost a third of which now comes from interest on the mortgages, Faqua again needs funds. The firm estimated it would need $50 million in new capital to finance its expansion over the next two years, $10 million of which would come from the internal operations of the firm. Again, they turned to the insurance companies who had loaned them money. The insurance companies agreed to loan the firm another $20 million in long term capital as of January 1, 1973, provided the firm raised another $20 million in common stock financing.

Under this demand, the firm went to its original underwriters and consulted with them on the sale of $20 million in equity financing. The underwriters looked at the situation and suggested several alternatives. The underwriters estimated they could sell the new issue directly to the public at $50 a share, $2 less than the present stock price of $52 a share, for a $5.00 per share commission.

Alternatively, the underwriters suggested that Faqua sell its stock on a subscription basis to its present stockholders. The underwriter estimated it could sell the necessary amount of stock at $45 a share with $1.50 commission on each subscribed share and $5.00 a share commission on each unsubscribed share. A third alternative would be to sell the new issue at $40 a share on a subscription basis, with a $1.00 a share commission on subscribed shares and a $5.00 commission on unsubscribed shares.

EXHIBIT 1

FAQUA HORSERY CO.

Balance Sheet, December 31, 1972

Cash ($000)	$ 4,300	
Accounts Receivable	15,400	
Inventory	17,600	
Total Current Assets		$37,300
Net Fixed Assets		40,400
Total Assets		77,700
Accounts Payable	4,000	
Note Payable	8,500	
Long Term Debt due within one year	2,000	
Total Current Liabilities		14,500
Long Term Debt —10% debentures		30,000
Stockholders' equity		
Capital Stock (10 million shares)		10,000
Additional paid-in capital		10,000
Retain Earnings		13,200
		$77,700

QUESTIONS

1. Assuming all shares are subscribed, what is the number of new shares under each alternative which must be issued to raise the $20 million? What is the number of rights required to subscribe to each additional share under each alternative? How many rights will a holder of 100 shares receive?
2. What is the value of a right under each alternative?
3. What will be the stock price of Faqua when it is first traded ex-rights under each alternative? Why does it change from the day before?
4. If Faqua raises the entire $50 million, assuming it earns 37% on its total assets including the $50 million for the entire year 1973 and it does not increase its current liabilities, compute the firm's earnings per share and stock price for 1973, assuming the P/E is constant. Assume the new equity is sold directly to the public.
5. Why is the commission higher on the unsubscribed shares than on the subscribed shares? What happens to the shareholder's subscription rights if he does not exercise them by their expiration date?

Case 35

TENMATE CORP.

Warrants

Mary Jones, a money manager for a group of wealthy private investors interested in speculative gains, is in charge of their SpecHedge Fund. She has been in charge since 1962, when the group offered her discretionary power to manage the fund. One of her first speculations had been in the warrants of the Tenmate Corp. at $2.00 a warrant. She had purchased 100,000 warrants for the fund and had seen the warrants rise to $41.00 a warrant by the end of 1972. Often, during the years, Mary had been very tempted to take her profit in the warrants, but always, after a careful examination of the prospects for the company and of the warrant itself, she decided not to sell.

From 1961, Tenmate has compiled an outstanding record of growth, first in juvenile clothes and then in double knit fabrics. The firm's first juvenile line had been based on the cute, stylish outfits of the comic strip characters and had sold extremely well. So well, in fact, that in 1963, the company issued a subordinated debenture with detachable warrants to raise funds for a large expansion program. It was these detached warrants which entitled the holder to purchase one share of Tenmate common at $20 a share until 1985 that Mary bought, when they were first listed on the American Stock Exchange in 1963. The expansion was just the first of many, and the firm grew from a small manufacturer with $10 million in sales and $750,000 in net earnings on 500,000 shares to one of the major importers and foreign textile fabricators with annual sales of over $250 million and earnings of $4.00 a share in 1972. As sales and earnings grew, so did the stock price and, consequently, the price of the warrant. From $15 a share in 1963, the stock rose to $60 in 1972, as shown in Exhibit 1. The warrant price rose from $2.00 to $41.00 in the same period.

Periodically, Mary had reviewed the investment in the warrants. She always computed the premium on the warrant which, in 1972, she found to have shrunk to $1.00. This was in contrast to the earlier years in which the premium had been substantial, but in keeping with the continuing decline in the premium which accompanied the rising stock price. Mary did not particularly like this shedding of the premium because it made the warrant price behave almost exactly like the stock price, instead of in the earlier years when the premium appeared to offer some resistance to sudden price reversals.

Mary had always used the Shelton model of premium evaluation, every time she reviewed the warrant investment. The model:

$$P = 4\sqrt[4]{\frac{M}{72}}\,(.047 - 4.25Y + 0.17L)$$

M = number of months remaining in the life of the warrant
Y = dividend yield on common stock
L = 1 if warrant listed, 0 if warrant not listed
P = premium

Mary figured the premium as the percentage difference between the upper limit on the warrant value (3/4 of the associated stock selling price) and the theoretical value of the warrant. She also considered her expectations for the stock price and its behavior over the last year in determining whether or not to liquidate the position.

EXHIBIT 1

	AVERAGE STOCK PRICE	DIVIDEND	WARRANT PRICE
1972	$60	$2.00	$41.00
1971	50-1/2	1.75	31-5/8
1970	40	1.50	23-1/4
1969	30-1/4	1	14-1/4
1968	28-3/8	1	12-1/2
1967	25-1/2	0	10
1966	22	0	7
1965	20-5/8	0	5
1964	18	0	3-1/8
1963	15	0	2

QUESTIONS

1. What is the theoretical value and the premium of the warrant in each year, 1963–1972, inclusive? Explain the downward drift in the premium.
2. Compare the 1972 premium as computed in Shelton's model with your 1972 premium computed in question 1. Comment on the difference. Also, comment on the model's assumptions which might lessen its applicability. Why does Mary consider each of the variables in the model as well as the other factors mentioned in evaluating the warrant?
3. Compare the profit Mary would have made if she had purchased $200,000 worth of the common stock in 1963 instead of 100,000 warrants. Draw conclusions; be sure to include risk consideration in your discussion.

Case 36

ARTHUR SCHWARTZ

Options

Art Schwartz is a wealthy private investor with a substantial portfolio of common stocks. Frequently, as a profitable extension of his investments, he "writes paper", i.e. sells options against the stocks in his portfolio. Sometimes, since he is so active and familiar with the option market he will go "naked" into the option market by buying or selling a call or put option on stocks which he does not have in his portfolio. However, most of the time Art covers his position, eliminating most of the risk of stock price fluctuations and taking only the option writing profit. Art is considered to be an aggressive option writer, and while he most frequently stays with the more common types of options such as calls, puts, and straddles, he has, on occasion, handled strips, straps, and spreads.

On January 27, 1973, Art sold a 95 day put on 100 shares of Artec Soda and Gas (ASG) to a broker for his client. The put was exercisable for $40 a share, the current market price at which ASG was trading, but ten points above the price Art had originally paid for the stock. Art received $300 for the put.

On the same day, Art also bought a 95 day call for his own account on 100 Standard Industrial shares, exercisable at the current market price of $40, for $325. Art had heard a rumor that the firm had struck oil in the back yard of its Alaskan subsidiary's packing plant and expected that the stock might respond. He subjectively estimated that the shares could rise to as high as $60 a share within 95 days, or, if the rumor was unfounded, could decline to the 30–35 price range where they were before the rumor started to circulate. Art subjectively gave the following tabulation of his expectations to his assistant:

Price	Probability of that price
30	5%
35	10
40	20
45	30
50	20
55	10
60	5

Art also knew that Standard Industrial shares were in small supply and very volatile; slight rumor could have a rather large effect on the stock price, which would allow Art to sell his option at a profit. Art suspected that there was already something afoot because the trading volume in the shares, while normally active had increased three fold in the last week. He felt the $325 he had paid for the option appeared very low, for the pricing rule of thumb on this type of option was 10% of the share value.

Art also saw an opportunity to profit on the conversion of a straddle being offered for sale by one of the option houses on the street. The option house was offering a 95 day straddle on 100 shares of ATZ, Inc. at the prevailing market price of $50 a share for $500. Knowing that he had a client interested in purchasing two calls for 100 shares each of ATZ at the prevailing price, but not owning any ATZ in his portfolio, Art simultaneously bought the straddle, sold two calls, one against his own account and one against the account of the person from whom he had bought the straddle, at $395 each, and bought 100 shares of ATZ, Inc. The transaction cost him $50 in commissions and 5% per annum to finance the purchase of the shares.

QUESTIONS

1. Distinguish among the various types of options mentioned in the case. Why should the volatility of the associated stock's price and the other factors considered by Art influence the option price?

2. Assuming ASG stock is selling at $42 a share on the expiration date of the put, what is the profit or loss to Art and to the purchase of the put? If the price were $38 a share on the expiration date would your answer be any different? What is Art's expected profit or loss on his 95 day call on Standard Industrial shares? Did he pay a "low" price for the call? What price would have been the upper limit he was willing to pay?

3. What is Art's profit from his conversion of the straddle?

Case 37

SPEIZMAN INDUSTRIES, INC.

New Issues

Mr. Dill, your stockbroker, is interested in selling you the shares of a company which his firm is underwriting. He has provided you with the preliminary prospectus, the body of which (all but the financial statements and the footnotes thereto) is reproduced on the following pages.

Preliminary Prospectus dated November 9, 1971

600,000 Shares

Speizman Industries, Inc.

Common Stock
without par value

Of the shares offered hereby, 225,000 shares are being sold by the Company and 375,000 shares are being sold by the Selling Stockholders (see "Principal and Selling Stockholders"). The Company will not receive any proceeds from the sale by the Selling Stockholders.

The Company intends to apply for the listing of its Common Stock on the American Stock Exchange.

THESE SECURITIES HAVE NOT BEEN APPROVED OR DISAPPROVED BY THE SECURITIES AND EXCHANGE COMMISSION NOR HAS THE COMMISSION PASSED UPON THE ACCURACY OR ADEQUACY OF THIS PROSPECTUS. ANY REPRESENTATION TO THE CONTRARY IS A CRIMINAL OFFENSE.

	Price to Public	Underwriting Discount (1)	Proceeds to Company (2)	Proceeds to Selling Stockholders (2)
Per Share	$	$	$	$
Total	$	$	$	$

(1) The Company and the Selling Stockholders have agreed to indemnify the several Underwriters against certain civil liabilities, including liabilities under the Securities Act of 1933.

(2) Before deducting expenses estimated at $ payable by the Selling Stockholders and $ payable by the Company.

Prior to this offering there has been no market for the Common Stock of the Company. The public offering price has been determined by negotiation among the Company, the Selling Stockholders and the Underwriters.

The shares of Common Stock are being offered by the Underwriters when, as and if delivered to and accepted by them, and subject to prior sale and to withdrawal of such offer without notice, and the approval of counsel and certain other conditions. It is expected that the shares will be ready for delivery on or about November . ., 1971.

Kidder, Peabody & Co.
Incorporated

The date of this Prospectus is November . ., 1971

IN CONNECTION WITH THIS OFFERING, THE UNDERWRITERS MAY OVER-ALLOT OR
EFFECT TRANSACTIONS WHICH STABILIZE OR MAINTAIN THE MARKET PRICE OF THE
COMMON STOCK AT A LEVEL ABOVE THAT WHICH MIGHT OTHERWISE PREVAIL IN
THE OPEN MARKET. SUCH STABILIZING, IF COMMENCED, MAY BE DISCONTINUED AT
ANY TIME.

THE COMPANY

Speizman Industries, Inc. and its subsidiaries are primarily engaged in marketing textile machinery manufactured by others and in the contract knitting of double-knit fabric for a major garment manufacturer.

Most of the machinery marketed by the Company is purchased for its own account for sale to its customers under exclusive arrangements with major European textile machinery manufacturers. The Company also acts as agent on a commission basis for other textile machinery manufacturers, sells used textile machinery and manufactures and sells specialized knitting and hosiery equipment designed and manufactured by it. Most of such machinery consists of new and used double-knit equipment.

Through The Contract Knitter, Inc., the operations of which were acquired by the Company on November 2, 1971, the Company is engaged in operating a knitting plant, established in 1968, which knits double-knit fabric primarily for one customer.

For the fiscal year ended July 3, 1971, approximately 75% of the Company's net sales and other operating revenues, including both sales of machinery and contract knitting, related to the double-knit industry. Double-knit fabrics are manufactured on machinery which came into prominence in the early 1960's and which by positioning needles on both sides of the fabric produces thicker, more stable fabrics than the lightweight fabrics produced by earlier knitting machinery having a single set of needles. Double-knit fabrics, which retain the give and resiliency of knits but which can also be used in place of traditional woven fabrics, have gained wide acceptance in women's apparel and are being used increasingly in the men's apparel field.

The Company, which was incorporated under the laws of North Carolina in 1967 to succeed to businesses founded by Morris Speizman and his family commencing in 1936, maintains its principal executive offices at 508 West Fifth Street, Charlotte, North Carolina 28201 (telephone: 704 372-3751). Unless the context otherwise requires, the term "Company" as used in this Prospectus refers to Speizman Industries, Inc. and its subsidiaries.

2

CURRENCY AND IMPORT CONTROLS

The Company's net sales and other operating revenues are derived largely from sales in the United States of textile machinery imported from abroad, primarily from Germany, and, therefore, are subject to currency fluctuations and import controls. Most of the Company's sales contracts permit it to recoup increased cost of goods resulting from exchange rate fluctuations. In addition, the Company hedges certain foreign currency transactions, principally in Deutsche Marks. As a result, currency fluctuations have not had a material impact on the Company's operations.

On August 15, 1971, the President of the United States announced a new economic policy to strengthen the United States economy. Included in such policy are a 10% additional import duty on the value of certain imports, including substantially all the products imported by the Company, a proposed 10% investment tax credit to purchasers of certain American-made machinery, including the machinery manufactured by the Company's domestic competitors, and wage-price controls. Substantially all the Company's backlog of orders for imported machinery at August 15, 1971, represented contracts pursuant to which the Company expects to recoup the major part of the additional import duty; the management of the Company does not, therefore, believe that the new economic policy will have any immediate material impact on the Company's operations. The management believes that it is too early to say whether the new economic policy will have a material adverse effect on the Company's future operations.

USE OF PROCEEDS

The net proceeds (estimated at approximately $) from the sale of the 225,000 shares offered by the Company will be applied first to repay indebtedness incurred in connection with the purchase of capital equipment for use in the operations of The Contract Knitter, Inc. and in connection with the financing of equipment leased by the Company to a lessee; the balance will be applied toward the reduction of the Company's bank debt.

The Company will not receive any proceeds from the sale of the 375,000 shares being offered by the Selling Stockholders.

DIVIDENDS

No dividends have been declared or paid by the Company on its Common Stock in the past. The Company at present intends to reinvest earnings in its business and hence does not expect to declare cash dividends on the Common Stock in the near future nor does the Company intend to pay cash dividends on the 5% Non-Voting Preferred Stock before January 1, 1974. Future dividend policy is subject to the discretion of the Board of Directors and will depend upon a number of factors, including future earnings, cash needs, business conditions and results of operations. The Company's ability to pay dividends is, in effect, limited by certain covenants in its short term borrowings commitment letter described in Note 13 to the consolidated financial statements. Under the most restrictive of such covenants, $35,407 was available for the payment of dividends at July 3, 1971.

CAPITALIZATION

The capitalization of the Company at July 3, 1971, and as adjusted to reflect the sale of the 225,000 shares being offered by the Company hereby and the application of the proceeds thereof, is as follows:

Title of Class	Outstanding	As Adjusted
INDEBTEDNESS:		
Short-Term:		
Collateralized Note	$ 60,000	(4)
Notes Due Banks and Bankers Acceptances—With interest at rates from 5.75% to 7.75% (2)	2,244,819	(4)
Total Short-Term	$2,304,819	(4)
Long-Term (including current portion of $1,343,805):		
Collateralized:		
Equipment Purchase Contracts—Payable in monthly installments including interest at rates from 11% to 14%	$1,514,287	—
Notes Due for Financing of Leased Equipment—Payable in monthly installments with interest at the rate of 5.5% above prime, but not less than 12%	591,819	—
Not Collateralized:		
Other Notes Payable—Payable in monthly installments with interest at rates from 0% to 7%	55,504	$ 55,504
Total Long-Term	$2,161,610	$ 55,504
STOCKHOLDERS' EQUITY:		
Preferred Stock, $100 par value (authorized 20,000 shares):		
5% Non-Voting Preferred Stock (non-cumulative) (outstanding, 10,488 shares)	$1,048,800	$1,048,800
Common Stock, without par value (authorized 3,000,000 shares(3)) (outstanding, 1,665,000 shares; outstanding as adjusted, 1,890,000 shares)	283,050	
Additional Capital	736	736
Retained Earnings	3,194,215	3,194,215
Total Stockholders' Equity	$4,526,801	$

(1) The information supplied in the above table has been retroactively adjusted to reflect a recapitalization of the Company effected on October 14, 1971, and the issuance on November 2, 1971, of 305,816 shares of the Company's Common Stock, without par value, in connection with the combination of The Contract Knitter, Inc., with the Company on such date (see "Management—Certain Transactions").

(2) All of such indebtedness has been incurred under a short-term borrowings commitment letter with North Carolina National Bank (see Note 13 to the consolidated financial statements).

(3) Of the authorized but unissued shares of Common Stock, 125,000 are reserved for issuance upon exercise of options which may be granted under the Company's Qualified Stock Option Plan adopted August 30, 1971.

(4) After payment of equipment purchase contracts, the collateralized note and notes due for financing of leased equipment, the remainder of the proceeds to the Company from the sale of the shares being sold by it hereby will be applied to payment of notes due banks.

For information concerning the obligations of the Company on long-term leases, see Note 12 to the consolidated financial statements.

4

SPEIZMAN INDUSTRIES, INC. AND SUBSIDIARIES

STATEMENT OF CONSOLIDATED INCOME

The following statement of consolidated income of Speizman Industries, Inc. and subsidiaries and predecessor corporations has been prepared to include the accounts of The Contract Knitter, Inc. and Morris Speizman (Canada), Ltd. which were combined with the Company in transactions more fully described in Note 1 to the consolidated financial statements. The statement has been examined by Haskins & Sells, independent public accountants, for the fiscal year ended July 3, 1971 as stated in their opinion, which is based in part upon the report of other accountants, and by Hertz, Herson & Company, independent public accountants, for the four fiscal years ended June 27, 1970. The opinions of these firms appear elsewhere in this Prospectus. This statement should be read in conjunction with its notes and the consolidated financial statements and related notes appearing elsewhere in this Prospectus.

	Fiscal Year Ended				
	6/30/67 (52 weeks)	6/30/68 (52 weeks)	6/28/69 (52 weeks)	6/27/70 (52 weeks)	7/3/71 (53 weeks)
Net sales and other operating revenues (Notes a, 1 and 3)	$ 7,812,173	$10,491,450	$11,350,922	$18,818,204	$28,757,639
Costs and expenses:					
Cost of sales and other operating expenses	6,157,901	8,630,471	9,480,675	14,845,157	21,665,197
Selling expenses	449,099	651,602	661,905	748,020	1,268,657
General and administrative expenses	491,845	733,795	731,293	1,108,132	1,460,889
Interest:					
Long-term debt	–	688	34,208	205,422	332,345
Other	66,666	123,353	153,915	227,345	196,678
Total	7,165,511	10,139,909	11,061,996	17,134,076	24,923,766
Income before income taxes and extraordinary items	646,662	351,541	288,926	1,684,128	3,833,873
Income taxes (Notes b and 8):					
Federal:					
Currently payable	214,758	166,715	192,254	763,175	1,557,230
Deferred	22,000	–	(72,100)	10,543	76,378
Other:					
Currently payable	37,897	44,961	31,745	155,851	329,300
Deferred	5,000	–	(16,750)	(4,790)	9,125
Total	279,655	211,676	135,149	924,779	1,972,033
Income before extraordinary items	367,007	139,865	153,777	759,349	1,861,840
Extraordinary items (Note c)	–	4,249	624,263	13,990	–
Net income	$ 367,007	$ 144,114	$ 778,040	$ 773,339	$ 1,861,840
Per share of common stock (Notes e and g):					
Income before extraordinary items	$ .25	$ .10	$ .09	$ .42	$ 1.04
Extraordinary items	–	–	.38	.01	–
Net income	$ .25	$ .10	$ .47	$ .43	$ 1.04

For numerical note references see notes to consolidated financial statements.

5

SPEIZMAN INDUSTRIES, INC. AND SUBSIDIARIES
NOTES TO STATEMENT OF CONSOLIDATED INCOME

(a) Net sales and other operating revenues and net income as originally reported for the years 1967 through 1970 and as adjusted, after giving retroactive effect to the transactions described in Note 1, are summarized as follows:

	1967	1968	1969	1970
Net sales and other operating revenues:				
As originally reported	$ 7,835,223	$10,382,699	$11,926,266	$16,965,438
Morris Speizman (Canada), Ltd.		194,045	327,143	576,953
The Contract Knitter, Inc.			336,331	2,310,420
Elimination of intercompany sales	(23,050)	(85,294)	(1,238,818)	(1,034,607)
As adjusted	$ 7,812,173	$10,491,450	$11,350,922	$18,818,204
Net income (loss):				
As originally reported	$ 357,733	$ 114,412	$ 907,755	$ 857,274
Morris Speizman (Canada), Ltd.	(112)	(2,600)	(32,486)	12,842
The Contract Knitter, Inc.			(24,581)	(65,665)
Elimination of intercompany profits			(79,953)	(427)
Restatement to give retroactive effect to adjustments resulting from income tax examination	9,386	13,994	7,305	(30,685)
Change of method of including 50% owned companies from cost to equity		18,308		
As adjusted	$ 367,007	$ 144,114	$ 778,040	$ 773,339

The $30,685 adjustment in 1970 resulting from an income tax examination was originally reported as an extraordinary item of $33,420, including $2,735 applicable to 1970.

Net sales and other operating revenues and net income for the fiscal year 1971 were increased by $4,439,840 and $580,570, respectively, as a result of the transactions described in Note 1.

Net sales and other operating revenues includes commissions on sales as agent for other manufacturers as follows: 1967, $17,688; 1968, $24,162; 1969, $100,050; 1970, $102,965; and 1971, $249,553.

(b) Federal income taxes are stated net of investment credits as follows: 1967, $5,000; 1968, $3,351; 1969, $1,365; 1970, $4,746; 1971, $35,168.

See Note 8 relative to the carryforward of unused investment credits.

(c) Extraordinary items consist of the following:

	1968	1969	1970
Reduction of provision for income taxes as a result of carryforward of net operating losses	$ 4,249	$ 34,681	$13,990
Gain from dispositions of investments, net of income taxes of $167,077		589,582	
Total	$ 4,249	$624,263	$13,990

6

SPEIZMAN INDUSTRIES, INC. AND SUBSIDIARIES

NOTES TO STATEMENT OF CONSOLIDATED INCOME

(d) Depreciation and amortization for each of the five fiscal years ended July 3, 1971 was as follows: 1967, $62,935; 1968, $90,295; 1969, $141,962; 1970, $600,880; 1971, $805,638. See also Note 5.

(e) The earnings per share of common stock have been computed based on the weighted average number of shares outstanding during each period after giving retroactive effect to the recapitalization and other transactions described in Note 1 to the consolidated financial statements. The average number of shares outstanding used in the computation of earnings per share of common stock for each of the five fiscal years ended July 3, 1971 were as follows: 1967, 1,477,168; 1968, 1,477,168; 1969, 1,663,682; 1970, 1,794,032; and 1971, 1,791,352. Since the preferred stock is non-cumulative, preferred dividends have not been considered (except for 1967 preferred dividends paid) in computing earnings per share of common stock.

(f) No dividends have been paid or declared by the Company. During the year ended June 30, 1967, predecessor corporations paid dividends of $4,085 on common stock and $516 on preferred stock.

(g) Assuming the issuance of 225,000 shares of common stock by the Company at the beginning of fiscal year 1971 and application of the net proceeds ($) to the retirement of indebtedness, net income per share of common stock for fiscal year 1971 would have been $

The decreases in income before income taxes and extraordinary items in fiscal 1968 and 1969 are primarily attributable to write-downs of work in process and parts inventories in connection with the phase-out of the manufacture by the Company of women's hosiery sewing and finishing equipment and to the relative unprofitability during such years of the Company's equipment rebuilding operations and, in 1969, to the costs associated with the introduction of imported knitting machinery and to the losses incurred by The Contract Knitter, Inc. during its initial year of operation. The extraordinary items which substantially increased net income for 1969 were the sale by the Company of its interest in a foreign corporation and receipt by the Company of an extraordinary cash dividend from a wholly-owned subsidiary subsequently disposed of by the Company. The foregoing financial statements do not include the results of operations of such two companies. The increases in profit margins in 1970 and 1971 are attributable to the substantial increases in sales in such years, which in turn were primarily due to the increased demand for double-knit machinery and, in 1970, for panty hose knitting machinery.

First Quarter Operating Results. The results of operations of the Company for its first fiscal quarter ended October 2, 1971 (thirteen weeks), and for the comparable period (fourteen weeks) in the preceding year are as follows:

	14 Weeks Ended 10/3/70	13 Weeks Ended 10/2/71
Net sales and other operating revenues	$6,294,518	$8,445,233
Net income	$ 339,482	$ 566,792
Average number of shares of common stock outstanding	1,798,275	1,665,000
Net income per share	$ .19	$ .34

These amounts, which are unaudited and not necessarily indicative of results for the entire year, include all adjustments (consisting only of normal recurring accruals) necessary for a fair presentation of results of operations.

BUSINESS

Lines of Business

The following table shows, for the indicated periods, the approximate amount of net sales and other operating revenues and income (loss) before income taxes and extraordinary items of the Company attributable to each line of business in which the Company is engaged:

Net Sales and Other Operating Revenues

Fiscal Year Ended (1)

Line of Business	6/30/67	6/30/68	6/28/69	6/27/70	7/3/71
Machinery and equipment sales	$ 7,812,173	$10,491,450	$11,014,591	$16,507,784	$24,501,306
Contract knitting (2)	—	—	336,331	2,310,420	4,256,333

Income (Loss) Before Income Taxes and Extraordinary Items

Fiscal Year Ended (1)

Line of Business	6/30/67	6/30/68	6/28/69	6/27/70	7/3/71
Machinery and equipment sales	$ 646,662	$ 351,541	$ 304,649	$ 1,717,535	$ 2,842,255
Contract knitting (2)	—	—	(15,723)	(33,407)	991,618

(1) The fiscal year ended July 3, 1971, covers a 53-week period whereas the other fiscal years as to which information is provided in the above table cover 52-week periods.

(2) Operations commenced in November, 1968, and were acquired by the Company on November 2, 1971 (see Note 1 to the consolidated financial statements).

The losses shown for contract knitting for the fiscal years ended June 28, 1969, and June 27, 1970, are attributed by management primarily to start-up costs and the use of the double-declining balance method of depreciation of machinery employed in this aspect of the Company's operations.

Machinery and Equipment Sales

The Company's principal business is the marketing of textile machinery, primarily in the United States. Through exclusive sales arrangements with European textile machinery manufacturers and, to a lesser extent, through sales of used and rebuilt machinery and through the manufacture of machinery designed by it, the Company is able to offer a broad range of machinery to textile manufacturers. Sales of textile machinery are concentrated in the outerwear and hosiery knitting, twisting and texturing, dyeing and finishing sectors of the textile industry.

Specific types of machinery and equipment offered by the Company include the following: circular knitting machines for double knit and also single knit cloth; heat setting, dyeing and finishing machinery for yarn and cloth; yarn texturing and spinning and twisting machines; ladies panty hose and stocking machines; men's and children's double and single cylinder knitting machines; laboratory knitting machines; special machines for knit-de-knit yarns used in the carpet trade, as well as for fabrics and hosiery; turning, sewing and inspecting machinery for panty hose and men's, children's and ladies' stockings; cloth inspection equipment and measuring machines; sweater fabric knitting machinery including border, collar and trimming knitters; solvent scouring and dry cleaning systems for synthetic and natural fibers and cloth; centrifugal extractors; package dye machines; high pressure dye machines for open width or tubular synthetic fabrics; air injection beam dyeing machines; thermo-printing machinery for cloth and cut out pieces; special machinery for folding, stacking and packaging ladies panty hose and stockings; machines for napping, brushing, inspecting, gumming, slitting and other processing

8

of greige as well as finished cloth; quilting machines; air pollution control equipment; high temperature jet cloth dyeing machines and certain types of machines for non-woven fabric formation. In addition, the Company sells needles, repair parts and supplies for knitting, dyeing and finishing mills.

During the fiscal year ended July 3, 1971, approximately 52% of the Company's net sales and other operating revenues consisted of sales of machinery purchased by the Company under exclusive arrangements with various machinery manufacturers. A substantial portion of such sales consisted of sales of double-knit machinery manufactured by C. Terrot Sohne, a leading West German manufacturer of double-knit machinery ("Terrot"). The Company has represented Terrot in the United States and Canada since 1959 and has the exclusive right to sell in the United States, in its own name and for its own account, all types of knitting machinery developed by Terrot since 1967, and machines to be developed by Terrot, under contractural arrangements which will expire, unless renewed by the parties, on December 31, 1979. Such arrangements are subject to termination by Terrot in the event that in any year the Company does not transact 80% of the average of its transactions in such machinery for the preceding three years or, at the option of the Company, if Terrot has not delivered machinery to permit the Company to achieve such level of business. The Company also represents ten other European (and one domestic) textile machinery manufacturers under similar exclusive sales arrangements. In addition, the Company recently entered into arrangements to act as sole distributor (excluding the Far East) of all of the dyeing and finishing equipment manufactured by Synalloy Corporation of Spartanburg, South Carolina. The Company also acts as the exclusive agent on a commission basis in the United States for five European (and one domestic) textile machinery manufacturers; during the fiscal year ended July 3, 1971, approximately 1% of the Company's net sales and other operating revenues consisted of commission income attributable to this aspect of its business. The Company also sells specialized knitting machinery manufactured by it.

In addition to sales of new machinery, the Company markets used textile machinery, most of which has been purchased abroad or taken as trade-ins from textile manufacturers in connection with sales by the Company of new machinery and rebuilt, where necessary, by the Company. During the fiscal year ended July 3, 1971, approximately 27% of the Company's net sales and other operating revenues consisted of sales of such machinery.

Terms of sales of the machinery marketed by the Company vary, but the Company typically receives from 20% to 33% of the sales price by the time of shipment with the balance in 30 days. Machinery is sometimes sold under conditional sales contracts which are discounted with various financial institutions, usually with limited or partial recourse to the Company. In addition, the Company has entered into equipment leases with one lessee for machinery having an original retail value of $997,126. These leases run for four-year terms, renewable at the option of the lessee for an additional one or two year term. The lessee also has the option to purchase the machinery after the expiration of the fourth year. See Note 3 to the consolidated financial statements.

The machinery marketed by the Company is sold to textile manufacturers throughout the United States and, to a lesser extent, in Canada, the United Kingdom and Mexico. During the fiscal year ended July 3, 1971, approximately 92% of the Company's machinery sales were made in the United States. During such year machinery was sold to over 1,030 customers, no one of which accounted for more than 7% of the Company's total machinery sales in such year, and the Company's five largest customers during such year accounted for approximately 27% of such sales.

Contract Knitting

The Company is engaged through The Contract Knitter, Inc. ("Contract Knitter"), a wholly-owned subsidiary acquired from stockholders of the Company on November 2, 1971, in manufacturing double-knit fabric on a contract basis (see "Management — Certain Transactions").

Contract Knitter commenced operations in 1968 and has agreed to furnish substantially all the productivity of its double-knit machines to Jonathan Logan, Inc. ("Logan") at a fixed price per pound (subject to adjustment by mutual agreement) of fabric through December 31, 1975. Under the terms of the contract Logan supplies all of the yarn processed for it by Contract Knitter and the yarn is processed to Logan's specifications. The contract may be extended for an additional three years at the option of Logan. Upon nine months' prior notice, Contract Knitter has the right to terminate the contract if it offers to sell to Logan at a formula price (in general, 20% of original cost) all of the machinery and equipment used to manufacture fabric pursuant to the contract. If Logan accepts the offer, then Logan will also be obligated to accept an assignment of the lease of the premises occupied by Contract Knitter. By December 31, 1975, the depreciated value of machinery and equipment of Contract Knitter, in place as of July 3, 1971, will be $502,552.

Backlog

The Company's backlog of unfilled orders for textile machinery to be sold by it for its own account, and deposits applicable to such orders, at the indicated dates were as follows:

	6/28/69	6/27/70	7/3/71	10/2/71
Backlog	$9,757,600	$14,204,000	$34,037,901(1)	$34,224,600(1)
Deposits	485,552	907,083	1,359,325	1,364,893

(1) Unadjusted to reflect any increases resulting from recoupment of the 10% additional import duty announced on August 15, 1971 (see "Currency and Import Controls").

Substantially all of such orders consisted of orders for Terrot double-knit machinery with an average delivery time of approximately two years per machine. The backlog at October 2, 1971, included an aggregate of $9,384,900 under two contracts with a major textile manufacturer deliverable at scheduled intervals through December, 1975. The contracts are terminable by such customer with respect to $5,483,400 and $3,475,800 of machinery, respectively, on six and 15 months notice, respectively, provided delivery is taken of all machines scheduled for delivery during the notice period. In the event of any such termination, the customer forfeits the deposit of $250,000 and $163,450, respectively, under the contracts. In addition, at July 3, 1971, and October 2, 1971, the Company had received orders for approximately $2,500,000 and $1,790,000, respectively, of equipment to be sold by it on a commission basis. Due to the extraordinary demand for double-knit fabrics over the past several years, the demand for double-knit machinery has been consistently greater than the productive capacity of textile machinery manufacturers; as more double-knit machinery is placed into production the Company anticipates that the demand for such machinery will decrease with a resulting decrease in the Company's backlog of unfilled orders.

Properties

The Company's principal offices are in Charlotte, North Carolina, where it also maintains warehouse and machinery rebuilding facilities. These offices and facilities consist of approximately 130,000 square feet, 100,000 of which are leased (see "Management—Certain Transactions"). Contract Knitter's manufacturing operations are conducted in a plant in Tuscaloosa, Alabama, consisting of approximately 40,000 square feet occupied under a lease expiring in February, 1975; Contract Knitter has an option to renew such lease to January 1, 1980. The equipment used in the operations of Contract Knitter consists of 106 double-knit machines and related peripheral equipment, most of which has been purchased by Contract Knitter under installment sales contracts. In addition, Contract Knitter leases approximately 16,000 square feet of warehouse space in Tuscaloosa. The Company also leases offices and

10

warehouse and shop facilities in Brooklyn, New York, which occupy approximately 16,000 square feet of space and owns offices and warehouse space in Leicester, England, occupying approximately 12,000 square feet of space. Sales and administrative offices are also leased in Montreal, Canada, and Mexico City, Mexico. Rentals for all space leased by the Company and its subsidiaries aggregate approximately $100,000 a year.

Employees

As of July 3, 1971, the Company (including Contract Knitter) employed 371 persons, 286 of whom were employed in production and customer service activities, 18 as salesmen and 67 in various administrative and executive capacities.

The Company has no agreement with any bargaining agent, has not experienced any work stoppage and believes its relations with its employees to be satisfactory.

Competition and Other Factors

The Company operates in highly competitive areas, competing with foreign and domestic manufacturers of textile machinery and their sales representatives, many of whom have substantially greater financial resources than the Company. In addition, the Company's operations are subject to the ability of its primary customers, United States textile manufacturers, to compete with foreign producers of textiles and to conditions in the textile industry in general.

MANAGEMENT

Executive Officers and Directors

The executive officers and directors of the Company are as follows:

Name	Position(s) with the Company
Morris Speizman	Chairman of the Board
Lawrence J. Speizman	President; Director
Robert S. Speizman	Executive Vice President; Director
Luther H. Hodges	Director
Addison H. Reese	Director
Theodore A. Valenstein	Secretary
Josef Sklut	Treasurer

With the exception of Mr. Sklut, each of the Company's executive officers has been engaged actively and continuously in the business of the Company and its predecessors for more than the past five years. Mr. Sklut joined the Company in December, 1967, and prior thereto was an executive with a textile manufacturer in Gastonia, North Carolina. Mr. Reese is Chairman of the Board of NCNB Corporation, Charlotte, North Carolina, and its banking subsidiary, North Carolina National Bank. Mr. Hodges, formerly Governor of North Carolina and Secretary of Commerce of the United States, is a director of several corporations.

11

Remuneration

Set forth below, on an accrual basis, are (i) the aggregate direct remuneration paid by the Company and its subsidiaries during the fiscal year ended July 3, 1971, to each director, and to each person who during such fiscal year was one of the three highest paid officers of the Company, whose aggregate remuneration exceeded $30,000, and to all persons, as a group, who were directors and officers during such fiscal year, (ii) the Company's contributions to its Profit Sharing Plan set aside or accrued during such year allocable to such persons and such group and (iii) the aggregate amounts set aside or accrued to July 3, 1971, for such persons and group under the Profit Sharing Plan.

Name	Capacities in Which Remuneration Was Received	Aggregate Direct Remuneration	Profit Sharing Plan Company Contribution	
			Amount Set Aside or Accrued During Fiscal Year Ended July 3, 1971	Total Amount Set Aside or Accrued to July 3, 1971
Morris Speizman	Chairman of the Board	$ 50,000	$ 2,031	$ 8,198
Lawrence J. Speizman	President	95,000	8,535	35,874
Robert S. Speizman	Executive Vice President	50,000	2,962	13,804
All officers and directors as a group (12 in number)		396,880	24,087	85,967

Profit Sharing and Stock Option Plans

The Company maintains a Profit Sharing Plan, contributions to which are borne entirely by the Company and participating subsidiaries, payable out of net profits in amounts to be determined by the Board of Directors. In general, employees become participants after three years of continuous employment and contributions begin to vest after five years of continuous employment. A trustee administers the Plan, which is qualified under applicable Internal Revenue Service regulations. (See Note 11 to the consolidated financial statements).

On August 30, 1971, the Company's stockholders approved a Qualified Stock Option Plan pursuant to which options for an aggregate of 125,000 shares of the Company's Common Stock may be granted to officers and employees. As of the date of this Prospectus, no options have been granted under the Plan. The Company's principal shareholders are not at present eligible to participate under the Plan (see Note 10 to the consolidated financial statements).

Certain Transactions

The Company was incorporated on July 3, 1967, to succeed to businesses theretofore principally owned by Morris Speizman and his sons, Lawrence J. Speizman and Robert S. Speizman. The following table shows the shares of stock issued in connection with the organization of the Company:

Name	7% Non-Voting Preferred Stock	Class A Common Stock	Class B Common Stock
Morris Speizman	7,658	561	93
Lawrence J. Speizman	–	561	374
Robert S. Speizman	–	561	374
Mrs. Morris Speizman	824	–	–
Sylval Corporation (1)	546	–	–
Theodore Valenstein	1,880	187	93
Totals	10,908	1,870	934

(1) Wholly-owned by Mrs. Morris Speizman.

The Speizmans and Mr. Valenstein may each be deemed a "promoter" of the Company as such term is defined in the Rules and Regulations promulgated under the Securities Act of 1933, as amended.

Subsequent to the organization of the Company, Mr. Valenstein acquired 240 of the shares of 7% Non-Voting Preferred Stock owned by Morris Speizman. On June 14, 1971, 131 of the shares of Class A Common Stock and all of the shares of Class B Common Stock owned by Mr. Valenstein were redeemed by the Company for $290,248. Of the shares of 7% Non-Voting Preferred Stock received by Morris Speizman in connection with the organization of the Company, 420 shares were given by him to The Speizman Foundation, Inc., a charitable foundation controlled by the Speizman family. Commencing in 1970, and terminating on June 8, 1971, the Company redeemed all of such shares of 7% Non-Voting Preferred Stock at the par value of $100 a share.

On July 3, 1971, the Company acquired all the stock of Morris Speizman (Canada) Ltd. from Morris Speizman in exchange for ½ share of Class A Common Stock of the Company. The Company's financial statements included herein have been restated to include the operations of such corporation, which were not significant.

On July 3, 1971, and immediately prior to the recapitalization of the Company effected on October 14, 1971, the outstanding capital stock of the Company consisted of 10,488 shares of 7% Non-Voting Preferred Stock, 1,739.5 shares of Class A Common Stock and 841 shares of Class B Common Stock. Pursuant to the recapitalization each such share of Class A Common Stock and each such share of Class B Common Stock was exchanged for 526.7134 shares of the Company's Common Stock, without par value, and each share of 7% Non-Voting Preferred Stock was exchanged for one share of 5% Non-Voting Preferred Stock.

Upon the recapitalization of the Company on October 14, 1971, the outstanding shares of stock of the Company were held as follows:

Name	5% Non-Voting Preferred Stock	Common Stock
Morris Speizman	6,998	344,734
Lawrence J. Speizman	–	492,477
Robert S. Speizman	–	492,477
Mrs. Morris Speizman	824	–
Sylval Corporation (1)	546	–
Theodore Valenstein	2,120	29,496
Totals	10,488	1,359,184

(1) Wholly-owned by Mrs. Morris Speizman.

Contract Knitter was organized on November 18, 1968, and in connection therewith Lawrence J. Speizman purchased 156¼ shares of its Common Stock for $15,625 and Robert S. Speizman purchased 93¾ shares of its Common Stock for $9,375. An employee subsequently purchased 12½ shares of Contract Knitter's Common Stock for $1,250, all of which shares were redeemed on June 12, 1971, for $105,000. On November 2, 1971, Contract Knitter was combined with the Company and promptly thereafter its assets and liabilities were transferred to a newly-formed subsidiary of the Company. In connection with such combination, Lawrence J. Speizman and Robert S. Speizman received 191,135 and 114,681 shares, respectively, of the Common Stock of the Company in exchange for the shares of Contract Knitter held by them.

From December 24, 1968, through July 3, 1971 the Company sold to Contract Knitter 53 double-knit machines and other equipment at an aggregate purchase price of $1,665,956. Such machines and equipment were sold at list prices current at the time the orders were placed except that certain machines which had previously been reserved for Contract Knitter's principal customer at a lower price (current at the time of reservation) were sold at the lower price. Substantially all the purchase price of such machines and equipment was borrowed by Contract Knitter; pursuant to the merger of Contract Knitter into the Company, the Company assumed the unpaid portion of such indebtedness. The Company has from time to time made interest-bearing demand loans to Contract Knitter in amounts up to $200,000. No such loans were outstanding at July 3, 1971, or subsequently.

From October, 1969, through October, 1970, the Company sold knitting machinery and other equipment to a corporation, 45% of the stock of which was owned in the aggregate by Messrs. Lawrence J. Speizman and Robert S. Speizman, for an aggregate purchase price of $1,106,425. Substantially all of such purchase price was financed through conditional sales contracts and chattel mortgage notes which have been discounted with partial recourse to the Company. All of such sales were made at ordinary retail prices. On October 15, 1970, the Messrs. Speizman sold their stock in such corporation to other stockholders thereof for a purchase price payable over five years and secured by a pledge of the stock being sold.

The Company's principal offices in Charlotte, North Carolina, occupying approximately 100,000 square feet of space, are leased under a ten-year net lease which commenced January 1, 1969, for a rental of $25,000 a year from a corporation owned by Morris Speizman's wife. The Company believes that such property is leased at a lower rental than the rentals prevailing for comparable property in the area. Such premises had previously been leased by the Company from the same corporation at an annual rental of $39,000.

The Company has an established line of credit with North Carolina National Bank of which Mr. Addison H. Reese, a director of the Company, is Chairman of the Board. At July 3, 1971, $2,244,819 was outstanding against this line.

PRINCIPAL AND SELLING STOCKHOLDERS

Morris Speizman and his sons, Lawrence J. Speizman and Robert S. Speizman, (the "Selling Stockholders") each own more than 10% of the Company's Common Stock and may each be deemed a "parent" of the Company as such term is defined in the Rules and Regulations promulgated under the Securities Act of 1933, as amended. The following table sets forth information as of November 9, 1971, as to the beneficial ownership of the Company's Common Stock by the Selling Stockholders, the number of shares of Common Stock to be sold by each of the Selling Stockholders and their holdings after completion of the offering and the beneficial ownership of shares of the Company's Common Stock by all officers and directors as a group.

Name and Address	Number of Shares Owned	Percent of Shares	Number of Shares to be Sold	Number of Shares to be Owned After Offering	Percent of Shares to be Owned After Offering
Morris Speizman 435 Colville Rd., Charlotte, N. C. 28207	344,734	20.70%	83,334	261,400	13.83%
Lawrence J. Speizman 16 Boxwood Lane Lawrence, N. Y. 11559	683,612	41.06%	184,060	499,552	26.43%
Robert S. Speizman 1909 Carmel Road Charlotte, N. C. 28211	607,158	36.47%	107,606	499,552	26.43%
All officers and directors as a group (including the above)	1,665,000	100.00%	375,000	1,290,000	68.25%

14

DESCRIPTION OF COMMON STOCK

All of the shares of Common Stock issued and outstanding on the date hereof are, and all of the shares of Common Stock covered by this Prospectus upon issuance will be, fully paid and nonassessable. Holders of Common Stock have no preemptive or subscription rights and are entitled to share ratably in all assets of the Company available for distribution to stockholders in the event of liquidation or dissolution after payment or provision for payment to the holders of any outstanding shares of the Company's 5% Non-Voting Preferred Stock, par value $100 a share, of an amount equal to the par value thereof plus accrued unpaid dividends, if any, thereon.

Dividend Rights. Holders of Common Stock are entitled to dividends if and when declared by the Board of Directors after provision for accrued unpaid dividends on the Company's 5% Non-Voting Preferred Stock, par value $100 a share (see "Dividends").

Voting Rights. Holders of Common Stock are entitled to one vote for each share held and have the sole right to vote for the election of directors and on all other matters requiring stockholder action. Holders of the Common Stock are entitled, upon the demand of any stockholder, to cumulate votes for the election of directors.

Miscellaneous

The foregoing summary of the terms of the Common Stock does not purport to be complete and is qualified in its entirety by reference to pertinent statutory and common law and to the applicable provisions of the Company's Certificate of Incorporation and By-laws, as amended.

Annual reports of the Company containing certified financial statements will be furnished to its stockholders beginning with the fiscal year ending July 1, 1972. The Company will also publish unaudited quarterly statements of results of operations beginning with the 13 weeks ended January 1, 1972.

North Carolina National Bank, Charlotte, North Carolina, is transfer agent for the Company's Common Stock.

UNDERWRITING

The Underwriters named below have severally agreed, subject to certain conditions, to purchase from the Company and the Selling Stockholders the aggregate number of shares of Common Stock set forth opposite their respective names below:

Underwriter	Number of Shares
Kidder, Peabody & Co. Incorporated	

TOTAL 600,000

16

The Underwriting Agreement provides that the several Underwriters are obligated to purchase all of the shares of Common Stock offered hereby, if they are obligated to purchase any. The Company and the Selling Stockholders have been advised by Kidder, Peabody & Co. Incorporated, as Representative (the "Representative") of the several Underwriters, that the Underwriters propose to offer the Common Stock to the public initially at the offering price set forth on the cover page of this Prospectus; that the Underwriters propose initially to allow a concession of not in excess of   cents per share to certain dealers, including Underwriters; that the Underwriters and such dealers may initially allow a discount of not in excess of   cents per share to other dealers; and that the public offering price and the concession and discount to dealers may be changed by the Representative after the initial public offering.

The Underwriting Agreement provides that the Selling Stockholders will not offer, sell or otherwise dispose of to the public Common Stock, other than that offered hereby, within 90 days of the effective date of the Registration Statement, without the consent of the Representative.

LEGAL OPINIONS

Legal matters in connection with the Common Stock covered by this Prospectus are being passed upon for the Company and the Selling Stockholders by Messrs. Weinstein, Sturges, Odom and Bigger, 426 North Tryon Street, Charlotte, N. C. 28202 and Messrs. Paul, Weiss, Rifkind, Wharton & Garrison, 345 Park Avenue, New York, N. Y. 10022 and for the Underwriters by Messrs. Sullivan & Cromwell, 48 Wall Street, New York, N. Y. 10005. Messrs. Paul, Weiss, Rifkind, Wharton & Garrison and Messrs. Sullivan & Cromwell may rely as to matters of North Carolina law upon the opinion of Messrs. Weinstein, Sturges, Odom and Bigger.

EXPERTS

The consolidated financial statements and schedules of Speizman Industries, Inc. and subsidiaries appearing in this Prospectus and in the Registration Statement have been examined by Haskins & Sells, independent public accountants, for the fiscal year ended July 3, 1971, and by Hertz, Herson & Company, independent public accountants, for the four fiscal years ended June 27, 1970, to the extent set forth in their respective opinions appearing elsewhere herein. As to amounts included for the Company's English subsidiary, the opinion of Haskins & Sells is based upon the opinion of A. C. Palmer & Co., chartered accountants. Such financial statements and schedules are included herein in reliance upon such opinions given upon the authority of such firms as experts in accounting and auditing.

ADDITIONAL INFORMATION

The Company has filed with the Securities and Exchange Commission, Washington, D. C., a Registration Statement under the Securities Act of 1933, as amended, with respect to the securities offered by this Prospectus. This Prospectus omits certain information in such Registration Statement. The Registration Statement may be inspected by anyone at the office of the Commission without charge and copies of all or any part of it may be obtained upon payment of the Commission's charge for copying. Reference is hereby made to the Registration Statement and the exhibits and financial statements and schedules filed as a part thereof for further information about the Company and the securities offered hereby.

17

OPINIONS OF INDEPENDENT PUBLIC ACCOUNTANTS

SPEIZMAN INDUSTRIES, INC.:

We have examined the consolidated balance sheet of Speizman Industries, Inc. and subsidiaries as of July 3, 1971 and the related statements of consolidated income, retained earnings, and changes in financial position for the fiscal year then ended (53 weeks), except as to amounts included for Speizman Industries (U. K.) Limited. Our examination was made in accordance with generally accepted auditing standards, and accordingly included such tests of the accounting records and such other auditing procedures as we considered necessary in the circumstances. As to amounts included for Speizman Industries (U. K.) Limited, which amounts represent 4%, 2%, and 1%, of consolidated assets, net sales and other operating revenues, and net income, respectively, we were furnished with the report of other accountants on their examination of the financial statements of such company.

In our opinion, based on our examination and the report of other accountants referred to above, the above-mentioned financial statements present fairly the financial position of the companies at July 3, 1971 and the results of their operations and the changes in their financial position for the fiscal year then ended (53 weeks), in conformity with generally accepted accounting principles applied on a basis consistent with that of the preceding fiscal year.

HASKINS & SELLS

Charlotte, North Carolina
August 30, 1971
  (November 2, 1971,
  as to certain information
  in Notes 1 and 13)

SPEIZMAN INDUSTRIES, INC.:

We have examined the statement of consolidated income for the four fiscal years ended June 27, 1970 and the statement of consolidated retained earnings and the statement of changes in consolidated financial position for the two fiscal years ended June 27, 1970 of Speizman Industries, Inc. and subsidiaries. Our examination was made in accordance with generally accepted auditing standards, and accordingly included such tests of the accounting records and such other auditing procedures as we considered necessary in the circumstances. The statements give effect to the recapitalization and reorganization as described in Note 1 to the consolidated financial statements.

In our opinion, the aforementioned consolidated financial statements present fairly the results of operations of Speizman Industries, Inc. and subsidiaries for the four fiscal years ended June 27, 1970 and the changes in retained earnings and financial position for the two fiscal years then ended in conformity with generally accepted accounting principles applied on a consistent basis.

HERTZ, HERSON & COMPANY

Charlotte, North Carolina
July 2, 1971
Relative to Note 1, November 2, 1971

18

OPINION OF INDEPENDENT CHARTERED ACCOUNTANTS

SPEIZMAN INDUSTRIES (U.K.) LIMITED:

We have examined the balance sheet of Speizman Industries (U.K.) Limited as of June 19, 1971 and the related statements of income, retained earnings, and changes in financial position for the 53 weeks then ended. Our examination was made in accordance with generally accepted auditing standards, and accordingly included such tests of the accounting records and such other auditing procedures as we considered necessary in the circumstances.

In our opinion, the above-mentioned financial statements (not presented separately herein) present fairly the financial position of Speizman Industries (U.K.) Limited at June 19, 1971 and the results of its operations and the changes in its financial position for the 53 weeks then ended, in conformity with generally accepted accounting principles applied on a consistent basis.

A. C. PALMER & CO.
Chartered Accountants

Court Chambers,
Friar Lane,
Leicester
July 2, 1971

QUESTIONS

1. Why must a prospectus be issued? What is its main purpose? What is the difference between the preliminary prospectus and a final prospectus? What is an indication to buy and a "when as and if issued order"?
2. Why has the Securities and Exchange Commission not approved the issue?
3. Who is selling the stock? Who is the underwriter? What is the proposed use of the proceeds from the sale of the stock?
4. What is the nature of the company's business? Who is the management? What type of stock is being sold?
5. Are the legal and accounting opinions of any value to your analysis of the company?
6. Do you believe you have sufficient information to make an informed investment decision? Would you like additional information? Do you believe you have been sufficiently alerted to the risks attendent to this stock?

Case 38

MUTUAL FUND PROSPECTUS

Mr. Horne is a family man in his mid forties who earns between $13,000 and $14,000 a year. For several years he has been accumulating savings in a savings and loan account at the rate of $50.00 a month. He has recently been told by a neighbor that he could put the same $50.00 a month into a mutual fund where there was a potential for earning more than the bank interest rate. The neighbor suggested Mr. Horne contact a mutual fund salesman to find out more about investing in mutual funds.

Mr. Horne did contact a salesman who came to the house to explain the workings of mutual funds. The salesman agreed that mutual funds offered a potentially higher return than the bank rate, but he also pointed out that a fund could return less than the bank rate or even result in a loss to Mr. Horne's original investment if the fund's stock portfolio shrank in value. He also gave Mr. Horne a prospectus, told him to study it, and to call if he had any questions. See cover to prospectus for additional information.*

The following pages contain excerpts from the prospectus Mr. Horne was given.

*The price to the public for shares offered by this prospectus varies with the fluctuations in the market value of securities owned by the Fund. It is computed at least once daily as of the close of the New York Stock Exchange, on each day the exchange is open for trading and

INVESTMENT OBJECTIVE AND POLICY

The objective of XYZ Growth Stock Fund is to provide long term growth of principal and future income rather than current income return. To achieve this objective it is the policy of the Fund to keep its assets invested, except for working cash balances, in the common stocks, or securities convertible into common stocks, of companies believed by the management to possess better than average prospects for long term growth, and this policy may not be changed without a vote of shareholders. Emphasis is placed on the selection of progressive, well-managed companies.

Since the shares of the Fund represent an investment in common stocks, shareholders should understand that the price of the Fund's shares will go up or down with changes in the market value of the stocks held by the Fund. Moreover any dividends paid by the Fund will increase or decrease in relation to the amount of dividends received from these investments. There is no guarantee that the objective of the Fund will be realized and its name does not imply an assurance that an investor's capital will increase.

INVESTMENT POWERS AND RESTRICTIONS

The Fund may not purchase the securities of any issuer if such purchase would cause more than 5% of its total assets taken at market value to be invested in securities of such issuer, other than U.S. Government obligations. The Fund may not purchase the securities of any issuer if such purchase would cause more than 15% of any class of securities of such issuer to be held in the portfolio and may not invest in the securities of companies which, including predecessors, have not been in continuous operation for at least three years, except that 5% of total assets may be invested in certain regulated public utility and energy transmission companies and venture capital investment companies not having a three-year record. The Fund may not purchase securities issues by investment companies except in the open market or in connection with a plan of consolidation or merger, nor may it purchase or retain securities of a company if one or more of the Fund's management owns one-half percent each and such persons own collectively more than 5% of the company's shares. The above restrictions may not be changed without a vote of the shareholders.

The Fund purchases securities primarily for investment, rather than with a view to trading profits. While the rate of portfolio turnover is not a limiting factor when management deems changes appropriate, it is expected that the

---

is the net asset value plus a sales charge equal to 8.5% (maximum) of the offering price, scaled down to 1 3/4% (minimum) depending upon size of purchase.

These securities have not been approved or disapproved by the Securities and Exchange Commission nor has the Commission passed upon the accuracy or adequacy of this prospectus. Any representation to the contrary is a criminal offense.

Fund's annual portfolio turnover rate generally will not exceed 50% in a particular year. The Fund owns foreign securities and may from time to time purchase such securities even though an interest equalization tax, presently a maximum of 11¼%, may be incurred. Such tax would increase the cost of such securities and correspondingly reduce the return on them.

It is not the policy to invest for the purpose of exercising control or management. It is not the policy to engage in underwriting securities (except insofar as the Fund may technically be deemed an underwriter in selling a portfolio security under circumstances which may require registration of the same under the Securities Act of 1933), to concentrate more than 25% of the assets (at market value at the time of each investment) in any one industry, to purchase or sell real estate, commodities, or commodity contracts. No margin transactions or short sales are permitted. The Fund may borrow money up to 10% and may pledge up to 15% of its gross assets at cost subject to a 300% asset coverage requirement (but only temporarily for extraordinary emergency purposes). The Fund may make call or six-month secured loans through notebrokers or banks. The restrictions in this paragraph may not be changed without a vote of shareholders.

SERVICES FOR SHAREHOLDERS

Lifetime Investing Account Every shareholder has a Lifetime Investing Account whereby he will receive after each share transaction a statement showing the cumulative activity in his account since the beginning of the year. At the end of each year he will receive a complete annual statement of share transactions as well as income tax information regarding dividends and capital gain distributions. Share certificates will not be issued unless requested. (Certificates for fractional shares are not issued in any case.)

DISTRIBUTION OPTIONS

The following distribution options are available to all Lifetime Investing Accounts with the exception of Check-a-month accounts (see below) and may be changed as often as desired. The current option will appear immediately following the account number on each confirmation statement:

Option A dividends reinvested; capital gains in additional shares.
Option B dividends in cash; capital gains in additional shares.
Option C dividends in cash; capital gains in cash.

Under Option A, dividends will be reinvested in additional full and fractional shares at the public offering price.

Under Options A and B, capital gain distributions will be paid in additional full and fractional shares at the net asset value applicable to each such distribution.

SERVICES FOR ACCUMULATION

The following services are voluntary, involve no extra charge other than the sales charge included in the offering price, and may be changed or discontinued without penalty at any time. Forms necessary to initiate bank draft investing and a Statement of Intention can be obtained through investment dealers.

Invest by Mail   for periodic share accumulation. Checks of $50 or more may be mailed directly to the Fund's Transfer Agent at any time—whether or not dividends are re-invested. The name of the investment dealer should accompany each investment.

Bank Draft Investing   for regular share accumulation. Cash investments of $50 or more made through the shareholder's checking account via bank draft each month or quarter.

Intended Quantity Investment, Statement of Intention   If it is anticipated that $12,500 or more of Fund shares will be purchased within a 13-month period, a Statement of Intention should be signed so that shares may be obtained at the same reduced sales charge as though the total quantity were invested in one lump sum. The Statement authorizes the Transfer Agent to hold in escrow sufficient shares which can be redeemed to make up any difference in sales charge on the amount intended to be invested and the amount actually invested. Execution of a Statement does not obligate the shareholder to purchase or the Fund to sell the full amount indicated in the Statement, and should the amount actually purchased during the 13-month period be more or less than that indicated on the Statement, price adjustments will be made.

SERVICE FOR WITHDRAWAL

Check-a-Month   to draw upon shareholdings conveniently. By a standard agreement, the Fund's Transfer Agent will send to the shareholder regular monthly or quarterly payments of any designated amount. The checks are drawn from income dividends (which are held in cash) and to the extent necessary, from share redemptions which would be a return of principal. Continued withdrawals in excess of current income will eventually use up principal, particularly in a period of declining market prices.

To use this service, at least $10,000 in cash or shares at the public offering price must be deposited with the Transfer Agent. The maintenance of a withdrawal plan concurrently with purchases of additional Fund shares would be disadvantageous because of the sales charge included in such purchases. A shareholder may not have a withdrawal plan in effect at the same time he is makinging recurring purchases of the Fund's shares. The cost of administering these plans for the benefit of shareholders who participate in them is borne by the Fund as an expense of all shareholders. The plans may be terminated at any time by the shareholder, the Fund or the Transfer Agent.

Full information on each of the above services and an application where required is available from your investment dealer.

PER SHARE INCOME AND CAPITAL CHANGES

(For a share outstanding throughout the fiscal years ended November 30)

	1961	1962	1963	1964	1965	1966	1967	1968	1969	1970
INCOME AND EXPENSES										
Income	$0.152	$0.157	$0.163	$0.180	$0.200	$0.204	$0.213	$0.215	$0.206	$ 0.255
Expenses	0.034	0.034	0.033	0.035	0.037	0.037	0.038	0.039	0.040	0.036
Net income	0.118	0.123	0.130	0.145	0.163	0.167	0.175	0.176	0.166	0.219
Dividends from net income	0.115	0.123	0.131	0.143	0.159	0.171	0.182	0.183	0.177	0.217
CAPITAL CHANGES										
Net asset value at beginning of period	$7.170	$9.375	$7.380	$8.230	$ 8.980	$10.780	$10.370	$12.750	$13.450	$12.620
Realized and unrealized net gains or (losses) on investments	2.447	(1.895)	1.041	0.848	2.006	(0.056)	2.661	0.908	(0.524)	(1,704)
Distributions from realized net gains	0.245	0.100	0.190	0.100	0.210	0.350	0.274	0.201	0.295	0.388
Net asset value at end of period	$9.375	$7.380	$8.230	$8.980	$10.780	$10.370	$12.750	$13.450	$12.620	$10.530
Ratio of expenses to average net assets	0.39%	0.45%	0.41%	0.42%	0.38%	0.35%	0.31%	0.31%	0.32%	0.34%
Ratio of net income to average net assets	1.35%	1.61%	1.62%	1.70%	1.67%	1.55%	1.43%	1.40%	1.33%	2.05%
Shares outstanding at November 30 (000 omitted)	62,076	73,252	76,075	77,873	80,795	85,877	92,960	97,635	97,732	101,294

The above table has been adjusted to reflect the 2-for-1 split on February 28, 1962.

EXCHANGE PRIVILEGE

Fund shares may be exchanged for shares of ABC Development Fund, Inc. and shares of that fund may be similarly exchanged for Fund shares at their respective net asset value per share beginning April 1,1971. They may also be exchanged for shares of those funds (and shares of "exchange funds" for which the Principal Underwriter acts as investment adviser) may be similarly exchanged for Fund shares at their respective net asset values per share. Each exchange must involve a minimum of $1,000 worth of shares, of which at least 80% must have been held for six months (twelve months in the case of "exchange funds"). These offers are available only in states where shares of the fund being acquired may legally be sold. These offers may be modified, superseded or terminated at any time without notice to shareholders. A transaction charge of $5 will be made. An exchanging shareholder will realize a gain or loss for Federal tax purposes. Prospectuses of the other funds are available from your investment dealer or from the Principal Underwriter.

REDEMPTION AND REPURCHASE OF SHARES

The shareholder has the right to redeem his shares by delivering to the Trust Company, Boston, Massachusetts 02106, either his certificates,or a stock power if no certificates have been issued, in good order for transfer, with a written request for redemtion. Redemption will be made at the net asset value next computed after such delivery. Good order means that certificates or stock power powers must be endorsed by the record owner(s) exactly as the shares are registered and the signature(s) must be guaranteed by a National Bank or Trust Company or a member bank of the Federal Reserve System (not a savings bank) or a member firm of the New York, American, Boston, Midwest, or Pacific Stock Exchanges. In addition, in some cases, good order may require the furnishing of additional documents. Payment will be made within seven days of the receipt of the aforementioned documents.

The Fund has authorized its Principal Underwriter to act as its agent in re-purchasing shares. The Principal Underwriter will normally accept order to repurchase shares by wire or telephone from dealers for their customers at the net asset value next computed after receipt of the order by the dealer if such order is received by the Underwriter prior to its close of business that day. These repurchase arrangements are for the convenience of shareholders and do not involve a charge by either the Fund or its agents; however, investment dealers may make a charge to the shareholder. Payment will normally be made within seven days of the receipt of an order to repurchase provided that the certificates, or a stock power if no certificates have been issued, have been issued, have been delivered to the Trust Company in good order as described above.

The right to redeem can be suspended and the payment of the redemption price deferred with the Exchange is closed, during periods when trading on the Exchange is restricted as determined by the Securities and Exchange Commission, or during any emergency as determined by the Securities and Exchange Commission which makes it impracticable for the Fund to dispose of its securities or value its assets, or during any other period permitted by order of the Commission for the protection of investors. The value of shares on re-demption or repurchase may be more or less than the investor's cost depending upon the market value of the portfolio securities at the time of redemption.

PRICING OF SHARES

The public offering price is the net asset value next computed after the sale plus a sales charge as follows:

Amount of Purchase	Sales Charge As Percentage of Offering Price
Less than $12,500	8.50%
$12,500 but less than $25,000	7.50
$25,000 but less than $50,000	5.75
$50,000 but less than $100,000	4.00
$100,000 but less than $250,000	3.25
$250,000 but less than $500,000	2.50
$500,000 but less than $1,000,000	2.25
$1,000,000 or more	1.75

The above scale is also applicable to (1) combined purchases of any of the funds referred to above through one dealer aggregating $12,500 or more made by any of the persons enumerated above within a thirteen-month period starting with the first purchase pursuant to a written Statement of Intention, in the form provided by the Underwriter, which includes provisions for a price adjustment depending upon the amount actually purchased within such period (a purchase not made pursuant to such Statement may be included thereunder if the State-ment is filed with 90 days of such purchase), or (2) purchases made by tax exempt charitable, religious, educational, and similar corporations, associations, or foundations described in Section 501(c) or (13) of the Internal Revenue Code or by tax exempt pension, profit shareing, or other employee benefit plans described in Section 401 of the Code, based upon the amount currently being purchased at the public offering price which would be applicable to that amount plus the total amount purchased at public offering prices subsequent to October 1, 1965 (at the price or prices paid), and still held in shares of the Fund, the funds referred to above or in shares received upon exercise of the exchange privilege.

Subject to the applicable provisions of the Investment Company Act of 1940, the Fund may issue shares at net asset value in the event that any other investment company or personal holding compnay is merged or consolidated with or acquired by the Fund, Shares may be sold to directors and officers of the Fund and to officers, directors and full-time employees of the Adviser and Principal Underwriter, who have been such for 90 days, or to any trust, pension profit-sharing or any other benefit plan for such persons, at net asset value, if such sales are made for investment purposes and provided the shares will not be resold except for the Fund.

DETERMINATION OF NET ASSET VALUE

The net asset value is determined once daily in the manner prescribed in the Articles of Organization. Briefly, this determination is made as of the cloase of trading on the New York Stock Exchange each business day on which the Exchange is open and is accomplished by dividing the number of outstanding shares of the Fund into its net worth (the excessof its assets over its liabilities). Securities held by the Fund which are appraised at market values (closing prices of securities listed on national exchanges and closing bid prices of unlisted securities) constitute the major portion of the Fund's assets. Securities for which market quotations are unavailable or which are restricted as to resale and other assets will be appraised at such value as is deemed to reflect fair value as determined in good faith by the Board of Directors of the Fund.

The public offering prices, based on the net asset value so determined, are effective for orders received by the dealer prior to the determination and received by the Underwriter prior to its close of business that day.

INVESTMENT ADVISER

Financial services, Inc, is the Fund's investment adviser. The adviser also serves as investment adviser to ABC Trust (assets approximately $2,200,000,000) and DEF Development Fund, Inc, (assets approximately $2,000,000,000). In addition, the Adviser acts as investment adviser to Massachusetts GHI Fund, Inc. a newly organized fund, the shares of which are initially being sold primarily to directors, officers, and employees of the Fund, the Adviser and the Principal Underwriter, although others are permitted to purchase shares. It is anticipated that when market conditions permit, a more general distribution of the shares of Capital will be made. The Adviser had contracted to serve as investment adviser to three substantial institutional clients in addition to its fund clients.

Subject to the supervision of the Directors, the Adviser is to furnish the Fund with overall investment, advisory, and administrative services, as well as supporting research and general office facilities.

The Adviser will pay all of the compensation of Directors (except Directors not affiliated with the Adviser who will each receive from $2,500 to $5,500 annually, depending upon attendance at meetings), officers, and employees. For these services and facilities the adviser receives a monthly fee computed on the basis of average daily net assets of the Fund. The effective rate of compensation of the Adviser is fixed by a formula as follows: The basic annual rate at which the monthly fee is computed is ½ of 1% of the average daily net assets of the Fund for the period. The basic rate applicable to the assets is cumulatively reduced in successive steps as the assets increase in size and exceed specific dollar amounts. The rate is reduced 9% for each $100 million of assets up to and including $600 million. The rate is further reduced 5 3/4% for each $100 million of assets in excess of $600 million up to and including $1.2 billion. Above $1.2 billion the rate is reduced to .217% of average daily net assets, the rate applicable at present Fund size. This fee arrangement resulted in fees of $2,404,000 to the Adviser for the fiscal year ended November 30, 1970. This amount will be reduced by the compensation paid by the Fund to those Directors not affiliated with the Adviser.

The Fund pays all its expenses other than those to be assumed by the Adviser, including without implied limitation, governmental fees, interest charges, taxes, membership dues in the Investment Company Institute allocable to the Fund, fees and expenses of independent auditors, of legal counsel and of any transfer agent, registrar and dividend disbursing agent of the Fund, expenses of repurchasing and redeeming shares, expenses of preparing, printing and mailing stock certificates, shareholders' reports, notices, proxy statements and reports to governmental officers and commissions, brokerage and other expenses connected with the execution of portfolio security transactions, insurance premiums, fees and expenses of the custodian for all services to the Fund, including safekeeping of funds and securities, keeping of books and accounts and calculation of the net asset value of shares of the Fund and expenses of shareholders' meeting. Expenses relating to the issuance, registration, and qualification of shares of the Fund and the preparation and printing of prospectuses are borne by the Fund except to the extent that its Distribution Agreement requires that firm to pay for printing in quantity and the qualification of Fund shares for sale in the various states.

The Agreement may be continued from year to year (after the initial two years) upon approval at least annually, by a majority of the Directors who are not parties to the contract or interested persons of any such party, or by vote of a majority of the outstanding shares of the Fund. The Agreement terminates automatically if it is assigned by the Adviser and may be terminated by either party on not more than sixty nor less than thirty days notice. If, while the Agreement is in effect, the Adviser proposed to amend its Articles of Organization in a manner which would permit (i) attribution of any value to the Agreement in computing the net asset value of the Adviser's stock, or (ii) sales

of its common stock by the Adviser or its shareholders at prices in excess of
net asset value determined as provided in said Articles as amended from time
to time, the question of approval or disapproval of such an amendement must
be submitted, to shareholders of the Fund and may not be made unless approved by the holders of a majority of the Fund's outstanding voting securities.
The Agreement further provides that the Adviser may render services to others.

PRINCIPAL UNDERWRITER

The Principal Underwriter, acts as principal in selling shares of the Fund to
dealers. The Principal Underwriter allows dealers discounts from the applicable
public offering price which are alike for all dealers. In the case of the maximum
sales charge the dealer retains 6½% and the Underwriter retains 2% of the
public offering price, except that these percentages are 6% and 2½% respectively
in the case of dividend reinvestments and subsequent investments under the
Lifetime Investing Accounts' Services for Accumulation. The underwriting
contract is renewable annually, upon approval by a majority of the Directors
who are not parties to the contract or interested persons of any such party, may
be terminated upon not more than six months written notice by either party,
and is automatically terminated upon assignment.

Neither the Principal Underwriter nor the dealers are permitted to withhold
placing orders to benefit themselves by a price change. The gross sales charges
for sale of shares of the Fund during the year ended November 30, 1970 were
$4,646,561 of which $1,811,847 was received by the Principal Underwriter and
$2,834,714 by dealers.

DIVIDENDS, CAPITAL GAIN DISTRIBUTIONS, AND TAX STATUS

The Fund's current policy is to pay quarterly cash dividends in the latter part
of March, June, September, and December which will be substantially equal to
all of its net investment income, if any, for its fiscal year ending November 30.
For Federal income tax purposes, such dividends (together with distributions of
any short-term capital gains) are taxable as ordinary income to the shareholder
and are expected to qualify in whole or in part for the $100 dividend received
exclusion. The net investment income will be distributed in full regardless of
capital gains and losses.

It is also the policy to distribute substantially all net long-term capital gains,
if any. It has been the practice to make such capital gain distributions payable
in shares of the Fund at net asset value or, at the election of each shareholder,
in cash. Approximately 31% of the net asset value of the shares as of November
30, 1970, represented unrealized appreciation. Net long-term gains on sale of
securities when realized and distributed are taxable as long-term capital gains
to the shareholder and do not qualify for the $100 exclusion. If the net asset
value of the shares is reduced below a shareholder's cost by distribution of gains

realized on sale of securities, such distribution will be a return of investment
though taxable as stated above.

For the year ended November 30, 1970 the Fund qualified as a regulated
investment company, and intends to do so in the current fiscal year and therefore was relieved of Federal Income Tax. The Fund will notify shareholders
whether distributions of any capital gains are to be treated as long-term or short-
term gains. Such distributions of gains are designated by the Fund as a "return
of capital or principal" to assist fiduciary shareholders in allocating them to
principal.

Any dividend or distribution paid shortly after a purchase of shares by an
investor will have the effect of reducing the per share net asset value of his
shares by the per share amount of the dividend or distribution. Furthermore,
such dividend or distribution, although in effect a return of capital, is subject
to income taxes.

ALLOCATION OF PORTFOLIO BROKERAGE AND PORTFOLIO TURNOVER RATE

The primary consideration in all portfolio security transactions is execution
at the most favorable prices and in the most effective manner possible. The
Trading Department of the Adviser, which also serves the other clients of the
Adviser, will at all times attempt to buy and sell in the best markets, and it will
have complete freedom as to the markets in which it seeks this result. When this
primary consideration has been satisfied, securities may be bought from or sold
to broker-dealers selling shares of fund clients, or broker-dealers who have furnished statistical and other factual information to the Adviser. In the case of
securities listed on national exchanges, where these exchanges provide the best
market in the particular case, the Adviser will seek to do business through home
broker-dealers, who have sold shares or furnished information, acting as agents, when
when they are capable of meeting its standards of execution as authorized by the
Agreement. In placing orders with such broker-dealers, the Adviser will, where
possible, take into account the comparative usefulness of such information.
Such information may be useful to the Adviser but its dollar value is indeter-
minable and it does not reduce the Adviser's normal research activities or expenses. The Agreement also authorizes the Adviser to consider sales of shares
of the Fund and any other fund clients of the Adviser in selecting broker-
dealers to execute portfolio transactions. In the case of securities traded in the
over-the-counter market the Adviser normally seeks to deal directly with the
primary market makers except in those circumstances where, in its opinion,
better prices and executions are available elsewhere. For the year ended November 30, 1970 the Fund paid total brokerage commissions of $2,290,709.
Of that total, commissions were paid to broker-dealers whose sales of shares
(43% of commissions) or furnishing of information (13% of commissions) were
factors in their selections. The balance of commissions paid were paid without

regard to the foregoing considerations, although selling group broker-dealers may have participated therein. Investment decisions for the Fund are made independently of other clients. The portfolio trading operations of the Fund and other clients are, however, conducted together, and occasionally they pay purchase or sell the same security. If this occurs, each day's transactions in such security will be averaged as to price and allocated between such clients in accordance with the total amount of such security being purchased or sold by each. The rate of total portfolio turnover for the year ended November 30, 1970 was 18.19%, for 1969 was 16.17%, and for 1968 was 11.88%.

LEGAL PROCEEDINGS

Certain shareholders of the Fund have brought civil actions in the U.S. District Court for the District of Massachusetts against the Directors of the Fund and the principal underwriter. The complains allege that the compensation of the Defendants, both directly and indirectly through the use of brokerage commissions on portfolio transactions, is excessive. The complaints seek recision of the Distribution Agreement, injunction of the conduct complained of, and damages. It is the opinion of the Fund's counsel that the suits are without merit. In the event that the plaintiff prevails, however, any monetary recovery will insure to the benefit of the Fund, or its shareholders, or both.

In December 1968, a action entitled Kauffman vs. The Dreyfus Fund, Inc., et al. was begun in the U.S. district Court for the District of New Jersey against some 65 named mutual funds, externally managed mutual funds "affiliated therewith or related thereto", the investment advisers of the named funds and certain affiliated individuals. A named defendant is the underwriter of the Fund. The complaint is brought representatively and derivatively and alleges conspiracies on the part of the defendants to restrain competition in management fees in violation of the anti-trust laws, to pursue certain brokerage and "give-up" practices in violation of the Investment Company Act of 1940, and to issue misleading proxy statements and other reports in violation of various Federal Securities Acts. The complaint seeks damages in an unspecified amount and injunctive relief. The course of litigation to date has involved plaintiff's alleged right to sue on behalf of more than the four funds of which he is a shareholder. The fund is not a party to said action nor, in the opinion of its counsel, is it within the class of funds on behalf of which or against that which the plaintiff alleges that such action has been brought.

INVESTMENTS — NOVEMBER 30, 1970

NUMBER OF SHARES	COST	MARKET VALUE
AEROSPACE — 0.4%		
225,000 Northrop Corporation	$ 8,784,955	$ 4,950,000
AIRLINES — 0.9%		
221,000 Delta Air Lines, Inc.	$ 5,923,884	$ 10,178,250
BANKS AND CREDIT COMPANIES — 3.4%		
150,000 Citizens & So. Nat'l Bank (Ga.)	$ 4,249,125	$ 4,350,000
100,000 Crocker National Corp.	3,275,000	3,225,000
341,000 Household Finance Corp.	7,286,714	14,407,250
245,000 Republic National Bank of Dallas	6,515,550	5,971,875
16,481 Third National Bank, Nashville	903,112	811,689
51,500 Wachovia Corporation	2,729,050	2,806,750
15,000 Wachovia Corporation $2.20 Cum. Cv., Ser. A Pfd.	779,389	885,000
150,000 Wells Fargo & Company	6,998,288	5,475,000
BUSINESS MACHINES — 16.9%		
250,000 Amer. Research & Develop. Corp.	$ 1,244,514	$ 12,968,750
150,000 Burroughs Corporation	15,418,281	16,387,500
265,000 Internat'l Business Machines Corp.	9,112,022	81,421,250
250,000 Moore Corp., Ltd.	2,899,077	7,875,000
285,100 Pitney-Bowes, Inc.	6,708,219	6,913,675
1,500,000 Rank Organisation Ltd., ADR	18,077,899	24,937,500
400,000 Xerox Corporation	3,730,337	35,750,000
	$ 57,190,349	$ 186,253,675
CHEMICALS — 1.9%		
200,000 Internat'l Flavors & Fragrances	$ 3,312,095	$ 13,125,000
213,700 Nalco Chemical Company	3,270,241	8,254,163
	$ 6,582,336	$ 21,379,163
CONSUMER GOODS AND SERVICES — 7.1%		
100,000 ARA Services, Inc.	$ 5,251,728	$ 11,350,000
350,000 Avon Products, Inc.	1,749,906	27,912,500
250,000 Holiday Inns, Inc.	5,709,434	9,062,500
349,800 Marriott Corporation*	4,765,645	9,094,800
200,000 Revlon, Inc.	10,686,760	13,675,000
175,000 Sperry & Hutchinson Company	$ 8,237,987	$ 7,525,000
	$ 36,401,460	$ 78,619,800
DRUGS AND MEDICAL — 10.7%		
100,000 Abbott Laboratories	$ 6,760,315	$ 7,487,500
225,000 American Home Products	13,039,961	15,131,250
154,000 American Medical Enterprises	4,271,545	3,360,375
225,000 Baxter Laboratories, Inc.	6,787,779	5,484,375
200,000 Hospital Corp. of America*	4,557,563	5,225,000
148,000 Johnson & Johnson	3,218,315	8,695,000
150,000 Lilly (Eli) & Co.	6,386,181	14,812,500
148,000 Merck & Co., Inc.	4,631,727	13,098,000
450,000 Schering Corporation	15,638,581	26,156,250
147,000 Searle, (G. D.) & Co.	6,087,182	7,405,125
300,000 Sterling Drug, Inc.	5,808,662	11,775,000
	$ 77,187,811	$ 118,630,375

INVESTMENTS — NOVEMBER 30, 1970 (Continued)

NUMBER OF SHARES	COST	MARKET VALUE
ELECTRIC UTILITIES — 2.4%		
90,000 American Elec. Power Co., Inc.	$ 3,084,424	$ 2,520,000
200,000 Central and South West Corp.	6,790,052	9,275,000
100,000 Gulf States Utilities Co.	2,230,800	2,337,500
250,000 Oklahoma Gas & Electric Co.	5,583,807	6,312,500
100,000 Texas Utilities Company	4,608,431	5,787,500
	$ 22,297,514	$ 26,232,500
ELECTRICAL AND ELECTRONICS — 10.7%		
520,400 AMP, Incorporated	$ 5,715,157	$ 29,272,500
450,000 Ampex Corporation*	11,421,416	7,875,000
100,000 Emerson Electric Co.	5,683,106	6,487,500
325,000 Internat'l Tel. and Tel. Corp.	11,080,523	14,828,125
150,000 Internat'l Tel. and Tel. Corp. $2.25		
Cum. Cv., Ser. N Pfd.	$ 7,357,325	$ 8,587,500
150,000 Magnavox Co.	4,602,811	5,531,250
180,000 Motorola, Inc.	9,272,403	9,360,000
200,000 Raytheon Company	6,748,157	4,475,000
317,590 Teledyne, Inc.*	16,305,470	6,589,993
225,000 Texas Instruments, Inc.	11,722,463	17,212,500
200,000 Zenith Radio Corp.	6,237,459	7,500,000
	$ 96,146,290	$ 117,719,368
ENTERTAINMENT — 1.0%		
275,000 Columbia Broadcasting System	$ 13,008,195	$ 7,975,000
141,750 Col. Broadcast. System (Cv. Pfd.)	2,279,878	2,657,813
	$ 15,288,073	$ 10,632,813
FOOD PRODUCTS — 2.5%		
50,000 Anheuser-Busch, Inc.	$ 3,254,453	$ 3,787,500
85,000 Coca-Cola Company	5,923,489	7,118,750
52,000 Pabst Brewing Co.	2,521,750	2,457,000
275,000 PepsiCo, Inc.	9,515,630	13,887,500
	$ 21,215,322	$ 27,250,750
FOREST AND PAPER PRODUCTS — 0.7%		
51,000 Boise Cascade Corporation	$ 2,075,084	$ 2,269,500
51,516 Georgia-Pacific Corp.	2,638,754	2,736,787
50,000 Weyerhaeuser Co.	2,472,555	2,656,250
	$ 7,186,393	$ 7,662,537
INSURANCE — 3.3%		
150,000 Aetna Life & Casualty	$ 6,175,469	$ 6,450,000
255,000 Gov't Employees Insurance Co.	11,485,027	11,538,750
225,000 Marlennan Corp.	3,141,337	10,968,750
280,280 NLT Corporation	8,528,871	7,847,840
	$ 29,330,704	$ 36,805,340
METALS AND MINING — 2.1%		
650,000 Newmont Mining Corp.	$ 8,976,768	$ 16,331,250
138,600 Utah Construction and Mining	5,645,890	7,068,600
	$ 14,622,658	$ 23,399,850

INVESTMENTS — NOVEMBER 30, 1970 (Continued)

NUMBER OF SHARES	COST	MARKET VALUE
OILS — 11.1%		
300,000 Amerada Hess Corp. (Cv. Pfd.)	$ 16,354,716	$ 29,100,000
100,000 Atlantic Richfield Company	9,018,589	6,237,500
200,000 Canadian Superior Oil Ltd.*	3,342,490	7,625,000
325,450 Kerr-McGee Corporation	12,232,684	34,253,613
300,000 Louisiana Land & Expl. Co.	7,173,026	18,150,000
125,000 Natomas Company	10,766,169	6,015,625
300,000 Pennzoil United, Inc.	19,486,658	10,012,500
65,000 Superior Oil Company	8,670,117	10,952,500
	$ 87,044,449	$ 122,346,738
OTHER PRODUCTS AND SERVICES — 6.1%		
75,000 Block (H&R), Inc.	$ 3,260,343	$ 4,612,500
510,000 Brunswick Corporation	9,424,541	8,988,750
160,000 Deltona Corp.*	5,038,473	4,620,000
412,000 Eastern Gas & Fuel Associates*	12,702,906	14,935,000
400,000 General Tel. & Electronics	10,944,133	10,950,000
85,000 Gould, Inc.	4,058,561	2,773,125
187,000 Mattel, Inc.	5,385,653	7,106,000
75,000 Minnesota Mining & Mfg.	1,119,074	6,740,625
300,000 United States Freight Co.	7,614,946	6,487,500
	$ 59,548,630	$ 67,213,500
PHOTOGRAPHIC PRODUCTS — 3.0%		
285,000 Eastman Kodak Company	$ 8,726,153	$ 19,807,500
175,000 Polaroid Corporation	4,513,524	13,059,375
	$ 13,239,677	$ 32,866,875
PRINTING AND PUBLISHING — 2.8%		
601,275 Donnelley, (R. R.) & Sons Co.	$ 10,860,821	$ 9,620,400
132,500 Dun & Bradstreet, Inc.	4,502,417	6,823,750
220,400 Grolier Incorporated	3,442,505	5,344,700
300,000 Scott, Foresman and Company	10,063,357	5,700,000
100,000 Times-Mirror Company	3,139,764	3,475,000
	$ 32,008,864	$ 30,963,850
STORES — 2.6%		
150,000 Dayton-Hudson Corp.	$ 4,451,206	$ 4,350,000
210,000 King's Department Stores	4,996,787	5,013,750
200,000 Kresge (S. S.) Co.	9,023,938	11,300,000
134,900 Morse Shoe, Inc.	4,943,092	3,203,875
200,000 Zayre Corporation*	7,367,162	5,250,000
	$ 30,782,185	$ 29,117,625

INVESTMENTS — NOVEMBER 30, 1970 (Continued)

NUMBER OF SHARES	COST	MARKET VALUE
SPECIAL HOLDINGS — 1.6%		
63,200 American Television & Comm.*	$ 875,385	$ 1,058,600
77,000 Amtel Inc.**	1,637,790	452,375
25,000 Bath Industries, Inc.*	566,224	437,500
75,000 Clorox Company	1,694,611	2,503,125
19,500 Energy Conversion Devices*	702,350	429,000
31,500 First Charter Financial Corp.*	1,098,495	1,287,563
10,000 Joy Manufacturing	449,339	472,500
30,000 Kenton Corp.**	1,161,645	399,375
35,000 Panhandle Eastern Pipe Line	1,304,022	1,443,750
25,000 Petrie Stores Corp.	741,116	875,000
15,000 Popeil Brothers, Inc.	268,275	232,500
11,100 Purolator, Inc.	659,115	732,600
75,000 B. F. Saul Real Estate Inv. Trust	881,250	1,106,250
50,000 Saxon Industries, Inc.*	1,051,891	962,500
20,000 F. & M. Schaefer Corp.*	657,630	635,000
24,800 Sonderling Broadcasting Corp.*	894,005	514,600
120,000 Swank, Inc.	1,870,367	1,965,000
40,000 Thompson (J. Walter) Company	1,521,844	1,145,000
20,200 USLIFE Corp.	493,202	616,100
25,000 Williams Brothers Company*	804,495	850,000
	$ 19,333,051	$ 18,118,338
MISCELLANEOUS SECURITIES — 0.6%	$ 6,886,346	$ 6,410,625
Total Stocks	$679,737,179	$1,014,684,536†
CORPORATE SHORT-TERM NOTES, AT COST PLUS DISCOUNT EARNED WHICH APPROXIMATES MARKET — 8.2%	$ 90,507,691	$ 90,507,691
TOTAL INVESTMENTS — 100%	$770,244,870	$1,105,192,227
Cost for Federal Income Tax Purposes	$769,807,239	

†Securities priced on the basis of over-the-counter bid prices totaled $79,806,629; all other items were at closing prices reported on national security exchanges.

*Non-income producing.

**At November 30, 1970, 77,000 shares of Amtel, Inc. and 22,500 shares of Kenton Corp., both acquired during January, 1969 were restricted as to resale. The fair values of such investments, aggregating $744,875 at November 30, 1970 and representing .07% of total investments, have been determined by the Board of Directors, after consideration of various relevant factors including the inherent value of the issuers, the basis of valuation of the securities at time of purchase, the current market valuation of unrestricted securities of the same class and information, if available, as to the price obtainable for such restricted securities, on the basis of 10% discounts from the market quotations for unrestricted shares (compared to discounts of approximately 7.5% at date of acquisition). In both cases the Fund has registration rights under the Securities Act of 1933 at the expense of the issuer.

QUESTIONS

1. What is the investment objective of the fund? How does the fund
intend to achieve its objective? Do all funds offer the same investment
objective, or are there other funds with different objectives?

2. Evaluate the investment restrictions of the fund. Do they lessen the
risk of investing in the fund? Do you feel they are too restrictive for
the fund to achieve its investment objective?

3. If the Securities and Exchange Commission (SEC) has not approved
the securities, what does the SEC have to do with the prospectus?

4. What are the possible effects of the different distribution options
on the future worth of any shares that Mr. Horne may purchase?

5. How much commission will Mr. Horne pay if he buys the shares?
If the fund were front-loaded, would that make a difference to the commissions Mr. Horne would pay?

6. If Mr. Horne elects to withdraw a fixed sum every month under
the fund's withdrawal service, what happens to the principal if the
designated monthly withdrawal is greater than the accumulated dividends?

7. From the statment of per share income and capital changes contained in the prospectus, comment on the efficiency with which the
fund is managed.

8. What is meant by the exchange privilege?

9. How does Mr. Horne redeem his shares and for what price?
Does he pay a commission for selling his shares?

10. What is the function of the principal underwriter?

11. What are the terms of the investment advisor's agreement with the
fund?

12. What are the tax status of dividend and capital gains distributions?
How does this affect Mr. Horne?

13. How might the legal proceedings, particularly the action filed in
Kauffman vs. The Dreyfus Fund, Inc: affect the relationship of the
investment advisor with the fund?

14. Do you think the fund should favor those broker-agents who provide it with investment information in placing orders to buy or sell
stock if the fund could get a lower commission rate from other broker-
agents who did not provide information?

Case 39

McCOIN FINANCIAL MANAGEMENT

SERVICE

Mutual Fund Performance Evaluation

Shortly after receiving his MBA from the University of Houston, Ken McCoin started the McCoin Financial Management Service. The intent of the service was to provide computerized analysis of mutual fund performance and to advise clients on the progress of their mutual fund investments. The service was registered with the Securities and Exchange Commission as a professional investment advisor. Mr. McCoin had developed a sophisticated statistical routine which ranked mutual funds by the volatility of their return in relationship to the return of the general market.

Mr. McCoin's technique correlated the individual fund's return to the S & B market index return. He discovered that, in general, mutual funds, because of their diversified portfolios, moved in tandem with the market. However, he had also discovered that the volatility of the relationship varied greatly among funds. The less risk averse funds were inclined to invest in more speculative stocks and to concentrate their protfolios in fewer issues and larger positions. As a result, the price of these "riskier" funds tended to be very volatile, surpassing the performance of the general market on the upswing and falling far short of the general market performance on the downturn. On the other hand, several more conservatively managed funds, which concentrated their portfolios in less speculative stocks and in a greater diversed list of securities, including bonds, performed better than the market average on the downswing but not as well as the market average on the upswing. Mr. Coin found that the extremes between the riskier and the more conservative funds were far apart. During the last market rise of 13%, some of Mr. McCoin's clients had as much as a 75% rise in the share price of their funds while others had experienced less than a 5% share price increase. By contrast, during the last market decline of 20%, some of the previously best performing funds had declined as much as 50%, while some of the previously less spectacular performing funds, fell less than 5%, and a few of the most conservatively oriented funds actually rose as much as 9%.

A careful examination of the funds in relation to their performances over the last market cycle, revealed that no fund performed ideally in the sense that its return fared better than the general market index in both the up and down phase of the cycle. Those which did better in one phase did worse in the other phase. A fund's stated investment objectives and other characteristics were no indication of how a particular fund was going to perform over the market cycle, although, in general, those funds with more conservative investment objectives fared better in the down phase. However, even among the only midly aggressive funds, Mr. McCoin found funds which fluctuated much more than the market in general.

Mr. McCoin, therefore, decided to apply his volatility ranking technique to determine the degree to which his rankings compared with the leading mutual fund advisory service's ranking and to see if volatility rankings could be used in conjunction with the risk free interest rate to select the best performing funds. Towards this effort, he gathered the return data, presented in Table 1 on each of the following three funds.

Fund A is rated by the leading mutual fund investment advisory service as a capital gains oriented fund which could be expected to exhibit higher than general volatility in relation to the market and, as a consequence, to have a higher than average risk factor. Total assets of Fund A are less than $100 million with all of the funds investments in common stocks, except for approximately 1% of its total assets which are in cash. The fund invests in many speculative situations and in the last market upswing was one of the top performers.

Fund B is rated by the leading service as a capital growth and income oriented fund, implying it is more diversified than Fund A and probably not as risky or volatile. In the broad and generalized range of funds it would fit in the average category of expected return and expected risk. Its portfolio was less heavily weighted towards stocks than Fund A but nevertheless had almost 80% of its assets in stocks. The portfolio was also more widely diversified in more seasoned issued than those of Fund A. Five periods ago the management had changed at the fund, when it failed to keep pace with the growth in the sale of new funds. The old management was accused of failing to provide sufficient performance to attract new customers and the new management had been installed. At that time the investment objective of the fund had been changed to its present one from the less aggressive income and capital growth objective.

Fund C is rated by the leading service as income and capital growth oriented, implying the fund is most likely to invest in stocks and bonds which promise good income first and capital gains second. During the recent market decline it had one of the best performances, rising almost 7%. It assets consist of almost 50% high grade corporate bonds, and the fund usually has a substantial amount of cash.

Once he has estimated the volatility of each fund, Mr. McCoin intends to select the best performing fund by comparing the calculated volatility to the U. S. Treasury bill rate of 6% which prevailed during the period of the data. Mr. McCoin believes that the best fund is that one which is the first to return at least the same as the bill rate. Mr. McCoin reasons that fund which takes the least general market rise to push its own return over the bill rate is in the best position over the market cycle.

TABLE 1
RETURNS

PERIOD	S & B INDEX	FUND A	FUND B	FUND C
1	10.0%	20.0%	10.0%	5.0%
2	8.0	16.0	8.0	4.0
3	6.0	12.0	6.0	3.0
4	3.0	6.0	3.0	1.5
5	2.0	4.0	2.0	1.0
6	− 1.0	− 2.0	− 1.0	− .5
7	− 3.0	− 6.0	− 3.0	− 1.5
8	− 8.0	−16.0	− 8.0	− 4.0
9	−10.0	−20.0	−10.0	+ .5
10	−20.0	−40.0	−20.0	+ 7.0
11	+10.0	+20.0	+15.0	+10.0
12	9.0	18.0	13.5	6.0
13	7.0	14.0	10.5	5.0
14	8.0	16.0	12.0	6.0
15	6.0	12.0	9.0	4.5

QUESTIONS

1. Graph the relationship in the return to the S & B market index and the return to each of the funds during the periods on which Mr. McCoin gathered data. Interpret your graph.

2. Classify each fund according to its volatility (i.e. the slope of the relationship line you have drawn in your answer to question 1). What is the implication for risk in your classifications? Do your volatility rankings agree with those of the leading mutual fund investment advisory service?

3. Which fund would be the first to return the bill rate in a market advance? Does this make it the best fund in terms of Mr. McCoin's criteria?

4. Comment on Fund B's volatility before and after the management shift. Can Mr. McCoin use his volatility rankings to detech such a shift and what are the implications for investment when such a shift occurs?

Case 40

CHARTING

PART A VERTICAL BAR CHARTS

Mr. Brads is a technical analyst for a large brokerage house. He is responsible for maintaining and interpreting vertical bar and point and figure charts on stocks which are of interest to the firm's clients. Mr. Brads has been charting the price movements of Telepoop, Inc., a highly volatile stock on the American Stock Exchange. He has gathered the following price and volume data:

DAY	HIGH	LOW	CLOSE	VOLUME (000)
1	75-1/4	72-3/4	73	125
2	74-7/8	73	73-1/2	75
3	76-1/4	73	76-1/4	125
4	78-7/8	74-7/8	75	150
5	74-7/8	73	74-7/8	60
6	77-1/2	75	75-1/2	70
7	74-7/8	72-1/2	73-7/8	190
8	74	73	73	80
9	75-1/8	73-1/8	75	100
10	77	74-7/8	75	110
11	76-7/8	75	75	85
12	82	75	81-3/4	445
13	82-1/2	79-1/2	79-1/2	290
14	79-3/4	76-3/4	76-3/4	80
15	77-3/4	76-1/2	77-1/2	50
16	80	76-1/2	80	110
17	82-3/4	80	82-1/2	165
18	82-1/2	79-7/8	81-1/2	110
19	81-1/2	77	77	80
20	79-1/2	77-1/2	79	90
21	82-1/4	78-7/8	82-1/4	110
22	85-1/4	83	84-1/2	310
23	86-1/2	85-1/2	85-5/8	160
24	86-1/4	81-1/4	81-1/4	140
25	83	80-1/2	80-3/4	90
26	80-1/2	78-1/2	79	70
27	83	78-7/8	80-1/4	180
28	82	80	80-3/4	50
29	81	78	78	40
30	78-1/8	77	77-3/8	30
31	79-1/4	77-1/2	78-1/2	40
32	80-1/4	78-1/2	79-3/4	105
33	81-1/2	79-3/4	80-1/8	125
34	82-7/8	79-7/8	82-7/8	60
35	85-1/2	84	84-1/4	85
36	87-1/4	84-5/8	85	130
37	88-1/2	84-3/4	84-3/4	200
38	86-1/4	84-3/4	86-1/4	190

DAY	HIGH	LOW	CLOSE	VOLUME (000)
39	88	86-1/2	86-1/2	60
40	86-3/4	82-1/4	82-1/2	150
41	85	82-7/8	84	235
42	85	83-1/2	83-3/4	105
43	84-1/4	83-3/4	84-1/4	55
44	84-1/2	83-1/4	83-3/8	45
45	84	81-1/2	82	55
46	84-1/2	81-3/4	84-1/4	155
47	86-7/8	84-1/2	85	130
48	84	80-7/8	81-1/4	120
49	81-3/8	77	77-1/4	130
50	81-1/2	79-1/2	81-1/4	240
51	81-1/8	79	79	100
52	79-1/2	79	79-1/2	115
53	82-1/4	79-1/8	82-1/4	40
54	84	82-1/2	82-5/8	25
55	84	82-7/8	84	55
56	81-7/8	85-3/4	82	55
57	81-3/4	79	81	50
58	82	81	81	170
59	83-1/4	81-1/2	82-3/4	60
60	83-1/4	82-1/2	82-7/8	35
61	82-7/8	81-3/4	81-3/4	55
62	82-1/2	80-1/4	80-1/4	10
63	79-1/2	77-1/4	77-1/2	20
64	78-3/4	76-3/4	78-3/4	40
65	81	78-1/4	78-1/4	125
66	79-7/8	75-1/8	76	55
67	78	75-7/8	77-1/8	110
68	78	77	77	180
69	77-1/2	75	75	55
70	75-3/4	74-3/4	74-7/8	25

QUESTIONS

1. Construct a vertical bar chart from the price data. Does the resulting chart resemble any recognizable chart pattern? If so, interpret the chart in terms of what it might mean to a chartist.

2. What underlying assumptions does the chartist make in interpreting his chart? Criticize and compare these assumptions to the random walk theory of stock prices.

PART B POINT AND FIGURE CHARTS

Mr. Brads was approached by one of the firm's clients and asked to const
and interpret a point and figure chart for a stock. Mr. Brads collected the follo
ing data:

DAY	PRICE (CLOSING)	DAY	PRICE
1	18-1/2	22	23
2	18	23	22-7/8
3	18-7/8	24	22-1/4
4	19	25	21-7/8
5	19-1/2	26	21-1/2
6	21	27	21-7/8
7	21-7/8	28	20-3/4
8	22	29	20-7/8
9	22-1/8	30	20-1/8
10	22-7/8	31	20
11	22-1/4	32	19-1/2
12	24	33	19-1/2
13	23	34	20
14	23	35	20-1/2
15	22-7/8	36	22
16	21	37	24-1/8
17	21-1/2	38	25
18	21		
19	22		
20	23		
21	24		

QUESTIONS

1. Using a three point reversal pattern, plot a point and figure chart for these data.
2. Compare the construction of the point and figure chart with that of the vertical bar chart. Do you find any differences?
3. Interpret the point and figure chart you have plotted. Do you find any break-outs? If so, what is your estimated price objective and how did you determine it?

INE

Relative Strength Trading Rules

James Blaine, a technical security analyst specializing in computer applications to security analysis, has developed some filter rules for his firm's clients who maintain active trading accounts. Jim believes that if he can detect price movements at an early stage in their development, he can offer a very profitable service to his clients. Every Monday morning Jim gets a computer printout of the price performance of the preceding week's trading for every stock on the New York and American Stock Exchanges. The raw price data have been fed into the computer during the weekend and run through Jim's filter routine. The program literally filters out all those stocks for which the price change has met Jim's criteria.

One of Jim's major filter programs is his relative strength index (R.S.I.). Jim has the computer compare the change in last week's price to a four week moving average of the price for each particular stock, such that he receives the value of the following formula for each stock:

$$R.S.I. = \frac{P_t - P_{t-1}}{\sum\limits_{t=1}^{4} \dfrac{P_{t-4}}{4}}$$

P_t = Price at the end of week t
P_{t-1} = Price at the end of the week $t - 1$

The computer then ranks each stock in descending order of its R.S.I. The stock with the highest R.S.I. is Jim's pick of the week.

Jim bases his relative strength index on the belief that it can detect, at a very early stage, a price movement from one equilibrium price to another. If this is so, the stocks with the greatest relative price change should be those just beginning their moves.

Jim also uses a 10% filter rule in trying to capture signs of the early part of a movement in stock price from one equilibrium position to another. Jim has had several unfortunate experiences where his R.S.I. has given false signals, such that a sudden increase in the stock price did not signal a further increase, but rather

172

was succeeded by a decline. He believes these arose because some random factor, rather than a specific change in the outlook for the company, caused a random price movement around the equilibrium price, which he mistook as the early stages of a change in the equilibrium price. In other words, the R.S.I. may be too sensitive. Jim, therefore, uses the 10% filter rule to confirm the R.S.I. If a stock rises (falls) 10% or more from its present price, Jim buys (sells) the stock until a 10% reversal in the trend of the price change occurs. Then he sells (buys) the stock.

The following information was compiled on three stocks:

STOCK PRICE DATA
End of Week

STOCK:	A	B	C
	$20	10	25
	21	11	24-1/8
	22-1/4	10-1/2	23-1/4
	23-1/2	10-1/2	25-3/8
	22-1/2	13	27-1/4
	21-1/2	15-1/4	26
	24	17	30-1/2
	23-1/2	20-1/2	31
	27-1/2	21-1/4	33-1/4
	29-1/2	19-3/8	29
	29	18	24-3/8
	31	17-1/4	28
	30-1/8	16	29-3/4
	27-5/8	15-3/4	34
	26-7/8	18-5/8	37-1/8
	24	23	31
	23	25	33
	24-1/8	24	32
	25-7/8	23-1/2	27
	26	23-1/2	26
	28	27-1/8	23
	29	26	21
	30	25	25

QUESTIONS

1. What is the relative strength index for each of the three stocks over the period of the data? Select the stock which is the most attractive as of the end of the data period under the R.S.I. criterion. Calculate the trading profit, assuming no transaction costs, which Jim would have made if he had always purchased the stock with the highest R.S.I. (assume he bought a 100 shares at a time) starting with the fifth week of the data. Compare that profit to the profit Jim would have made in each stock if he had simply bought 100 shares of each stock at the beginning of the data period and held it to the end of the data period.

2. Using a 10% filter rule for each of the stocks, pinpoint the trading prices for each stock. What, if any, is the profit from the 10% trading rule, assuming Jim bought 100 share lots only. Compare that profit to the buy and hold strategy for each of the stocks, as calculated in your answer to question 1.

3. Assuming a $40 commission each time Jim bought or sold 100 shares, recompute your profit calculations for the 10% filter rule and the R.S.I. Draw conclusions.

Case 42

POOR, SOPHISTICATED INVESTOR

Portfolio Construction

Steve Allsod, a finance major, has just completed his first course in investments and with the $2,000 he has accumulated wants to buy stocks. He has carefully examined several issues using the techniques he has learned and has decided to concentrate his investments in the shares of Local Lighting and Power, Inc., a conservatively financed and well run electric utility serving Steve's hometown and Grayson Foundries, Inc., a small producer of standard iron forgings which is very prone to cyclical fluctuations. Steve has ruled out any short sales in his portfolio until he feels the market is about to decline. However, he has decided that he might keep some of his portfolio in cash instead of buying one of the stocks if his analysis showed this would be advantageous.

The share of both companies were presently selling at $10 each on the American Stock Exchange when Steve made the following projections about each company's expected performance during the next year, the period over which Steve expected to hold the stocks he purchased. He projected a rising economy in which companies such as Grayson have historically done well. In comparison to last year's earnings per share of $1.00 Steve estimated the following probability distribution for Grayson's earnings per share:

Earnings per Share	Probability
$ .90	10%
1.25	20
1.50	40
1.75	20
2.00	10

He also estimated that while the stock was presently selling at ten times earnings, it would sell at 12 times estimated earnings during the next twelve months because of improved market conditions. Per share earnings for Local Lighting and Power were expected to continue to grow from last year's $.50 at the same 20% a year growth that had prevailed in the past decade, although there was a 50% possibility that a rate increase would soon become effective which would increase earnings growth to 36% per year.

Steve also examined the past price action of the two securities and found the following:

Grayson	Local L & P
8	8
7	8¼
6½	8½
6	9
7½	8½
9	9
8½	8½
9	8½
10	9
11	9
9	9
9	8½
9	9½
10	10

Steve expected the price action of the two securities to be similarly related in the future.

QUESTIONS

1. Formulate the probability distribution of expected prices for each stock based on Steve's projections.

2. Compute the expected value (mean) and the standard deviation for each stock, based on your answer to question 1.

3. Compute the correlation coefficient between the price activity of each stock. What is the correlation between each stock's price activity and Steve's cash reserve?

4. Determine the expected return and the standard deviation for each of the following possible portfolios:

Grayson	Local L&P	Cash
50 shares	150 shares	$ 0
100	100	0
150	50	0
200	0	0
100	0	1,000
0	100	1,000

Do any of the portfolios dominate any other portfolio? Which portfolios comprise the attainable set? Construct the efficient frontier and interpret it.

Case 43

ACORN FINANCIAL ADVISORS, INC.

Utility Functions

John Jones, a young investment advisor with Acorn Financial Advisors, Inc., had been in consultation with several new clients and was attempting to determine their attitudes toward risk. In addition to conversations with the clients, the company had devised a little quiz which attempted to reveal the client's attitude toward risk.

John's first client was Mrs. Sara Beerbottom, whose husband was a very successful dress manufacturer and a client of Acorn. Although 60 years old Mrs. Beerbottom was very spirited and with her bridge club had formed an investing group which, in her own words, "was to give us something to do and something we can have in common with our husbands." It was quite obvious that Mrs. Beerbottom and her group were exceptions to the rule. All were very wealthy and were apparently willing to undertake substantial risk as long as they could out perform their husband's investment club.

John showed Mrs. Beerbottom the Acorn Risk Quiz and asked her to fill it out. Here are her answers:

Is there any minimum amount of income you need from your investments?   NO

Assuming you have $100,000 to invest, would you invest it in a stock which had a 50% chance of rising to $130,000 and a 50% chance of falling to $70,000?   YES

Would you trade the above investment for one which had a 50% chance of rising to $150,000 and a 50% chance of falling to $50,000?   YES

Assuming the $100,000 had a value of 5, assign from 0 to 10 a value to each of the other possible outcomes below:

$ 50,000	1
70,000	3
100,000	5
130,000	8
150,000	10

Assign a descending order of preference to each of the three investments mentioned in the quiz.

$50,000–150,000	1
70,000–130,000	2
$100,000	3

John's other client was Mr. Monery, a distinguished looking businessman, who has four children, two approaching college age, and supported a rather high life style in the suburbs. Mr. Monery told John he wanted to invest his funds for supplemental income purposes during his retirement years and wanted John's professional management to make the nest egg grow, especially to counter inflation. John asked him to fill out the quiz and here are his answers:

Is there any minimum amount of income you need from your investments?   YES

Assuming you had $100,000 to invest, would you invest it in a stock which had a 50% chance of rising to $130,000 and a 50% chance of falling to $70,000?   NO

Would you trade the above investment for one which had a 50% chance of rising to $150,000 and a 50% chance of falling to $50,000?   NO

Assuming the $100,000 had a value of 5, assign from 0 to 10 a value to each of the other possible outcomes.

$ 50,000	0
70,000	2
100,000	5
130,000	7
150,000	8

Assign a descending order of preference to each of the three investments mentioned in the quiz.

$50,000–150,000	3
70,000–130,000	2
$100,000	1

QUESTIONS

1. Assuming the assigned values represent units of utility, graph the implied utility functions of both Mrs. Beerbottom and Mr. Monery.
2. Comment on the risk tolerance of each in light of the utility function you have drawn. How do they differ? What implication does the shape of the utility function have for appropriate investment policy.

Case 44

MR. SCHWARTZ'S TRIAL PERIOD

Portfolio Management

You are a financial advisor, and Mr. Schwartz has come to you for investment management of his $10,000 account. He is prepared to place the entire sum in an account under your sole discretion for a one year trial period, at the end of which, if you have done well, he will seriously consider retaining your services for his entire $250,000 portfolio.

Mr. Schwartz is presently a robust man of fifty, with two unmarried daughters and a wife who depend on him for their sole support. He has thoughtfully named them his beneficiaries in his $300,000 face value of life insurance. However, he would still like to leave them a reasonably sized legacy of stocks and bonds. In fact, he has turned to you because he wants you to increase the value of his portfolio for that purpose. He has limited interest in receiving dividends, because his dress manufacturing business provides him with sufficient current income.

Mr. Schwartz is very optimistic about the future of the American economy and believes that stocks provide him with the best investment opportunity to participate in this expected growth. However, Mr. Schwartz is not unsophisticated, and he realizes that there are risks as well as returns when one buys stocks. In fact, he has mastered the concepts of risk, return, and diversification and requires that you inform him of the risk and return you expect from the entire portfolio.

Knowing that in the trial period you will have to perform at least as well as the market in general and that you cannot afford high transaction costs which will cut into your performance, you have selected equal dollar amounts of two stocks which you intend to hold for the entire period unless your opinion changes. You have selected F. W. Valco (FWV), a large major retailer, and M & M Medico (MMM), a small, but well-established and growing health care concern. The prospects for both companies are, in your opinion, very bright. FWV should continue the earnings improvement that was started several years ago when new management took over and modernized the firm's operations. With a favorable economic climate, earnings, in your estimation, could climb from the $3.00 per share of last year to the $3.30–$3.50 range this year. Some further geographical diversification of the firm's outlets into more rapidly growing areas of the country and into the European Economic Community could lessen the firm's dependence on the cyclical income patterns of the highly industralized cities where the majority of present stores are located. FWV has no long term debt, because most of the stores are leased, although even considering the leases, the firm's total debt to equity ratio is very low.

MMM experienced a rapid expansion in its sales and earning with the advent of Medicare and the growing utilization of medical facilities by the consumer. You estimate the firm could continue the slightly over 20% growth in earnings that it has had in the last few years, and earnings per share could rise to the $3.00–$3.10 range. The prospects for any change in the firm's operating environment from its present favorable state appear slim, and the firm's capital structure is very reasonable by industry standards.

The most important consideration for you, however, is that any portfolio you select must perform as well as the market average, during the trial period, whether the market rises or falls. You expect that if the market were to rise, both FWV and MMM would rise, and if the market were to fall, both would decline. You estimate the market stands a 50–50 chance of falling to 90.00 or rising to 120.00 on the S & B index from its present level of 100.00. In your analysis you have gathered the following information on the historical price performance of both stocks in relation to the S & B market index:

HISTORICAL PRICE PERFORMANCE

	S & B MARKET AVE.	F. W. VALCO (FWV)	M & M MEDICO (MMM)
1961	75.0	$40	$25
1962	67.50	38	20
1963	80.00	42	29
1964	81.00	42	30
1965	89.00	44	36
1966	106.00	47	45
1967	96.00	43	40
1968	86.00	41	31
1969	95.00	45	37
1970	100.00	50	50
1971 (Est.)	90.00–120.00		

	FWV	MMM
	1970	1970
Sales	$275,000,000	$55,000,000
E. P. S.	$3.00	$2.50
Dividends	1.00	0
Est. E. P. S. (1971)	3.30–3.50	3.00–3.10

If past relationships hold true, the stock prices of FWV and MMM should rise and fall in the same proportion to the market's movements.

In fact, you have intentionally selected the two securities for their relationship to general market movements, in order to minimize the chances of not doing as well as the market.

QUESTIONS

1. Why, if the companies' prospects are favorable, would you have to worry about general market performance?
2. Graph the relationship between the return to each stock and the S & B index in each period. Use a separate graph for each stock. From your graphs determine which stock is the "riskier", explain your reasoning.
3. If the S & B market index fell to 90.00 by the end of the trial period, what would you expect the price of FWV and the price of MMM to be? If the index rose to 120.00, what would the expected prices be then?
4. Comment on the nondiversifiable risk for each stock. How would you measure it? Comment on the diversifiable risk for each stock. How would you measure it?
5. Graph the relationship between the return to the market index and the return to a portfolio which is comprised of an equal dollar amount of each stock. From your graph comment on what has happened to the return and the risk when the two stocks were combined into a portfolio.
6. Discuss the problems you may encounter when using historical data for your analysis of market based relationships.

Case 45

THE WIDOW WHIRL

Portfolio Management

When Mr. Whirl died at the age of fifty-five he was survived by his wife of 30 years, Martha, and two children, John, 20, a junior at the state university and Mary, a married daughter. Wilson Whirl had met Martha when he was just beginning his career at the local bank, the organization he had been employed at for the rest of his life and of which he was vice president at the time of his death. Martha was fifty at the time of her husband's death, and although deeply grieved, she was otherwise in good health. For a while she went to live with Mary and her husband Herbert, a rising young lawyer in the community, and their two children. However, Martha was determined not to become dependent on Mary for support and refused to accept the offer of an upstairs bedroom and the accompanying babysitting chores, claiming fifty was not old.

After the funeral, Mrs. Whirl sat down with Herbert to take stock of her position. Mr. Whirl had left his entire estate to her. Mrs. Whirl received $30,000 from the group life insurance policy that Mr. Whirl had at the bank. This was paid directly into the estate in one lump sum. During the 30 years Mr. Whirl had worked at the bank, he had contributed regularly to the bank's pension plan and at his death had accumulated pension benefits which Mrs. Whirl was entitled to receive at the rate of $3,000 a year for the actuarially estimated remaining thirty years of her life. Under the social security laws Mrs. Whirl would receive benefits of $100 a month as long as John was in school and until he reached the age of twenty-two and then would receive no benefits until she reached 62 years of age. At 62, Mrs. Whirl could expect to receive social security benefits of $177.00 a month. There was no medical insurance since Mr. Whirl's group policy at the bank expired when he did. The state in which Mrs. Whirl lived had no inheritance taxes but Herbert estimated that the federal estate taxes would be 25% of the estate's value after the $60,000 exemption and all legal, administrative, and final health and funeral expenses were deducted. Since Mr. Whirl had died slumped over his desk, the final expenses were only the $2,000 burial fees. Herbert donated the legal and administrative fees. Besides the insurance proceeds and the pension plan, Mrs. Whirl also inherited the home she and her husband had jointly owned and occupied for over 20 years. The latest appraised value of the home was $45,000 but there was an $8,000 balance on the 8% mortgage which was payable in equal monthly installments of $113.34, including interest and principle, for the next 8 years. The upkeep on the home amounted to $20 a month in utilities and $250 a year in school and property taxes. Mrs. Whirl had also been left two cars, a new four door sedan, on which $100 a month for the next three years was due and which had a resale value of $3,000 and a somewhat older car, worth $500, which was in perfect running order and free of debt. Other than the mortgage and the car installment loan, Mrs. Whirl inherited no other outstanding debts.

In addition, Mrs. Whirl inherited a portfolio of securities, which is summarized in Table 1. Around the bank Mr. Whirl had been known as somewhat of a swinger and had occasionally relied on tips for his investments, although, to his credit, he never used the same investment procedure for his clients. Mr. Whirl had not given much attention to his portfolio and he had not fared well, although someday he had always expected to make that killing in a security.

THE ESTATE OF WILSON WHIRL

Stocks

NO. SHARES	NAME	DIVD.	TOTAL INCOME	YLD	COST	MARKET VALUE PER SHARE	TOTAL VALUE
100	SCM	–	–	–	$22.00	$15.00	$ 1,500.00
100	Control Data	–	–	–	85.00	35.00	3,500.00
50	Natomas	$ .25	$ 12.50	0.4%	75.00	65.00	3,750.00
50	Houston Ltg. & Power	1.33	66.50	2.9	20.00	46.00	2,300.00
200	Sea Containers	–	–	–	8.00	10.00	2,000.00
400	KDI Corp.	–	–	–	5.00	2.00	800.00
500	Greyhound wts.	–	–	–	5.00	7.00	3,500.00
100	Dayton-Hudson	.50	50.00	1.4	33.00	36.00	3,600.00
			$129.00				$20,950.00

Bonds

S&P RATE	FACE VALUE	NAME	CURRENT YIELD	YLD TO MAT.	COST	MARKET VALUE PER SHARE	TOTAL VALUE
BB	$10,000	General Instrument 5% cv sub deb '92	8.20%	8.75%	50 points	60	$ 6,000.00
–	5,000	Norlin 9% sub deb '88	10.59%	10.96	60 points	85	4,250.00
							10,250.00

Checking account	400.00
Savings Account (5% annual interest)	1,300.00
Real Estate: 50% interest in a partnership	10,000.00

The real estate partnership is in the process of being dissolved and Mrs. Whirl should receive her late husband's $10,000 share within the year.

Mrs. Whirl has told Herbert she would like to remain active, despite her husband's death. She had always been used to an active social life and had been quite a party giver in her day. She had also worked for charities and before she retired to the life of a housewife, she had worked as a secretary at the bank. She also said she did not consider 50 years too old to remarry and that if the right man came along she would consider marriage. Herbert even suggested a cruise to relax her after the sudden passing of Mr. Whirl. She told Herbert she needed $5,000 per year living expenses in addition to her car and home payments.

QUESTIONS
1. Analyze Mrs. Whirl's financial and personal position. Define appropriate investment objectives for her, justify your answer.
2. Prepare a balance sheet of her assets and liabilities. Estimate Mrs. Whirl's present and future income needs.
3. Evaluate Mrs. Whirl's inherited portfolio in light of the investment objective you have defined for her.
4. Suggest an appropriate portfolio for Mrs. Whirl. Be sure to reconcile your estimate of her income needs with your portfolio recommendations.

Case 46

THE ACORN LIFE INSURANCE

CO.

Institutional Portfolio Management

Mr. Jones has recently been hired as executive-vice president in charge of investments by the Acorn Life Insurance Co. Prior to coming to Acorn, Mr. Jones had been an investment trust officer in one of the largest banks in the state. He had started his career in investments immediately upon receiving his M.B.A. from the state university as a security analyst for one of the brokerage houses, and it was there that he had also gained experience in investment banking.

Mr. Jones had been recruited for the Acorn position after the former vice president, Mr. Kelly, had retired. Acorn, founded in 1909, was a relatively small life insurance underwriter operating solely within the one state in which it was domiciled. Mr. Jones was expected to operate the investment portfolio with the small staff that he had been provided. Most of the personnel had been with Acorn for a substantial length of time and were concerned with the bookkeeping and mechanical maintenance of the portfolio, although one or two had actually done some field interviews in connection with investments for Mr. Kelly.

Within the Acorn corporate structure, the investment division had always been regarded as a strong contributor to the firm's earnings and a store of liquidity to tap when the payment of benefits was to be met. The firm offered no types of insurance other than life insurance and the board of directors had no intention of diversifying into any other area of the insurance industry or into any other industry, although the board had become concerned recently with the increased competition which had been reported by the salesmen. The competition was offering similiar policies but a higher interest on the accumulated premiums. Nevertheless, new sales of policies were running at a steady pace of $10 million dollars of face value annually. Acorn already had $800 million insurance in force, most of it whole life.

Premium income from the policies averaged $150 a year per $10,000 of face value and was expected to hold at that pace in the foreseeable future. Of the premium income, one-third goes to the salesman for his commission and one-third goes to operating expenses. The actuarial department estimates from the state insurance agency mortality tables that Acorn will have to pay $10 million a year in death benefits for at least the next 10 years.

One of the few disconcerting practices of the company which Mr. Jones discovered when he arrived was the low interest rate of 5% at which policy holders could borrow against the equity in their policies. He was surprised to learn that the last time interest rates on U.S. Treasury bills had risen above 6% almost $10 million was borrowed, placing a great strain on the investment portfolio to meet this demand. He had suggested to the board of directors that this interest rate be increased, and they were presently considering the matter.

The state insurance agency under which Mr. Jones would have to operate had relatively strict rules as to the investment practices of life insurance companies under its jurisdiction. While it allowed life insurance companies to invest all reserves, it restricted them from investing more than 30% of the company's assets in common stocks or other equity securities or in securities with less than a Standard and Poor's rating of A or above. Further, the agency was very insistent in its demand that death benefits be paid immediately, otherwise it would stop the firm from doing business. The agency also insisted that expenses be subtracted from income as they occurred, so that salesman's commissions and other costs were recorded as the premium income came in. No expenses were allowed to be deducted from investment income or profits.

Mr. Jones found the following investment portfolio at Acorn when he arrived:

ACORN'S PORTFOLIO

AMT. (mil)	ISSUE	S + P RATING	COST	CURRENT PRICE	CURRENT YIELD	YIELD TO MATURITY
5	Amer. Brands 5-7/8s 1992	AA	100	86-1/2	6.8	7.2
10	Amer. Tel. & Tel. 3-1/4s 1984	AAA	100	68-1/4	4.8	7.0
3	Columbia Gas Sys. 8-3/4s 1995	A	100	105-1/2	8.3	8.2
5	National Tea Sub. deb 3-1/2s 1980	BB	100	60-1/2	5.8	10.05
5	Liggett & Myers 6s 1992	A	100	86-3/4	6.9	7.3
10	Standard Oil (N.J.) 6-1/2 1998	AAA	100	95-1/4	6.8	6.9
10	Gull Oil 6-5/8s 1993	AAA	100	96	6.9	7.0
2	Atlantic Richfield 8-5/8s 2000	AA	100	108-1/2	7.9	7.6
10	Loans to policyholders at 5%					
5	U. S. Treasury bills due in 3 months		99	99-1/2	—	—
5	U. S. Treasury 4-1/4s 1992		100	80	5.35	5.95

	Convertible Bonds	S + P RATING	COST	PRICE	CURRENT YIELD	CONVERSION PRICE
10	Houston L+P 5-1/2 1985 cv. deb	AA	100	110-1/2	4.98	44.00

Preferred Stocks

SHARES (000)	ISSUE	RATING	COST	PRICE	DIVIDEND	YIELD
10,000	Liggett & Myers 7% cm (NC)	A	100	100	$7	7%
10,000	Ohio Power 7.6% cm	A	100	100	7.60	7.6

Common Stocks

20,000	Amer. Tel. & Tel.	A+	20	41-3/4	2.60	6.2
5,000	Puget Sound P+L	A—	22	28-3/8	1.84	6.6
10,000	Standard Oil (N.J.)	A+	50	68-7/8	3.90	5.7
20,000	Lone Star Gas	A—	15	25-5/8	1.36	5.4

QUESTIONS

1. Construct a schedule of cash inflows and outflows for Acorn, include both premium and investment income.

2. Discuss the implications of the schedule you have constructed in question 1

for Acorn's investment policies, particularly on liquidity and risk considerations.
3. What legal constraints should Mr. Lewellen consider in his investment policies?
4. In light of your answers to the above questions, comment on Acorn's present
investment portfolio and make appropriate suggestions for any changes in policy
which might be beneficial to Acorn.

Case 47

H. HOUR INVESTMENT FUND

Portfolio Size

You have just been hired as the portfolio manager for the newly formed H.
Hour Investment Fund, created and organized by Mr. Hour and four of his associates for the purpose of taking large investment positions in a limited number of
stocks. The fund's investment objective is capital gains, although all of the associates agree that the fund should not invest in very speculative or venture capital
situations. Current income is of no importance to the fund.

Each associate contributed $100,000 to the fund, and the plans call for no
further contributions. The associates feel that in the long run, the value of the
fund should increase because of their favorable expectations for the American
economy and for stock prices, but they are unwilling to suffer a large loss in the
initial periods of the fund's operations. Mr. Hour has specifically stated that he
does want the actual return to be more than two standard deviations from the
expected return at the beginning of the period.

The fund is organized with three levels of authority. A security analyst has
been hired by the group to maintain a constant surveillance on a selected list of
stocks and to provide you with a constantly updated report on each stock's expected price performance over the next holding period. As portfolio manager,
you represent the second layer of authority. Your responsibility is to choose,
from the list provided by the security analyst, the combination of stocks which
will be the most suitable to Mr. Hour, who makes the final decision to accept
or reject your suggested portfolio. The approved list is as follows:

Stock	Present Price	Expected Return	Expected Return Variance
Medicon, Inc.	$30	10%	.03
Balls Express	25	12	.05
Argonair, Inc.	35	13	.06
John J. Jones, Inc.	50	10	.05
Eranone, Inc.	20	8	.02
General Colonel's Chick.	70	7	.01
Hillview Village	10	0	.02
Short Short	60	10	.04
General Aloe	65	10	.03
Aszor Foods	30	10	.02

From the list provided you have selected Balls Express, Argonair, Inc., General Colonel's Chicken, and Aszor Foods, as candidates for your portfolio. Further, you have decided you will invest equal dollar amounts in those stocks which finally are included in your portfolio. As the next step in your analysis, you have estimated the relationship of each stock's past price performance to the general market index and found the following results:

Stock	Regression Coefficient	Standard Error of the Estimate
Balls Express, (BE)	1.3	9%
Argonair, Inc. (AIR)	2.0	10
General Colonel's Chick. (GCC)	.7	4
Aszok Foods (AF)	.5	2

The various portfolios available from among the selected stocks reveal the following historical price relationship to the market index:

Portfolio	Regression Coeff.	Standard Error
1 BE + AIR + GCC + AF	1.0	25 %
2 BE + AIR	1.8	3.25 %
3 BE + GCC	.9	1.05
4 BE + AF	1.1	1.09
5 BE + AIR + GCC	1.2	1.25
6 BE + AIR + AF	1.4	.835
7 BE + GCC + AF	.9	.900
8 AIR + GCC	.7	.890
9 AIR + AF	1.2	1.300
10 AIR + GCC + AF	1.3	1.200
11 GCC + AF	.5	.705

Your investigation reveals that if you purchase the shares in orders of $150,000, you can arrange for a block transaction. If the order is less than $150,000, the transaction cannot be handled as a block. The block commission rate is 1.0% of the total value, while the non-block rate is 1.5% of the total transaction value.

QUESTIONS
1. Why did you, as portfolio manager, choose certain stocks as portfolio candidates?
2. Rank each of the 11 portfolios in descending order of expected return. Can you eliminate any from consideration?
3. Rank all the portfolios in descending order of the standard error. What can you say about the relationship of the number of stocks and diversifiable risk?
4. Using Mr. Hour's criterion that he does not want a portfolio which may be more than twice the standard deviation from the expected value and considering transaction costs which portfolio is the best?
5. Can your optimal portfolio have fewer than four stocks and a higher standard error than the least standard error portfolio available? Why or why not?

Case 48

MR. AVON'S PORTFOLIO REVIEW

Portfolio Readjustment

Mr. L. Smith, a portfolio manager with a large investment management firm, has been in charge of Mr. Avon's portfolio for almost ten years. The relationship has been a satisfactory one, and Mr. Avon's portfolio has grown nicely. Each year about this time Mr. Smith prepares an annual review of the portfolio and makes suggestions for its improvement.

At the beginning of last year, Mr. Smith had purchased the capital growth portfolio recommended by the firm's security analysts for clients in Mr. Avon's risk category. The expected risk and return to the portfolio, which at that time, lay on the efficient frontier, were .05 and .09, respectively. At that position on the efficient frontier, Mr. Avon was fully invested in stocks, but had undertaken no margin or lending, and his portfolio return and risk were identical to that expected for the market portfolio. At this review, one year later, Mr. Smith's firm is again estimating that the market portfolio has an expected return of .09 and an expected risk of .05. The firm also expects the yield on Treasury bills to be 6% during the coming year.

The original portfolio had done well during the year, and the firm's analysts expect that most of the gain they had anticipated for the portfolio has been realized. They estimate that the expected risk and return to the original portfolio, if held, would only be .03 and .03, respectively. Three of the original ten issues in the portfolio have realized what the analysts believe are their full potential gain and should be sold. At Mr. Smith's request they have recommended three stocks, which they believe have good potential and which could replace the three sell recommendations. If Mr. Smith were to replace the three sell recommendations with the three new buy suggestions, he estimates Mr. Avon's portfolio would have an expected return of .10 and an expected risk of .0625. Mr. Smith also expects that the interest rate at which Mr. Avon could borrow would be 6% during the coming period.

Mr. Smith's firm has a definite policy of portfolio readjustment to which he must adhere in revising Mr. Avon's portfolio. The first principle of readjustment according to the firm is not to increase the client's risk exposure above the original level, which in Mr. Avon's Case was .05. While the firm does not specifically prohibit the taking of large losses in an effort to readjust a portfolio, it does not allow its portfolio managers to sell securities on which the firm's analysts have not issued a sell recommendation. In the case of Mr. Avon that means Mr. Smith can sell only the three stocks recommended for sale by the analysts. In the readjustment, the objective is to give the maximum return at the risk exposure which prevailed in the original portfolio. Borrowing and lending may be used to reach that objective, and transaction costs may be ignored. Further, portfolio allocation among issues should be in equal dollar amounts. The dollar amount of borrowing or lending should also be in units proportional to the number of stocks in the original portfolio. For example, in Mr. Avon's ten stock portfolio, one unit of borrowing would be 1/10 of the portfolio's value.

The firm's analysts have provided Mr. Smith with their annual selected portfolios for the five risk categories used by the firm. Each portfolio is designed to give the greatest expected return at that particular risk level. The parameters of the portfolios are given in the following table.

Portfolio	Expected Return	Expected Risk
A	.15	.14
B	.115	.075
C	.09	.05
D	.07	.03
E	.065	.01

If a new client were to start now he would be assigned by the portfolio manager to one of the selected portfolios, according to his level of risk aversion.

The analysts also tell Mr. Smith that they expect short term interest rates over the period to be approximately 6%. They further estimate that the prevailing risk function will be linear, in the form $R_p = R_f + b(\sigma \rho)$.

Where R_p is the expected return to the portfolio
R_f is the risk free rate
b is the risk coefficient
σ_ρ is the standard error risk measure of the portfolio

The market analysis section of the firm estimates that b should be .6.

QUESTIONS
1. Construct the prevailing efficient frontier, and compare the present position of the original portfolio to the frontier. Why is the original portfolio no longer on the frontier?
2. Is the available portfolio, after Mr. Smith replaces the sell recommendations with the buy recommendations, on the efficient frontier? Under the policy of the firm can Mr. Avon's portfolio get back on the efficient frontier during the coming period?
3. Considering the possibility of borrowing and lending with Mr. Avon's portfolio, can Mr. Smith return it to the original risk level? How would he go about doing this? How many units of borrowing or lending (a unit is 1/10th of the portfolio) must Mr. Smith borrow or lend to return to the former risk level? What is the expected return to the portfolio after the borrowing or lending has brought the portfolio back to its former risk level?

Case 49

MR. SWAYER

Dollar Cost Averaging

Mr. Swayer is the sole owner of a tavern in a working class neighborhood. He has been in the same location for almost ten years and has built a steady clientele and a respectable income from the business. He is well-liked in the neighborhood, and he and his wife and three children live in the apartment above the bar. While he works hard, opening the bar at 11 A.M. and not closing until 2 A.M. the next morning, he is very satisfied and sees no reason why he and his family should move from the area or why he should not remain in the same spot he is now for the rest of his working days.

Mr. Swayer, now 35, had originally moved into the area after his discharge from the Army and had taken a day shift job as a welder at the nearby boiler manufacturer. During his stay there he had grown unhappy working for some-one else and had decided to put some of his Army severance pay to work for him. A salesman at the plant had told him of a small electronics firm, and Mr. Public had purchased some of the stock only to find he had lost almost 1/2 his original investment in a matter of a few months. Salvaging what was left of his capital he opened the tavern.

Skiddish from his first and disastrous brush with stocks, Mr. Swayer had vowed never to buy stocks again. However, wiser with the business experience of the last ten years, Mr. Swayer had decided to build a retirement fund for himself. He had seen an ad in the local paper for the 2 John St. Fund which had stressed that he could build a retirement fund at the rate of up to $2,500 a year tax-free, if he were self-employed. Mr. Swayer had sent the paper clip-ping to the fund to ask for more information. A prospectus arrived in the mail a few days later.

Mr. Swayer read that under the Koegh plan, he could set up a retirement plan with the fund which would be tax free. All Mr. Swayer had to do was to invest a fixed amount at regular intervals. The fund, in turn, would invest the money in a diversified portfolio of stocks and bonds which they hope to make grow and which could provide Mr. Swayer with a comfortable retirement nest egg. The prospectus also stated that the fund would charge a fee for the professional in-vestment management it provided but that it would not charge any sales com-mission because it did not have a sales force and no salesman would call. Mr. Swayer was just as happy no salesman would call because he had had enough of salesmen from his last experience with stocks. Mr. Swayer asked the advice of his accountant who encouraged him to open a Koegh plan.

Mr. Swayer contracted with the fund to invest $625.00 the first of every quarter, starting with January 1 of next year, in the fund. He also made arrange-ment that any dividends which he was entitled to would be automatically re-invested for him in more shares of the fund by the fund, but that at no time was his investment, including dividends, to exceed $2,500 a year.

Mr. Swayer made the following payments during the next three years:

Date	Price of Fund Shares
January 1, 19XX	$15.00
April 1, 19XX	12.50
July 1, 19XX	10.00
October 1, 19XX	12.50
January 1, 19XX	15.00
April 1, 19XX	17.50
July 1, 19XX	20.00
October 1, 19XX	18.00
January 1, 19XX	19.00

Date	Price of Fund Shares (Continued)
April 1, 19XX	21.00
July 1, 19XX	22.00
October 1, 19XX	20.00

QUESTIONS

1. How many shares of the fund did Mr. Swayer purchase during the three years?
2. What is the average price per share paid by Mr. Swayer for his shares? What has been the average price of the fund during the three years? Why is the latter higher?
3. If Mr. Swayer sold his shares today, what would be his profit?
4. If the fund had charged a 10% sales commission, what would be your answers in questions 1,2, and 3?

Case 50

ARTHUR COCOA'S PORTFOLIO

Geometric Mean Evaluation

Art Cocoa is a 45 year old dress manufacturer. He has been working at various aspects of the business since he was 15, and, despite his lack of formal education, he has become quite successful, eventually owning his own firm, Suzy Quzy, which produces inexpensive cotton fashions for young misses. Despite being a little overweight, Mr. Cocoa is in the finest of health and a man of almost boundless energy. He has a wife and two unmarried daughters of whom he is extremely fond and has thoughtfully provided enough health and life insurance so that in the event of his death or disability the family would be financially secure. Obviously, his current income is more than sufficient for his needs, but he has begun to worry about his estate. For years he has dabbled in the stock market, playing hunches here and tips there; sometimes making money but more often than not losing money. In the process he has ended up with a relatively speculative portfolio of stocks worth about $50,000 in today's market. Mr. Cocoa has decided to seek professional investment management for his portfolio.

Mr. James Lewellen, a portfolio manager with Lionel D. Tranes and Co., is the person to whom Mr. Cocoa was referred. Mr. Lewellen determined, in talking with Mr. Cocoa, that his portfolio objective was capital gain with the purpose of accumulating an estate. Dividends or any form of current income were of no importance to Mr. Cocoa. Mr. Cocoa provided Mr. Lewellen with the following list of his present holdings:

Abbott Corona   Mr. Cocoa had originally purchased 1,000 shares of this small jewelry manufacturer on a tip from one of his friends. The purchased price was $12.50 a share, but the stock had not done well and was presently selling for $5.00 a share in the over-the-counter market. The Lionel D. Tranes security analyst has evaluated the position and prospects for Abott Corona and informed Mr. Lewellen that the stock had a very small floating supply outstanding and as a consequence was a rather volatile stock, capable of as much as a 50% increase in price if the market should rise and as much as a 40% decrease in price if the market should slide.

Alice MacFay   Mr. Corona had purchased 500 shares of this manufacturer of children's dresses when it had first sold stock to the general public at $20 a share. The stock is now selling at $10 a share. Mr. Cocoa was personally familiar with the management of this company and had thought its prospects were excellent. However, shortly after the public sale, the family which was in control and was running the firm had had an argument and the dynamic younger members had split off to form their own firm, crippling the operations of Alice MacFay. Lionel D. Tranes' security analyst for this area had looked at the company and reported that prospects remained reasonably favorable for the company. In an up economy and market, he could see the stock rising as much as 40% from its present level, although a down market and economy could depress the stock as much as 30%.

M. J. Winston and Co.   Mr. Cocoa had purchased this established publisher of trade journals and textbooks because his neighbor's college age son had said they were the most popular books on campus. Mr. Cocoa had originally purchased 400 shares at $35 a share, and they were now selling at $50. The Tranes' analyst estimates that in a good market the stock could rise to $80 and in a bad market could rise to $60 a share.

Electronic Vasbators, Inc.   Mr. Cocoa had originally purchased 800 shares of this research and development oriented company at $40 a share. However, several products on which the company was working were not commercial successes, and the depressed shares are currently selling at $25 a share. The Tranes' security analyst estimates that earnings for the company could turn around from the present $1.00 a share to $1.25 in the coming year and that the stock could, in a good market rise 45% or in a bad market fall 10% from its present level.

Fred James   Mr. Cocoa had just recently purchased the stock of this retail dress chain and its current price was identical to $10 a share he had paid for the 1000 shares in his portfolio. The security analyst in the retail area has estimated a reasonably good recovery in disposable personal income could push Jame's earning and stock up almost 35%, while a continuation of the present recession could see James's stock price rise only 10% from its present level.

Mr. Lewellen had consulted the economic and market forecasting unit at

Tranes and was given the official thinking that the firm estimated a 50-50 chance of a good market and an economic recovery occurring in the next year. Mr. Lewellen was told to evaluate his client's portfolio prospects and to make his recommendations in light of this estimate. The economics forecasting unit also suggested that all portfolio managers consider high grade bonds which were presently yielding 9%, just about equal to what the economics forecasting unit anticipated as the long run return to common stock portfolios.

QUESTIONS

1. Construct a payoff matrix, which Mr. Lewellen might use in his presentation, for Mr. Cocoa's present stock portfolio and for a bond portfolio, assuming there is a 50% chance of a good market and a 50% chance of a bad market.

2. Compute the expected return and the standard deviation for each of the two portfolios in the matrix. Compute the geometric mean of the two portfolios. (Hint: the geometric mean (G) is the product of each return raised to its probability (P_j) of occurrence multiplied by each other return raised to its P_j

$$G = \prod_{j=i}^{n} \left[(Return_{i_j})^{P_j} \right]$$

3. Compare the expected return to the geometric mean return. Comment on the implied risk element in the geometric mean return as compared to the standard deviation of the expected return.

4. In light of Mr. Cocoa's investment objective and financial position, do you think the all bond portfolio is appropriate for him?

5. Assuming the payoff matrix is constant and that last period was a good market and that next period is a bad market, compute and compare the geometric return and the expected return over the two periods.